FIELDING
TRAVEL GUIDES

NEW ZEALAND
1994

Current Fielding Titles

Fielding's Australia 1994

Fielding's Belgium 1994

Fielding's Bermuda/Bahamas 1994

Fielding's Brazil 1994

Fielding's Britain 1994

Fielding's Budget Europe 1994

Fielding's Caribbean 1994

Fielding's Europe 1994

Fielding's Far East 1994

Fielding's France 1994

Fielding's The Great Sights of Europe 1994

Fielding's Hawaii 1994

Fielding's Holland 1994

Fielding's Italy 1994

Fielding's Mexico 1994

Fielding's Scandinavia 1994

Fielding's New Zealand 1994

Fielding's Spain & Portugal 1994

Fielding's Switzerland & the Alpine Region 1994

Fielding's Worldwide Cruises 1994

Fielding's Shopping Europe 1994

Fielding Travel Guides

New Zealand
1994

The Adventurous
Guide to What's Up
Down Under

by
Zeke Wigglesworth
and
Joan Wigglesworth

Fielding Worldwide, Inc.
308 South Catalina Avenue
Redondo Beach, California 90277 U.S.A.

Fielding's New Zealand 1994

Published by Fielding Worldwide, Inc.

Text Copyright ©1993 Zeke Wigglesworth and Joan Wigglesworth

Maps, Icons, Illustrations Copyright ©1993 FWI

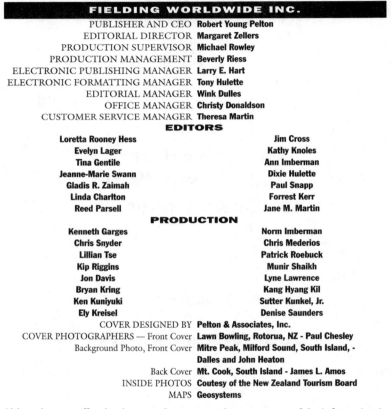

FIELDING WORLDWIDE INC.

PUBLISHER AND CEO **Robert Young Pelton**
EDITORIAL DIRECTOR **Margaret Zellers**
PRODUCTION SUPERVISOR **Michael Rowley**
PRODUCTION MANAGEMENT **Beverly Riess**
ELECTRONIC PUBLISHING MANAGER **Larry E. Hart**
ELECTRONIC FORMATTING MANAGER **Tony Hulette**
EDITORIAL MANAGER **Wink Dulles**
OFFICE MANAGER **Christy Donaldson**
CUSTOMER SERVICE MANAGER **Theresa Martin**

EDITORS

Loretta Rooney Hess	**Jim Cross**
Evelyn Lager	**Kathy Knoles**
Tina Gentile	**Ann Imberman**
Jeanne-Marie Swann	**Dixie Hulette**
Gladis R. Zaimah	**Paul Snapp**
Linda Charlton	**Forrest Kerr**
Reed Parsell	**Jane M. Martin**

PRODUCTION

Kenneth Garges	**Norm Imberman**
Chris Snyder	**Chris Mederios**
Lillian Tse	**Patrick Roebuck**
Kip Riggins	**Munir Shaikh**
Jon Davis	**Lyne Lawrence**
Bryan Kring	**Kang Hyang Kil**
Ken Kuniyuki	**Sutter Kunkel, Jr.**
Ely Kreisel	**Denise Saunders**

COVER DESIGNED BY **Pelton & Associates, Inc.**
COVER PHOTOGRAPHERS — Front Cover **Lawn Bowling, Rotorua, NZ - Paul Chesley**
Background Photo, Front Cover **Mitre Peak, Milford Sound, South Island, - Dalles and John Heaton**
Back Cover **Mt. Cook, South Island - James L. Amos**
INSIDE PHOTOS **Coutesy of the New Zealand Tourism Board**
MAPS **Geosystems**

Inquiries should be addressed to: Fielding Worldwide, Inc., 308 South Catalina Ave., Redondo Beach, California 90277 U.S.A., Telephone (310) 372-4474, Facsimile (310) 376-8064, 8:30 a.m. - 5:30 p.m. Pacific Standard Time.

ISBN 1-56952-017-8

Printed in the United States of America

Dedication

For Andrea, who plays the world like an Irish fiddle—a little harsh, a little mellow, a little sad, but always in tune.

In 1946, Temple Fielding began the first of what would be a remarkable new series of well-written, highly personalized guidebooks for independent travelers. Temple's opinionated, witty, and oft-imitated books have now guided travelers for almost a half-century. More important to some was Fielding's humorous and direct method of steering travelers away from the dull and the insipid. Today, Fielding Travel Guides are still written by experienced travelers for experienced travelers. Our authors carry on Fielding's reputation for creating travel experiences that deliver insight with a sense of discovery and style.

Zeke and Joan Wigglesworth spent 10 years laying the painstaking foundations for this entertaining and informative guide to the "other" land down under. They've traveled to all the undiscovered treasures of this panoramic island nation so you won't miss a thing that wild, wonderful New Zealand has to offer. They've done a superb job of guiding the adventurous traveler to the country's natural wonders. And the Wigglesworths' delightful intimacy with New Zealand's history, people, and culture will make your trip to the land of the kiwi unforgettable.

In 1994, the concept of independent travel has never been bigger. Our policy of *brutal honesty* and a highly personal point of view has never changed; it just seems the travel world has caught up with us.

Enjoy your New Zealand adventure with the Wigglesworths and Fieldings.

Robert Young Pelton
Publisher and C.E.O.
Fielding Worldwide, Inc.

Fielding Rating Icons

The Fielding Rating Icons are highly personal and awarded to help the besieged traveler choose from among the dizzying array of activities, attractions, hotels, restaurants and sights. The awarding of an icon denotes unusual or exceptional qualities in the relevant category. We encourage you to create your own icons in the margin to help you find those special places that make each trip unforgettable.

Fielding Selection	Author Selection	Money Saver	Expensive	Quality	Warning
Homey	Luxurious	Rustic	Simple	Scenic	Business
Great Scenery	Picturesque	Beaches & Resorts	Spectacular Cuisine	Romantic	Relaxing
Museum/ Art Gallery	Artistically Important	Architecturally Interesting	History	Book Reference	Musically Interesting
Shopping	Festivals	Nightlife	Wine Tasting	Crafts	etc.
Cycling	Hiking	Golf	Tennis	Strolling	Horseback Riding
Cross-country Skiing	Downhill Skiing	Deep-sea Fishing	Fresh-water Fishing	Snorkeling & Diving	Sailing
Arrival & Departure	By Bus/Local Transportation	By Air	By Road	By Water	By Rail

TABLE OF CONTENTS

NEW ZEALAND

INTRODUCTION

Lawn Bowling at Baths

Mother England had two children Down Under, one boisterous and often uncouth, the other more gentlemanly and decorous. In many ways the two—Australia and New Zealand—are very similar.

They are both countries stuck far out in the Southwest Pacific. They both have a mostly Anglo-Scottish-Irish culture superimposed on an older indigenous population. They are both former colonies of the British Empire, and thus are culturally, politically and philosophically attuned to Great Britain. They play the same games, enjoy the same cultural events, tell the same jokes, have roughly the same accent (at least to a North American ear). They are economically intertwined; if the Australia market gets a cold, New Zealand gets pneumonia. The citizens of both countries migrate back and forth continually, depending on which society seems to have the most jobs or the most promise at any given moment. They fight wars together, and they die far from home together.

GREEN AND PASTORAL

But there are vast differences, as well. The major one is attitude, probably created by the differences in geography. Most of the population of Australia clings to the southeastern coast because most of the interior of the country is relentless desert. This huge area, the same size as the United States, gives Aussies a decided frontier outlook in many ways. On the other hand, New Zealand is a gentle country, even in the South Island where there are extremes of cold and heat. There is a famous poem in Australia, written by Dorothea Mackellar, that says: "I love a sunburnt country." But in New Zealand, like Ireland, the overwhelming image is green—paddocks filled with sheep and deer, green bushlands clinging to the sides of green fjords, green rain forests swathing the bases of glacier-covered mountains. *The green of New Zealand has made the Kiwis more pastoral, more tranquil, less involved with taming a rugged landscape.* They seem, on the whole, to be quieter and less strident than their Australian brothers and sisters, a bit more sedate and at ease with themselves. The New Zealanders, after all, had nothing to prove to the English—unlike the first colonists to Australia, taken to Sydney in chains, the Kiwis came to their land as free citizens, on an equal footing with Great Britain from the first.

CULTURE

There are also some profound cultural differences. Modern-day Australia, while it has come a long way since the days when the official government policy was "Whites Only," still carries the burdens of a racist society. Part of the reason is historical. It is estimated that only 300,000 Aboriginals lived in the vast expanse of Australia when the Europeans arrived. They were primitive hunter-gatherers, totally unprepared for the incursion of a technically superior society. The fate of the Aboriginals was never in doubt from the first. Today they comprise only about one percent of the total population and have little political power.

THE MAORIS

In New Zealand, it has been a different story. Europeans encountered a well-organized (if violent) Polynesian society when they landed in the 1820s. The Maoris, as they are called, were more than a match for the Europeans, and despite numerous bloody clashes between the two societies, New Zealand has been a dualistic nation for more than a hundred years. In truth, this does not mean the two peoples have lived in complete harmony or that racial biases are unknown. But compared to Australia, New Zealand is a well-integrated and tolerant society. Part of the reason, of course, is that the Maoris are not the same subjugated people as the Australian Aboriginals. The Maoris have political clout, growing land rights and make up a third of the population.

AUSTRALIA AND NEW ZEALAND

Too often, visitors to the Antipodes link Australia and New Zealand closer than they really are. They are both unique cultures, both worthy of attention, both worthy of examination. And, too often, because of money or time constraints, the two are linked together on a whirlwind tour that does justice to neither. It's much like somebody coming to North America and trying to see Canada and the United States on one trip. There is also a common assumption that the two countries are right next to each other. They are close, but not that close—*1,300* miles of ocean separate them.

We urge those with the time and the wherewithal to allow enough time on a single trip to do both countries properly, or lacking that, do them one at a time. Having said that, and knowing the realities of travel, we have tried in this book to offer our thoughts about how to get the most out of a trip to New Zealand. We first arrived here thinking the country was just another state of Australia, another Tasmania, perhaps—off the beaten path from Sydney and a long way from Los Angeles. What we found is a society that clings to what we in the United States used to call "old-fashioned values." *Some observers think New Zealand is in a time warp, a society living 50 years in the past, and in some ways they might be right.* What we do know is that the country is a vacationer's dream. Every possible activity is available, and the range of choices is from international, 5-star quality down to Mom-and-Pop shoestring. We know of no country that surpasses New Zealand in its ability to take care of tourists, especially middle-income travelers and those who see the sights from beneath a backpack. Many hotels, and even some international-class hotels, have baby-sitting services, something unheard of in most places. There are special backpackers' passes, there is excellent, modestly priced bus and train service, and there are also lodges where you can blow US $500 a night—without meals.

ABOUT US

We think, to judge the observations contained in this book, you should know a bit about us. This is our second guide book (Fielding's *Australia* was the first). Travel journalism is not new to us, however, nor is travel. The male member of the outfit is the travel editor for a well-respected newspaper in the Bay Area of California. The female half has been his research assistant, fellow writer and traveling companion for more than 30 years. Together or separately, we have been all over the world, from Teheran to Casablanca to Prague to Khabarovsk to Vietnam to the Greek Islands—and the list goes on. We say this not to dazzle you with our expertise, but to alert you to that fact that we have made just about every stupid mistake you can make and still live to tell (or write) about it. We have been confused and lost in so many places so many times we lost count, and the number of fights we've had about directions, plans, hotel choices and menu translations make Divorce Court look like a kindergarten class.

WHAT TO EXPECT

Travel books, like any form of journalism, carry with them the biases of their creators, some subtle, some obvious. Over the years and over the miles, we have developed habits and patterns of enjoyment and methods of criticism that we apply to our travels, our selection of accommodations, our fancies in food, our methods of conveyance. There is nothing wrong with this, certainly, as long as these biases are made plain—which we have tried to do here.

We are, first and foremost, Americans, which designation carries with it hordes of prejudices concerning clean toilets, potable water supplies and legal rights. But more, we are Northern Californians, which means we have certain outlooks normally found only on the West Coast, including a tendency to scoff at wines not produced in Napa or Sonoma counties, coupled with an irresistible urge to devour tons of fresh artichokes and eat tons of fresh garlic. (There is no such thing as too much garlic).

We are both Greenies, having seen examples all over our planet of our species slowly fouling its own nest, and we have little regard for societies which forget that people are the first order of business, not political or monetary agendas.

We like isolation and wildernesses, and camped more than our share back when the kids were small and even a Motel 6 was financially impossible. But we also like cities and have a real fondness for paved streets and flush toilets. While we are not reluctant to sup with strangers when necessity or instant friendship arises, and have been known to take bus tours and actually enjoy them, we prefer doing things on our own. We have learned to be patient and flexible, having discovered early on that Murphy was indeed an optimist.

Given a choice, we ignore timetables, try not to adhere too closely to itineraries. Trains have their place; so do buses and guided tours. But for our tastes, the only way to travel is by personal vehicle, be it camper van or car—we are too lazy for bikes, too conventional for motorcycles. Money and time often make such independent travel impossible, but whenever possible, we are on the road, enjoying the freedom of being able to stop where and when we want, of taking any back route that comes along, of making our days as long or as short as we choose. We think this is essential to your enjoyment of New Zealand. On the one hand, the country is small enough to easily allow such freedom. And on the other, and more important, hand, the New Zealanders make it very easy to travel independently—in fact, they encourage it.

A few things about how to use this book: *Because New Zealand is on the decimal system using dollars and cents, there can be confusion when discussing prices. In almost all cases, we have quoted prices in New Zealand dollars so you can use current exchange rates to estimate expenses.* The rate over recent years has hovered around 50-60 US cents to the Kiwi dollar.

Also, our thanks to the New Zealand tourism office in Los Angeles. And special thanks to Paul and Carolyn Snyder for their help, and Matt Nauman for all his assistance. It really was a possum, Matt.

THE EXPLORERS

Captain Cook's Statue and Young Nick's Head

The two Lands Down Under—Australia and New Zealand—primarily owe their discovery by European explorers to a philosophic quest for balance. By the beginning of the 17th century, most of the major land masses on the planet had been outlined, although vast interior areas were still unexplored. But it seemed to European philosophers and cartographers that such an ideal form as a sphere required an ideal balance of masses. Europe, North America, India, Cathay, the lands of the Near East—all lay to the north of the equator. There were the masses of sub-equatorial Africa and South America, to be sure, but a sense of harmony insisted that there should be at least one more great continent in the south, a mythical land mass that came to be called "terra australis incognita" in Latin, "the unknown southern land."

The island continent of Australia had been nibbled at for centuries, but was thought to be just an extension of New Guinea, not the mythical missing land, so the search for the great southern land mass continued well into the 18th century.

THE FIRST DISCOVERY

The credit for the first European investigations of any part of Australia fell to the Dutch, who had by the beginning of the 17th century taken firm hold of Indonesia. Ships sailing south and east from Batavia—modern Jakarta—chanced upon the mostly inhospitable west, south and north coasts of Australia. Throughout the 1600s, Dutch traders and explorers flushed out their charts of Australia but sailed past, seeing little to attract colonization or trade.

In the slow process of wooden-ship exploration, Dutch sailors apparently were the first to discover one of the southern hemisphere's little gifts to navigators: the Roaring Forties. From the tip of Cape Horn, east past the Cape of Good Hope, south past Australia, great winds blow almost constantly around and around the planet, like a giant merry-go-round. If you catch a ride between 40 degrees and 50 degrees south latitude, you can sail the vast stretches between land masses with a constant, predictable, strong west wind at your back.

THE DUTCH

One of the most successful of the Dutch explorers—at least in terms of discoveries—was Abel Janszoon Tasman, a Dutch East India Company captain. In 1642, he was given orders to sail well south of the East Indies to near the Antarctic Circle to look for that elusive and as yet undiscovered great southern continent. He sailed Aug.14, and by October was far to the southwest of Australia at about 49 degrees south latitude, a record at the time. He never found land, only fog and heavy seas, so he decided to sail back to about 45 degrees south, then head east until he reached the approximate longitude of New Guinea, then head north. It was a route that almost guaranteed he would hit land.

On Nov. 24, he sighted what would later become Australia's main penal colony and only island state, naming it Van Dieman's Land in honor of Anthoonij van Dieman, governor-general of the East

Indies. It would be well into the 19th century before the island would be known by its modern name: Tasmania. He sailed north along the island, but storms forced him east before he got to what would later be named the Bass Strait, the often turbulent stretch of water separating mainland Australia from Tasmania. After leaving the island, he sailed across the waters east of Australia (now called the Tasman Sea) until Dec. 13, when he ran into a big landmass sitting right square on top of the Roaring Forties.

New Zealand had been discovered. Again. But this time by a European sea power, 1,000 years after the Polynesians. Tasman apparently first sighted New Zealand, which he named "Staten Landt," in the vicinity of modern Hokitika on the west coast of the South Island. He sailed north in an effort to determine if the land mass was an island, and actually sailed into the narrow strait separating the two islands. Bad sea conditions forced him back, so he continued on north, passing and naming Three King Islands where the South Pacific and the Tasman Sea meet.

In all, he spent less than a month in New Zealand waters. He had less than a pleasant experience with the locals, who killed several of his crew and were less than hospitable. Winds carried him to the northeast, where he eventually made landfall in Tonga. After puttering around in the Solomon Islands and the Bismarck archipelago, he returned to Batavia in June 1643 after sailing about 5,000 miles. The Dutch East India Company was not much taken with his performance (no trade possibilities had arisen), but the voyage did prove Australia/New Guinea was not connected to any missing landmass. The Dutch started calling Australia "Nieuw Holland" and Tasman's "Staten Landt" eventually became listed on naval charts as "Nieuw Zeeland," named after Zeeland, the maritime province of the Netherlands west of Antwerp.

CAPTAIN JAMES COOK

For reasons best left to Dutch historians, none of their bold sailors ever made thorough enough investigations of the east coast of Australia or New Zealand to recommend colonial establishments. It would be more than 125 years before Europeans showed any interest in the two lands beneath the Southern Cross. It again fell to a single naval captain to write the next chapters. But the captain who arrived off New Zealand in 1769 was no Abel Tasman—he was

James Cook, without doubt one of the most successful mariners in the history of Pacific Ocean exploration.

In the summer of 1769, there was to be a transit of the planet Venus—Venus would pass between the earth and the sun—which was an astronomical event of some importance. The Royal Navy, also still concerned about *terra australis incognita* (and rumors that the Spanish and French were sniffing around), decided to kill two birds with one stone and dispatch a ship to watch the heavens and also look for the missing continent.

Their Lordships had a spare ship—a beamy, bulky, shallow-draft former coal-ship named the *Endeavor*—and they had a spare naval lieutenant, one James Cook. The *Endeavor*, about 100 feet long, carried a crew of 94. In addition to Cook, there were several scientists, including an astronomer and two botanists, Joseph Banks, a fellow of the Royal Society, and Daniel Carl Solander, a pupil of the great Swedish botanist, Carolus Linnaeus. Cook was ordered to go as far south as 40 degrees latitude, then sail around until he either found the missing continent or reached New Zealand, which, as we have noted, had been ignored for more than a century following Tasman's discovery. Cook did his Venus-transit job while enjoying the attractions of Tahiti, then headed south for the second part of his duties. In Tahiti, he was joined by a local chief, Tupaia, who came along for the ride and to help translate. Cook sailed 1,500 miles southwest from Tahiti, failing to find anything faintly resembling a continent. He then headed for New Zealand. *At about 2 in the afternoon on Oct. 7, 1769, one of the ship's boys, 13-year-old, Nicholas Young, spied land—what is now called Young Nick's Head near Muriwai on the north-central coast of New Zealand's North Island.*

Cook's orders from the Admiralty also instructed him to parley with any New Zealand natives he met and see if he could work out a real estate deal of some benefit to His Majesty's Government. Cook exceeded that brief somewhat by simply claiming the whole thing for good King George III. He had also been given orders to survey New Zealand and chart its waters. *Cook, with his usual careful attention to detail, spent almost six months charting almost 2,500 miles of Kiwi coastline, a survey job that to this day is a marvel of accuracy and detail.*

A VIOLENT INTRODUCTION

Cook made landfall Oct. 9 in a bay lying north of Young Nick's Head, near the modern-day city of Gisborne. It was not a good beginning. Cook went ashore hoping to get water and fresh food. He also took Tupaia, who, to Cook's delight, was able to converse with the local residents. Despite the conversations, violence broke out, resulting in one Maori being shot and killed. When a war canoe filled with irate Maoris tried to attack the *Endeavor,* the crew shot and killed four more warriors. The harbor soon was full of very irate New Zealanders, and Cook, who abhorred violence and was dispirited by the deaths, decided to avoid further bloodshed and sailed Oct. 11, naming the harbor Poverty Bay because, he said, "it afforded us no one thing we wanted." (These days, Poverty Bay might be more to Cook's tastes—it's a major wine-growing and agricultural area).

He sailed south, but finding no good anchorages—or friendly locals—changed his course back north at a point he called Cape Turnagain. He continued north to a harbor he called Mercury Bay (he observed a transit of Mercury there), then went north around North Cape, sighted Tasman's Three Kings Islands, then passed down the west coast. Along the way, he sighted and named Mount Egmont, the 8,261-foot dormant volcano that serves as New Zealand's Mount Fuji. He then sailed through the strait, named after him, that separates the North and South Islands. He went north again as far as Cape Turnagain to prove North Island was indeed an island, then sailed south to circumnavigate the South Island. He passed by the Southern Alps, but clouds obscured the 12,350-foot mountain later named after him—just as clouds had obscured Tasman's view of 11,470-foot Mount Tasman the century before. The Maori name for New Zealand—Aotearoa: *the Land of the Long White Cloud*—was living up to its name.

Cook's survey proved that New Zealand was two islands, not part of any great southern continent. He left New Zealand on March 31, 1770 and sailed for home—via Australia and some very hairy experiences on the Great Barrier Reef. He reached Batavia Oct. 10, 1770, where many of his crew—including Tupaia, his Tahitian translator—died of land-based diseases. He finally returned to England on July 13, 1771.

THE MISSING CONTINENT

The Admiralty was greatly pleased by Cook's accomplishments; so much so, that within months, he was presented to George III at court, promoted and given orders to return to the South Pacific to continue his search for the missing continent—and while he was at it, stake a claim to whatever he could because the French and Spanish were apparently still muddling around out there, as well. He left England again in July 1772, this time with two ships, his own *Resolution* and the *Adventure*, commanded by Capt. Tobias Furneaux. The old *Endeavor*, battered but not beaten, had been sent off to the Falkland Islands as a supply ship.

Cook's strategy for his second voyage was simple: sail to a point as far south of 40 degrees latitude as possible, then sail east in a giant circle from south of the Cape of Good Hope to New Zealand then to Cape Horn and back around to the Indian Ocean. This way, he figured if there was a great missing continent down there, he should find it. He planned to try his great circle route during two southern summers, spending the winters exploring in the vicinity of Tahiti.

THE "FILTHY FIFTIES"

By December, he was near 57 degrees in what folks in the navy trade call the "Filthy Fifties," where he encountered storms, fog, icebergs—and no land. One startling discovery was made—iceberg ice, melted, became fresh water; the notion that icebergs came from fresh-water glaciers was apparently unknown at that time.

CROSSING THE ANTARCTIC CIRCLE

On Jan. 17, 1773, Cook and Furneaux crossed 66.33 degrees south latitude, becoming the first men to cross the Antarctic Circle. A few days later, he reached 67.15 degrees south, 39.35 east, a point just 75 miles north of present-day Enderby land and the closest he ever came to Antarctica. Early in February, the two ships were separated in a fog, but Cook and Furneaux had made arrangements to rendezvous at Queen Charlotte Sound, the beautiful fjord-like harbor on the northeast tip of the South Island, now used by *inter-island* ferries.

Cook and *Resolution*, having sailed almost 11,000 miles without seeing land, hauled into Dusky Sound, one of the isolated fjords on the southwestern coast of the South Island, on March 27. Cook and crew rested for about six weeks, then went on to their meeting with

Furneaux at Queen Charlotte Harbour. After a winter of fun in the sun (including a relaxed visit with the good folks in Tonga), the two captains headed for the Antarctic again, intending to stop at Queen Charlotte. On the way, the ships became separated again in a storm. Cook stayed at the harbor until November 1773, then left, leaving a note to Furneaux in a bottle (plus a sign on a tree: "Look underneath"). Furneaux and crew, battered by the storm, arrived a few days later and met with a disaster. (See the discussion of cannibalism in the Maori section.)

Cook, meanwhile, was heading toward the ice again. On Jan. 30, 1774, he and his crew became the first recorded humans to pass south of 70 degrees, but he was still far from land—where he was, the Antarctic landmass lies at about 75 degrees. Having by this point had his fill of ice and storms, he sailed north to Easter Island, then to Tahiti. He returned to Queen Charlotte Sound in October (after charting Easter Island, New Caledonia, the New Hebrides and the Marquesas), then sailed for England, having circumnavigated (but never seen) Antarctica.

COOK'S LAST VOYAGE

He visited Queen Charlotte Sound one more time, on his third and last great voyage of exploration. He arrived in mid-January 1777, and left at the end of March. The intent of this voyage was to find a northwest passage between the Pacific and the Atlantic somewhere in the Arctic. Cook sailed north, discovered the Hawaiian Islands, mapped the coast of Alaska and Siberia, then returned to the Hawaiian Islands in October 1778. In February 1779, on the Big Island of Hawaii, Cook was killed by the islanders. He was 50.

WAR AND PROGRESS

In the years following James Cook's explorations, New Zealand was visited by a mob of explorers, English and French, and growing numbers of seaman came to hunt seals, and later, sperm whales. By the 1820s, one of the first European settlements had been started at a place called Kororareka in the Bay of Islands on the North Island. Today, the settlement is called Russell, and is a quaint little tourist and fishing town. But in the whaling days, it was known as the "Hellhole of the Pacific," an epithet used with glee today by tourism boosters. It was made the first capital of the fledgling colony in 1840, an honor that lasted less than a year.

By as early as 1830, things were pretty raunchy in some parts of New Zealand, which was getting a bad reputation sailing circles and government offices, especially back in England. The general view was that law and order were virtually non-existent; many of the country's resources were being pillaged, Maoris were being killed and exploited. Protests began, from missionaries in New Zealand as well as social activists in England, insisting that something had to be done to protect the Maoris and their land rights—as well, of course, to Anglicize the country so colonists could live in some sort of peace.

And what better way to protect the Maoris than by simply taking control of the country? Although Cook had claimed New Zealand for the British crown on his first voyage, the islands had for the most part been ignored in the years following. The English seemed to be more intent on making Australia a working proposition than paying attention to the colonization of New Zealand.

TREATY WITH THE MAORIS

In 1840, an English representative, William Hobson, met with about 50 Maori chiefs at a place called Waitangi, not far from Russell in the Bay of Islands. In the treaty signed there Feb. 6, the Maoris recognized the sovereignty of Queen Victoria, and the queen in return recognized Maori rights to land, fishing, forests and other property. Further, it was agreed that only the crown could purchase Maori land. Not all the Maoris, including several major chiefs, were willing to sign the document. But In the end, about 500 or so chiefs accepted the treaty. The Treaty of Waitangi officially opened the doors to English colonization, which was sporadic. At first, colonists were vastly outnumbered by the Maoris, and for the first years of their history, colonial New Zealanders were, as one historian put it, living in "mere encampments on the fringe of Polynesia." Feb. 6 is now a national holiday in New Zealand.

Until 1852, New Zealand was directly governed by the crown—or at least the ministers working for the crown. In that year, a constitution for New Zealand was approved by the British Parliament. The document set up a governor appointed by the British, plus an upper house appointed by the governor and a locally elected lower house. Final veto over legislation passed in New Zealand remained in London, even if it had been approved by the governor. That system lasted, with a few changes, until 1947 when New Zealand was given the final legal powers to amend its own constitution and thus become a fully independent nation.

A MODEL FOR CHANGE

In the late 19th century, New Zealand became internationally famous among political theoreticians as a sort of modern test tube for social change. In the 1880s, the country had a severe depression, resulting in a movement toward left-wing political parties and welfare legislation. In 1890, the Liberal Party took control, a tenure that lasted until 1912. During those two decades, universal suffrage was introduced—women got the vote in 1893—and compulsory arbitration of labor disputes was enacted, land reform was introduced, minimum wage laws were passed, old age pensions were begun. In 1935, after a period of conservative control, the Labour Party, philosophic heirs to the Liberals, took control again and ushered in New Zealand's modern welfare state. The country soon had free health care, free education, welfare benefits, low-cost housing, the 40-hour week and many socialized industries. In recent years, there has been a trend toward decentralized government, with some backlash against government ownership and control of industries and utilities. Some industries have been sold to private companies, and some New Zealanders feel the only way to get the economy bubbling again is to get into a free market system. New Zealand, always experimenting with government, is still at it.

WORLD WAR II

From the time the country was colonized, until after World War II, the Kiwis, like their cousins in Australia, constantly rallied to the defense of Mother England, sending troops to die in wars thought essential by London. And like the Australians, they paid dearly for the privilege. Something like 3,000 Kiwis died in the mismanaged, ill-advised Gallipoli campaign in 1915. They were part of the Australia-New Zealand Army Corps—the Anzacs. Like Australia, April 25, the day the troops landed in 1915, is celebrated as a national holiday. In all, about 100,000 New Zealanders went off to World War I. Casualties were staggering: 45,000 wounded, 16,000 killed.

World War II was a great blow to New Zealand-Great Britain ties. The mighty British navy, supposedly the backbone of the Empire's defenses, was knocked out of the Pacific war early, and the attack at

Pearl Harbor meant the Kiwis and the Aussies were all alone and virtually unprotected against the Japanese. In the end, of course, the reborn United States Pacific fleet prevailed, and after the Japanese surrender, New Zealand, like Australia, formed attachments with the new Pacific power, the United States. About 28,000 Kiwis were killed or injured in the war.

ANTI NUCLEAR PIONEERS

Ties with the United States were so strong following the war, in fact, that New Zealand joined with Australia to form ANZUS, one of the Cold War-spawned mutual defense treaties. That lasted until the early 1980s when New Zealand again made international headlines with a bold anti-nuclear stance. It refused to allow any ships with nuclear weapons to enter New Zealand waters, which immediately caused Washington to dump the Kiwis from the ANZUS organization. A decade of chill settled over New Zealand-U.S. relations, not helped by America's refusal to confirm or deny if its ships were carrying nukes. Things have thawed a bit, but remember, New Zealand is still "Clean, Green and Nuclear Free." Most New Zealanders seem to genuinely like Americans—U.S. military and foreign policies, on the other hand, are not much accepted. Relations between France and New Zealand are even icier, however.

The French, for reasons not understood by anyone in the South Pacific, continue above-ground nuclear tests. Greenpeace, which has been trying to stop these tests for years, sent one of its protest ships, the *Rainbow Warrior*, to Auckland harbor in 1985. *The French, in a truly stupid move, sent secret agents down to blow it up. The sinking of the* Warrior *caused an international scandal and to this day, the French are less than welcome in New Zealand.* The *Rainbow Warrior* is still in New Zealand—it was towed to a spot near the Bay of Islands and scuttled to make an artificial reef. It's popular with scuba divers. Actor Jon Voight made a movie of the affair, shot on location in New Zealand. Look for it: **"The Sinking of the Rainbow Warrior."**

THE MAORI

Maori waka paddling at Turangawaewae

Imagine a huge triangle cut into the surface of the Pacific Ocean, with the base running roughly north-south from the Hawaiian Islands to New Zealand; its sides running east to Easter Island. This is the great Polynesian Triangle, a huge expanse larger than several of the continents; more than 5,000 miles on each side, a total area of something like 14 million square miles. It has been the site of one of the boldest migrations in human history. Among the societies contained within the boundaries of the triangle, in addition to Hawaii, Easter Island and New Zealand, are the Cook Islands, the Marquesas, Tonga, Tahiti and the Samoas.

It seems strange now, looking at the snow-capped Southern Alps, or driving by the carefully cropped sheep paddocks of modern New

17

Zealand, to remember that until the late 18th century, this mostly Caucasian nation was Polynesian. The usual concept of a Polynesian island is palm trees, warm breezes, bananas, tropical coral lagoons—a far cry, indeed, from the temperate to chilly climate found in New Zealand. But Polynesian it was, the southern territorial limit of the peoples who began their immense migration east across the Pacific more than 2,000 years before Europeans came calling. In fact, *95 percent of all the land mass in Polynesia is comprised of New Zealand.*

THE GREAT MIGRATION

There seems to be general agreement that the ancestors of the Polynesians who discovered New Zealand began their great migration from Southeast Asia maybe 4,000 or 5,000 years ago. By around 1,500 B.C., they had expanded through Indonesia to New Guinea, and by 1000 B.C. were in Tonga and Samoa. During the next 1,000 years, the societies in what is now called Western Polynesia thrived, evolved a distinct culture and set of languages and began expanding east. The last great discovery for these wide-ranging peoples was the two major (and one minor) islands that are now called New Zealand.

It was, by any measure, an incredible expansion of humans. Indeed, until the explosive European migrations that followed the discovery and eventual domestication of the New World, no peoples on earth were as wide-spread as the Polynesians.

The ability of the Polynesians to travel great distances across open oceans and establish permanent colonies was greatly aided by their ability to construct large, sea-going canoes, sometimes more than 60 feet long. Using such craft, often double-hulled, they were able to carry along the tools, animals, plants and equipment they needed to become self-sufficient on strange new islands. As they slowly made their way eastward, these great explorers discovered many islands basically void of food supplies, so they lived on the staples they brought with them—coconut, taro, sweet potatoes, breadfruit, bananas; plus domesticated pigs, dogs and chickens.

ARRIVAL IN NEW ZEALAND

Some paleontologists think the first Polynesians arrived in New Zealand between 700 and 1100 A.D. The consensus seems to be that these Polynesians—today called the Maori—are descendents of a group that almost certainly came from Eastern Polynesia—likely candidates being Tahiti, the Marquesas or the Cook, Society or Austral islands. At any rate, several sites in New Zealand have revealed artifacts similar to those found in Eastern Polynesia. Some historians believe that the island-hopping explorations by the Polynesians were accidents, that canoes were caught in storms or blown off course. Others believe that the exploration was intentional, a sort of Pacific manifest destiny, and that the degree of expertise exhibited by Polynesian navigators was nothing less than phenomenal. Current theory lumps all of Maori history in New Zealand into a single millennium-long event, but divides it into two distinct eras, the Archaic (hunter/gatherer) and the Classic.

When the first Polynesians arrived in New Zealand, they found a climate unlike anything they had come across on their oceanic travels: often cold, blustery, highly changeable, ranging from sub-tropical to sub-antarctic. Their traditional food trees could not survive in most parts of the islands, and even the normally hardy taro plants were at risk. But unlike many other Pacific islands, New Zealand was full of stuff to eat—the forests were filled with birds, and the shores and river estuaries were rife with seals, shellfish and other seafood. Several native plants turned out to be good food sources, and after some experimentation, the Maori discovered ways of keeping kumara (sweet potatoes) sheltered during the harsh winters.

THE ARCHAIC PERIOD

The major settlements during the Archaic period seem to have been along the northeastern shore of the South Island. At the time of the first settlements, the climate in New Zealand was warmer, and the South Island was not as intemperate as it can become these days. The abundance of non-agricultural food allowed the early Maori to migrate with the seasons, and apparently it wasn't until the climate cooled and population pressures built that the Maori were forced north and began establishing the semi-permanent farming and fort-like sites that were a hallmark of the Classic period.

The Maori were not always kind to their adopted land. Because of their isolation, the islands of New Zealand evolved a huge variety of birds which thrived until human contact. Because there were no predators on the islands, many species of birds were flightless, fulfilling the evolutionary niche filled elsewhere by foraging animals. Because of their lack of mobility, these birds were easy targets for hungry hunters—thus *it is estimated that the bulk of the 13 known moa species (large flightless birds similar to emu and ostriches) had been hunted to extinction by 1300, as were perhaps 20 species of flying birds.* Maori hunters also made massive dents in the seal populations and thousands of acres of forests were stripped, causing erosion and loss of wildlife.

THE CLASSIC PERIOD

The shift between the Archaic and Classic periods was not abrupt; the transition came faster is some parts of the islands than others. There is also evidence that agriculture was practiced to some degree during the Archaic period.

At any rate, by the time of the **first European contact** (Tasman in 1642, Cook in 1769), the Maori had evolved a complex, war-like society. One of the main hallmarks of the Classic period was the construction of fortified defensive positions called "*pas*," and intertribal wars and skirmishes, fought in hand-to-hand combat, were common. Almost 6,000 *pa* sites have been discovered in New Zealand, the bulk of which are on the North Island. By the late 18th century, the greatest number of Maori lived on the coastal fringes of the North Island. Most of the peoples living on the South Island and the isolated Chatham Islands (500 miles southwest of Christchurch) were fishers and birders. *The total Maori population in 1770 is estimated to have been between 100,000 and 150,000.*

By Pacific standards, the Maori were quite advanced. They had evolved intricate houses, finely carved and utilitarian, with internal hearths, windows, sliding doors and porches. Special birthing and funereal houses were constructed, as were separate cooking quarters, storehouses and tribal meeting houses.

Facial tattooing was common, as it was in a few other Pacific societies. For men, it was extensive on cheeks, nose and foreheads and showed warrior status; women normally only tattooed their chins. In Maori society, women were the main food gatherers and crop tenders. Men were thus free to build houses and boats, carve sculptures and make war. The concept of "*utu*," or revenge, was central to Maori society, and almost any insult could lead to warfare. Usually, such wars of revenge took place in the non-planting season when there was free time for outdoor activities.

THE MAORI MYTHOLOGY

Maori creation beliefs and tribal lore are complex and similar to those of other Polynesian societies. In the Maori version of discovery, a bold navigator named Kupe sailed from the homeland, a place called Hawaiki, and found New Zealand. He returned to Hawaiki (now thought perhaps to be Tahiti) and gave the people instructions about how to get to the two large islands he had discovered far to the southwest. Some centuries later, because of wars and population pressure, the ancestors of the Maori set sail to find New Zealand. They arrived in the islands in a series of great canoes, and modern Maori tribes trace their ancestors back to one of those specific canoes. It is generally conceded in most Maori accounts that the first landfall was at the **Bay of Plenty** on the North Island, usually Whangaparaoa in the East Cape region. While this seems logical if the first settlers came from Eastern Polynesia, there is also some evidence to suggest that the first settlements were on the South Island, but that northern Maoris conveniently forgot this later and changed the location to fit in with their own tribal lore.

CANNIBALISM

It turned out that the often-brutal Maori were also cannibalistic, as apparently were the residents of the Marquesas, the islands where they might have come from. The first evidence that the New Zealanders dined on one another was gathered by Cook during his first voyage, 1769–71. His favorite anchorage in New Zealand was Queen Charlotte Sound at the northern tip of the South Island. Here he made friendly contact with the locals, who were not reluctant to discuss their food habits with Cook and his scientists. One day, in a cove near his anchorage, Cook saw Maoris cooking up a stew and recognized human arm bones. He named the place **Cannibal Cove**. Also on this trip, he bought a gnawed-on arm bone to prove to the outside world that cannibalism did exist; Joseph Banks, one of the scientists on the trip, bought a preserved head. Banks thus apparently became the first tourist to snap up that particular type of New Zealand souvenir. The next century, so many whalers, sealers and passersby were buying preserved heads that local chiefs were hard put to keep up with the demand. *There's a combination museum/tattoo parlor in the red light district of Amsterdam, for example, where one of the most popular exhibits is a heavily tattooed, preserved Maori head*, brought back, no doubt, by one of those early travelers.

The Maoris told Cook that enemies were eaten to absorb the courage and spirit of the fallen.

Maori cannibalism became personal for Cook on his **second voyage,** 1772-1775. With him was a second ship, the *Adventure,* commanded by Capt. Tobias Furneaux. During their explorations, the two ships became separated, and in November 1773, Cook sailed on, leaving instructions for Furneaux at the Queen Charlotte Sound anchorage.

When Furneaux finally arrived, battered and soaked from a storm, he decided to rest awhile before sailing on to join Cook. He sent a party of 10 men out for food; they never returned. A second party came upon the remains of the first—the head of a ship's servant, the tattooed hands of two seamen, five shoes and several baskets filled with human flesh ready for cooking. *Figuring enough was bloody enough, Furneaux decided not to rendezvous with Cook, but instead sailed off to Cape Horn and then to England via the Cape of Good Hope, becoming the first man to go around the world west to east.* He arrived back in England in 1774, and was promptly sent off to America to deal with the uppity Yankees.

In another incident on the second voyage, Cook grossed out his whole crew. Noting a freshly killed Maori corpse ashore, he decided, for the sake of science, to see the thing done up close. He was, he said, *"filled with indignation against these Cannibals,"* but ordered a piece of the flesh roasted and brought on board, whereupon one of the Maoris aboard *"eat it with a seeming good relish before the whole ships company (and it had) such an effect on some of them as to cause them to vomit. That the New Zealanders are Cannibals can no longer be doubted."*

On Cook's third voyage, a Queen Charlotte area chief named **Kahoura** came aboard ship and confessed he had been in charge of the Maoris who had killed the Furneaux party. Apparently, the incident occurred when a trigger-happy crewman shot and killed two Maoris in a scuffle over some ship's biscuits. Cook, who by this time in his career was taking an anthropologist's approach to cannibalism, took no action. In fact, Kahoura asked for, and was granted, permission to sit for a portrait by John Webber, an expedition artist. The portrait still exists.

A FIERCE TRIBE

The Maori were, in all, a daunting people. Not only were they fierce, they looked fierce, with tattooed faces, colorfully decorated nose holes, vivid feathered cloaks and large hand weapons.

Maori challenge

They further disconcerted the English with a bizarre dance-greeting for both friend and foe—they rolled their eyes and stuck out their tongues in an effort to terrify their intended victims—which they did. This display (dancing, tongues, rolling of eyes) is called a "*haka*" and not only serves to rattle the opposition, but limbers up the body for the forthcoming warfare. There is a tale, probably true, that during World War II, a Maori battalion decided to stage a *haka* on Crete prior to a bayonet attack. The Wermacht troops took one look at this horde of crazy New Zealanders sticking out their tongues and generally acting like Maori warriors and took off for the hills.

It took less than a generation for the effects of European contact to shatter much of traditional Maori society. *Like other islanders throughout the Pacific, the Maori paid dearly for being discovered. European diseases killed them by the thousands.* Maoris who resisted incursions by greedy whalers were shot and killed. Alcohol and prostitution took their toll. And, perhaps worst of all, Maoris were introduced to modern weapons of war, especially the musket. A series of inter-tribal wars began, and where once such combat was fought hand to hand with relatively light losses, muskets brought wholesale slaughter. Some estimates say as many as 60,000 Maoris died in such clashes in the 1820s.

MISSIONARIES

And, as in other cases throughout the Pacific rim, missionaries came to tell the locals that most of their culture was wrong. Clothing styles, art work, the basic beliefs of a long oral tradition, all wrong. And also, as in other parts of Polynesia, the missionaries were quite successful. Christianity has planted deep roots in contemporary Maori society.

One fascinating thing about this period in English colonial history is the contrast between treatment of the Maoris in New Zealand and the Aboriginal peoples of Australia. In Australia, there was never very much concern shown for the land rights of the Aboriginals. In fact, the English simply declared that Australia was a vacant land, and as such, was wide open to colonization.

In New Zealand, faced with a much more advanced indigenous population—as well as a native population that had shown itself capable of forcefully dealing with strangers—the tack was entirely different. Most everyone involved, including some Maoris, thought the only way to preserve Maori land rights and culture was for England to take control of things. This was good imperialistic logic, which served the English well around the world during the heady days of the Raj.

A CLASH OF CULTURES

It was probably inevitable, given the two divergent cultures sud-denly thrust together, that violence would break out. The English colonists, for their part, saw the open stretches of land around the islands as fertile farm and ranch land just waiting for the plow and cattle. The Maoris, whose concept of life held that many areas were "*tapu*," or off-limits because of religious reasons, thought in the beginning that when they signed the Treaty of Waitangi ceding con-trol of New Zealand to the British crown, they were simply giving Queen Victoria the "shadow of the land," a sort of long- term lease, and that full ownership would always remain in their hands. In addi-tion, of course, there was the European notion that treaties signed with non-European peoples were just so much hot air and didn't really count, anyway. It was an outlook accepted by the French,

English and Americans in North America, and by the British in Australia and New Zealand.

Fighting broke out in the early 1840s, beginning what is called in New Zealand history the "**Land Wars.**" English settlers would move into lands owned by the Maori, the Maori would fight back. The end result of the wars, which lasted off and on until the 1870s, was that the Maori lost and the colonists became the dominant culture in New Zealand. Part of the problem was that the colonists were more or less unified, but the Maori, traditionally a tribal culture, had no country-wide, unifying force. Indeed, during the wars, Maoris fought Maoris to the benefit of the English. Some of the lands taken by force or deceit in those days are at the heart of present-day Maori land claims.

MAORI ART

During their millennium-long development before arrival of the Europeans, Maori artists created a distinct form of Polynesian art, primarily in wood carvings, but also in their use of "**greenstone**" or nephrite and bowenite, two forms of jade mined in the valleys of the Taramakau and Arahura rivers on the west coast of the South Island.

Maori arts at Art Centre in Christchurch

Some of the finest wood carving was reserved for meeting houses, called "*whare runanga,*" with intricate interlacings and decorations and typical grotesque masks with abalone-shell eyes and huge distended tongues. In the later Classic period, extensive carving was also done on the interior panels of the meeting houses. Excellent carvings were also done on the prows of war canoes, treasure boxes and other household items. *A definitive look at the greenstone and wood-carving skills of the Maori is offered in the book,* "Te Maori," written in 1984 and published by Harry N. Abrams Inc. in association with the American Federation of Arts. *(In Maori, "te" means "the," a word you'll see all over the country in town and city names.)* Greenstone was highly prized and used for ceremonial adzes, figures, pendants and war clubs. Some of the pieces are delightfully intricate works of art. Some anthropologists thought it would not have been possible for the Maori to develop such sophisticated art by themselves, and that the islands must have been visited by peoples who taught them the art forms. This view is pretty well ignored today.

Compared to Australia, which has had, over its 200-year history, many periods of overt, government-sponsored racial prejudice against the dark-black aboriginal people, the lighter-skinned Maoris have in the main been treated much better in New Zealand. Racial harmony is part of the country's ethic; indeed, when 5,000 or so American troops came to train and recuperate during World War II, the many incidents of G.I. and Marine Corps bigotry toward Maoris appalled New Zealanders, both Maori and *pakeha*, or non-Maoris. *There has been enough intermarriage, in fact, that there are few full-blooded Maoris today, and something like 10 percent of all New Zealanders have some Maori blood.*

PRESERVATION OF TRADITION

Again in contrast to the Australian Aboriginals, the Maoris were able to preserve much of their oral tradition and history in written form. Due to efforts of some early missionaries, especially a ne'er-do-well named Thomas Kendall, *the Maori language was given a written form, and much of the oral traditions were retained and are available for 21st century Maoris.* The Treaty of Waitangi, for example, was written in English and Maori. In Australia, even today, almost all of the ancient tribal customs and mores are passed on orally.

This is not to say that Maori-*pakeha* relations have been all roses. Maoris have been cheated out of their lands and properties, relegated in many instances to second-class citizenship and pushed out of the mainstream, their 1,000-year culture suppressed and ignored. But, like the Aboriginals in Australia, there is growing awareness of native rights and heritage, as well as growing political pressure to address what many Maoris see as a long record of mistreatment and dishonesty. *Today, the once-vilified Maori language is protected, and "language nests" have been set up to teach and preserve the Maori tongue, much the same as the Irish have set up "gaeltecs" in Ireland to preserve Irish Gaelic.* In addition, the Treaty of Waitangi, never completely implemented and often simply ignored, has been reaffirmed, with major land rights ceded back to the Maoris. In 1975, the government set up the Waitangi Tribunal to examine Maori land claims and violations of the treaty. As a result, Maoris have been given 10 percent of the national fishing quota and major mineral rights. If treaty rights are fully implemented, the Maoris could end up owning more than three-quarters of the South Island—a vast acreage that contains six national parks and such lucrative tourist properties as the world-famous Milford Track. Unlike Australia, where vast chunks of land have been ceded back to the Aboriginals—and then been closed to the white majority—*the prevailing attitude among the Maoris seems not to be an attempt to shut off public access to their lands or create a separate Polynesian country.* But they make no bones about wanting the income that such lands generate. The fishing quota alone, which Maori tribes can sell to private companies, is worth millions of dollars. The hope is that the additional income realized from control of their treaty lands will enable many Maoris to break the poverty cycle, and as a result, eventually bring Maoris and pakehas to an economic and racial balance, which is what New Zealand is supposed to be all about to begin with.

"GO HOME QUEENIE"

Like any other group of humans, however, there is not complete agreement about the progress of Maori affairs in New Zealand, as Queen Elizabeth discovered in 1990. She and Philip came to Waitanga in February to celebrate the 150th anniversary of the treaty signed by her great-great-grandmother, Victoria. As the royals stepped ashore, a group of Maori protestors shouted "Go home, Queenie," and heckled her during a speech: "You already have everything. What more do you want, Elizabeth?" The ultimate insult came as the queen's motorcade passed. A young Maori student threw a wet, black T- shirt at the queen's car as a symbolic gesture to protest New Zealand's treatment of the Maoris. The shirt did not hit the queen, but she looked startled as it landed in her car. (The girl was arrested and sentenced to several months of public service).

But the queen was also given a friendly Maori greeting by warriors with temporarily tattooed faces who said howdy by dancing forward, jabbing the air with spears, rolling their eyes and sticking out their tongues in the traditional haka. Also, an estimated 100,000 Maori population took part in building or restoring 21 giant war canoes for the occasion. The canoes, built and navigated using traditional Maori methods, commemorated the Maori discovery of New Zealand.

The queen, for her part, said that she acknowledged that the treaty stipulations had not always been followed. Later, she met with some of the descendants of the original chiefs who had signed the treaty. All seemed sweetness and light.

The process of Maori participation in modern New Zealand is not completely smooth, of course, despite Maoris being in Parliament, in seats of power, in the arts, in business, in all walks of life. There are scandals yet today in the way Maori affairs are being handled, and the dragging economy of New Zealand is making progress—for all New Zealanders—sometimes slow and painful. It does seem, however, that some sort of line has been drawn for Maori rights that cannot easily be erased.

The New Zealand government also recognizes the potential tourist interest in Maori culture, and has put together a brochure listing companies in the country which specialize in tours to important Maori sites, plus shopping excursions for Maori art and cultural performances. The guide is available from the New Zealand Tourism Board in Santa Monica.

THE LAND

Lake Matheson, Westland

GEOLOGY

As we write this, we are sitting about a 3-iron shot from two major California earthquake faults; one, the infamous San Andreas and the other, the lesser known but no less dangerous Calavaras Fault. From time to time, the faults around San Francisco Bay let go with a shaker of some size, reminding us always that our planet is still very much alive and kicking. We raise this only to show that some Americans have this, at least, in common with the folks in New Zealand. The tectonic activity that gives the coast of California its reputation —justified—for the shakes, is the very process that has created New Zealand.

New Zealand sits on the southwestern edge of a huge floating piece of earthly crust called the Pacific Plate, which is slowly grinding against another piece of crust called the Indian-Australian Plate. California sits at the northeastern edge of that same Pacific Plate, grinding against the American Plate. As the residents of either Wellington or Santa Cruz can tell you, all that grinding results in constant earthquakes, most small, some deadly. Both the Pacific Coast and New Zealand are part of the so-called "Ring of Fire," the vast area of tectonic activity that circles the Pacific Basin. New Zealand, geologically young and active, has little in common with Australia, an ancient, weathered continent that sits in the middle of the Australian Plate, relatively free of tectonic troubles.

WHERE PLATES COLLIDE

The present shape of New Zealand is about five million years old. *As Pacific islands go, New Zealand is unusual.* Most Polynesian islands are basaltic rock extruded from ancient volcanoes. New Zealand, however, is mostly the result of the earth's crust being heaved up, higher and higher as the two plates collide. Much of the base rock of the New Zealand islands is sedimentary, left over from the ancient proto-continent called Gondwanaland. It is estimated that the flat, lowland mass of New Zealand separated from Australia and Antarctica about 80 million years ago, then began its uplifting by tectonic forces about five million years ago. The North Island is the youngest of the two; rocks on the South Island date to between 400 and 600 million years old, twice as ancient as those of the North Island.

The fault lines that mark the meeting of the two crustal plates in New Zealand run through the heart of both islands. In the north, they have created the **Taupo Volcanic Zone,** which runs from the Bay of Plenty to the Tasman Sea, a belt that has created the popular thermal tourist resorts around Rotorua and Lake Taupo. *The North Island is also full of volcanoes,* from the west coast (dormant and lovely Mt. Egmont), to the active volcanoes of Tongariro National Park in the center and White Island, an active volcano about 30 miles north of Whakatane in the Bay of Plenty. This belt of volcanoes continues north all the way to Tonga and Samoa. The Tongariro volcanoes erupt periodically, scattering ash as far south as Wellington. But the peaks, in a display of both fire and ice, are also popular skiing destinations. *Earthquakes, too, are common in New Zealand, espe-*

cially near the fault zones. This century, there have been some biggies (7 or 8 on the Richter scale). One, on the North Island in 1931, raised a huge chunk of the harbor at Napier above sea level, creating 15 square miles of new land and killing about 160 people. New Zealanders seemed to have adopted the same fatalistic attitude about earthquakes as residents of California. They're just waiting for "the Big One." *In an official earthquake preparedness brochure issued by the New Zealand government, we have this nice bit of shaky logic: "The best answer for when the next major earthquake will occur in New Zealand is 'eventually.' "*

THE MOUNTAINS

It's no problem figuring out where the plates are meeting in the South Island: just take a look at the Southern Alps. The fault lines run basically from near Picton south along the west coast, and the 400-mile-long row of mountains is the boldest evidence of the continental masses being thrust upward; *there are more than 15 mountains in the range that are at least 10,000 feet high.* The Alps are not volcanic—instead, ancient seabeds have become towering peaks buried beneath a permanent cover of snow. The mountains of the South Island have a long history of glaciation. Several large glaciers remain today, and the evidence of ice at work in the past is evident all along the fjord-cut southwestern coast, which looks much like southern Norway. Here you find New Zealand's most famous fjord: Milford Sound.

The mountains split the South Island into three climatic zones. Prevailing weather patterns run west-east (remember the Roaring Forties), which make the west coast wet and windy. *It's not unusual for the coast to get 160–170 inches of rain a year, and gale-force winds can whip up any time.* The mountains themselves offer a true alpine ecosphere, with glaciers, hanging valleys, ice-melt rivers and stands of firs and other alpine plants. To the east of the mountains are the broad plains that comprise the South Island's agricultural zone. Warmer and dryer, the east coast is cut in many places by wide river valleys that have carried millions of tons of gravel down from the mountains. Indeed, *some the of gravel- river plains in New Zealand are among the largest in the world.*

The climate in the North Island tends to be warmer in general than the South Island, although snow still covers the tops of the volcanic mountains and it can rain heavily at times. Auckland is usually warmer than Wellington, which has the advantage (or disadvantage) of sitting on the Cook Strait. *The strait acts as a funnel for the wester-lies roaring through, and if a really serious blow comes along, the ferry trip from Wellington to the South Island can be very rough, sometimes impossible.*

PLANTS

New Zealand seems to be very keen on protecting its most valuable natural resource—trees. You'll see this almost anywhere you travel in the country. On one hill, you'll see evidence of clear-cutting through a forest, which is the timber industry's equivalent of an A-bomb, but just around the corner, you'll see another hill that has been completely replanted. They do harvest trees in New Zealand, but they also have a vigorous program of reforestation. It's a delicate balance —on the one hand, you have one of the most environmentally sensitive populations in the world. And on the other hand, you have a struggling timber industry in a country beset by economic problems. We read in a local newspaper of a woman, almost 80, who stepped in front of a bulldozer that was mistakenly clearing native bush from the wrong parcel of land. And in the same paper was an appeal for more people to invest in forestry industries.

CLEAN AND VERY GREEN

New Zealanders, like most everybody else in the world, have not always been sensitive to the environment and long-range problems caused by short-term goals. When the European settlers started arriving in number after 1840, they were less than pleased by the land—thorny shrublands, bleak grasslands, dense forests. Their solution was twofold: first, introduction of many species of European plants and animals (so they felt more at home), and, worse, a process they called "winning the land." This meant clearing large areas of land to make room for sheep and cattle. Often, that led to disaster as soil erosion set in. The land in many places in New Zealand is steep, so when it rains on unprotected soil, the result is predictable. Early settlers, either ignorant or uncaring, burned the native brush and planted grass—along came heavy rains, good-bye grass and soil. The denuded land also contributed to the loss of bird species and insects.

After World War II, New Zealanders decided enough was enough, and have become very protective of their lands and forests, something we cannot say about the Australians, who still haven't caught on that even renewable resources must be handled with care.

There are still many chunks of subtropical forests in New Zealand—which, if you're a plant freak, is the place to hang out. *There are 150 species of ferns, from 2 centimeters across to 50-foot-high man-ferns.* The country's national symbol is the **silver fern**, which is the emblem their beloved rugby team, the All Blacks, wear on their jerseys. Another species, the bracken fern, was used by the Maoris as a food source.

McKellar Saddle, Fiordland

Despite massive harvesting in the 19th century, there are still more than 100 species of native trees, mostly conifers and flowering hardwoods. The trees are more similar to species found in South Africa, Malaysia and South America than the next-door neighbor, Australia. But like Australia, New Zealand was cut off from the rest of the world, resulting in some species of plants found nowhere else. One of the real treasures are the vast beech forests, dense and dark, which you can see around the big lakes of the South Island. Also abundant are **podocarps**, species of broadleaf trees with a thick ground cover of pines, ferns, mosses and orchids.

One of the great ecological disasters in New Zealand was the wanton destruction of the islands' *kauri forests.* **Kauris** (*Agathis australis*) are the redwoods of the Southern Hemisphere. Once these great trees covered vast areas of the country, but their very nature spelled their doom. They grow slowly, maturing over centuries, and grow tall and straight. The Maoris used the kauris to build their long war canoes. *As they grow, kauris shed their lower branches, meaning they make perfect masts for sailing ships.* The whalers first recognized their worth, and later the lumbermen moved in. In the space of about 40 years, most of the forests had been destroyed. In addition, at the base of the trees, large deposits of resinous sap gathered, which turned out to be an excellent source of varnishes. Between the lumbermen and the hordes who came to harvest the resin, the result was disastrous, leaving barren, eroded land in their wake. It was only in the late 1950s that the last stands of kauri were protected by legislation. The oldest tree in the country is thought to be more than 2,000 years old. Kauris are also found in Queensland, and have suffered much the same fate. In New Zealand, they only grow above 38 to 39 degrees latitude, so *the best place to see them is in one of the protected forest parks on the North Island.*

Two of the more common plants you'll see touring around New Zealand are flax and cabbage trees.

Flax was to the Maori what the yucca was to the tribes of the Southwestern United States. It's actually a lily, not a member of the linen flax plants found elsewhere. They used it to make clothing and to braid strong ropes. At one time, there were about 50 varieties. Californians, never a group to miss a trick, are now using several species of imported Kiwi flax plants as landscaping plants. When first imported, they carried such names as Maori Maiden, Maori Sunrise and Maori Queen. Sensitivity to Maori concerns has changed the names, however. Now you look for species with "rainbow" names—Rainbow Maiden, Rainbow Sunrise, etc.

If they hadn't picked the silver fern as the national plant, the Kiwis might have picked the **cabbage tree**, a ubiquitous member of the agave family. Maoris used it for food (edible taproots, stems and leaf-shots). It produces large, scented flowers in the spring when it blooms, and the leaves grow in tufts, giving it a distinctive shape. They look a lot like giant palmettos, usually growing up to about 40 feet high.

Another plant you can't avoid seeing is the **tussock**, for lack of a better comparison, the Kiwi equivalent of sagebrush or Australian spinifex. It's actually a grass that grows in clumps, and various species are found from alpine areas to the lowlands. The biggest tussock plants can grow up to three feet high.

New Zealand is a flower lover's paradise, with some 500 species of alpine flowers found nowhere else in the world. There are, for example, more than 60 species of **mountain daisies,** one of which produces a bloom 10 centimeters (about four inches) across. There is also a **New Zealand eidelweiss,** not a close relation but similar in bloom. You'll also see 40 species of **buttercup,** including the Mount Cook lily. We were also pleased to see **ice plant**, which graces the dunes along the California coast. New Zealand even has its own version of Spanish moss called Old Man's Beard, a parasitic plant you'll see all over trees in the Milford Sound area.

*Count on also seeing lots of introduced plants—***oaks, eucalyptus, cedars, redwoods, elms** *and that most noxious of plants—and a real menace to farmers—***gorse**, *a native of Scotland.*

If you want to get a close-up view of New Zealand's special native plants, check out the **Otari Native Plant Museum** in Wellington, which raises and preserves 1,200 species of indigenous plants. While you're out on the road, stop at the offices of national parks and preserves around the country which usually have a supply of local plant guides for sale.

Frolicking gannets at Cape Kidnappers

ANIMALS

If you were a bird, and worried about getting through life without becoming some other animal's dinner, for millions of years, New Zealand was the place to be. No predators, no mammalian or reptilian egg-snatchers. It was a great life—that is, until humans arrived. What happened after that, for birds, was an ecological disaster. When the Maoris populated New Zealand about 1,000 years ago, they brought pigs, dogs and rats, none of whom were kind to the original residents. Because of the lack of native predators, many species of New Zealand birds had lost the ability to fly, and were easy targets for hungry Maori hunters. In fact, several types of flightless birds were hunted to extinction, including the **moa**, the New Zealand equivalent of the ostrich or emu. One type of moa stood 10 feet tall.

EUROPEAN IMPORTS

As if the Maoris weren't bad enough, European settlers completed the destructive process by bringing along a whole cast of nasties, including **stoats, possums, cats** and **ferrets**. One of the first callers, Capt. James Cook, a farsighted sort, often left pigs behind at anchorages where he was likely to return. *That's what they call feral pigs in New Zealand these days: Cap'n Cookers.* Not, of course, that he's responsible for all the wild pigs running around. But with one thing and another, it is estimated that 70 percent of the original bird species have been wiped out. Not satisfied with killing off all the birds, the settlers also brought along rabbits, deer and chamois which chewed the country into severe ecological problems. *All the introduced animals, especially rats, stoats, possums, ferrets and feral cats, continue to be a major threat to New Zealand birdlife.*

MAMMALS

The only mammals "native" to New Zealand are bats, seals and sea lions. By native, we mean pre-human, because it is generally agreed that almost all of the original bird species in the country flew in from somewhere else, as did the bats. The seals and sea lions migrated in, as well. There are two species of bats—the short-tailed and the long-tailed. The seals and sea lions are the fur seal and Hooker's sea lions, a very rare species found only in the southern islands of New Zealand.

LIVING FOSSILS...

One of the more fascinating true native animals is a small reptile, an actual living fossil called the **tuatara**. *Here's an animal which can trace its family tree back 200 million years to the Lower Triassic. They are extremely rare, and can live to at least 150 years of age. They mate when they're 20, stop growing when they're 50.* They eat insects, shed their skins once a year, hibernate when it gets cold and can swim easily. Up close, if you're lucky to see one in captivity, tuataras look like small iguanas. It is thought they arrived in New Zealand in the Jurassic Period about 130 million years ago when the islands were still part of Gondwanaland. They once roamed all over New Zealand, but because of human intervention and introduced predators, have retreated to a few off-shore southern islands.

The best place to see a tuatara is at the tuatarium at the Southland Museum and Art Gallery in Invercargill. The big draw at the museum used to be George, a tuatara who was, by tuatara standards, a giant—about 600 millimeters long (nearly 24 inches). He died in 1969 at the tender age of 150. Some of the new kids on the tuatara block at the Invercargill facility are Henry (he's 100 years old); Albert, 45; Lucy, 35, and Mildred, 30. We saw Henry, a rare treat. He ignored us. Admission to the museum and tuatarium is free, but donations are welcome.

New Zealand has three species of native frogs, unique in the world because they do not have a tadpole stage—they are born live as miniature mirrors of their parents. And the New Zealand form of the **gecko**, unlike geckos in other parts of the world, is also born live without hatching from an egg. The geckos live throughout the country, including higher mountain elevations.

GIANT INSECTS...

Three species of insects worth a mention are the **katipo**, the **glow worm** and the **weta**. Katipos are spiders, related to North American black widows or **Australian redbacks.** They are found mostly on the west coast of the north island, and are the only animals in New Zealand that are a threat to humans. **Glow worms** are the larval stage of a fly found in limestone caves on the North Island. They have chemical body lights, very much like our fireflies. They are a big tourist attraction, drawing visitors to caves at Te Anau and Waitomo. The insects coat the ceilings of caves, then drop long sticky filaments to catch flying insects. They stay in the larval stage about nine months. The weta is a primitive beastie, very rare, found in mountainous areas. One type, the **giant weta,** *is one of the heaviest insects in the world, weighing as much as a small bird.* They look like big, nasty versions of a cricket. They have jaws that can pierce skin, spikes and spines and, all in all, are not very social. Wetas often have a tough time surviving because they are eaten by rats.

FOUR FOOT EELS...

The country is also home to a fish called the New Zealand **long-finned eel**, found in fresh water rivers and lakes. The three- to four-foot-long eels can live up to 80 or 90 years and weigh up to 50 pounds. Some New Zealanders feed the eels in an effort to make pets of them. The eels return to the ocean to spawn, then die.

STRANGE AND BEAUTIFUL BIRDS...

The most famous animal in New Zealand is also the national symbol and the national nickname—**the kiwi**. Kiwis are flightless, nocturnal, very shy and omnivorous. Their bodies are round and they have spiky feathers that resemble fur—they look, in fact, like giant Chinese gooseberries, a tasty morsel known in most countries as the kiwi fruit. They have enormously long, sensitive beaks they use to snuff through ground debris, lousy eyesight and a great sense of smell. The male can make an ungodly shriek called the "kiwi call," but mostly they're quiet and elusive. *Your chances of seeing one in the wild are almost nil,* but there are plenty of zoos and nocturnal displays around the country. There are three species of kiwis, the largest being maybe two feet long.

New Zealand Kiwi.

One bird you probably won't have any trouble seeing at all is the **kea**, a pesky alpine parrot that fills the New Zealand niche reserved for uppity North American blue jays. They are curious and sneaky birds, and no tour bus is safe from them. They hang around tourist areas and mooch food and generally raise hell. There are signs here and there imploring you not to feed the keas, which is not only bad for them, but just encourages them to further mischief. You only find them in the South Island in areas between forests and alpine meadows. Keas are fairly large birds, growing up to 20 inches high, with strong beaks and brownish-green feathers. They were once hunted because farmers thought they attacked and killed small sheep. They will eat carrion, but there is no solid evidence proving that they will attack a healthy sheep.

Not satisfied with having one of the peskiest parrots around, *the New Zealanders also claim the world's largest parrot*, the extremely rare, very noisy **kakapo**, which is also the world's only flightless parrot. About the size of a small owl, the kakapo is on the verge of extinction in New Zealand. *Another extremely rare bird is the colorful* **takahe**, *another flightless animal. It was believed to have been extinct by 1898, but a small colony was found in 1948 near Lake Te Anau.* Takahes have been bred in captivity, but the numbers are still very small. Their decline, as with other native birds, was mostly due to introduced predators.

All in all, the combination of surviving New Zealand species plus the many types introduced by the settlers makes New Zealand a birdwatcher's delight. Some of the rarer birds are in aviaries, but many of the really endangered ones exist only in the wild and are heavily protected. But among the many birds you'll see driving around, in addition to the keas, are **black swans** (imported from Australia); pukekos, which look something like a takahe but aren't as rare; **the Australian harrier; the New Zealand gray duck** (looks like a female mallard); **oystercatchers** (almost any beach); **magpies** (another Aussie immigrant), the **Indian myna bird**; the **tui**, a white-wattled, very noisy forest dweller, and shags, a cousin to the North American cormorant.

Several popular species of birds are found only at certain locations around the country. For example:

The **royal albatross,** a huge seabird, nests in a colony at Taiaroa Head, about 20 miles from Dunedin on the South Island. Tours are available; the nesting season starts in November.

Yellow-eyed penguins are also found near Taiaroa Head, as are fur seals. The penguins come ashore to tend their nests in the afternoon; they are best seen June-August.

There is a **white heron** sanctuary near Whataroa on the west coast of the South Island near Franz Josef. The nesting season is November-February.

The only on-shore rookery for **gannets** in the southern hemisphere is located at Cape Kidnappers near Napier on the North Island. The males arrive in July to claim nesting sites. The birds mate for life and may live up to 20 years. The cape was named by Capt. Cook because the Maoris tried to kidnap a Tahitian on board his boat.

...AND OF COURSE SHEEP

Lastly, but certainly not leastly, there is no way you will avoid seeing that most ubiquitous of New Zealand critters, the **sheep**.

Sheep Shearing

New Zealand is the largest wool, lamb and mutton exporting nation in the world because of the huge flocks of sheep, which are found from island tip to island tip. In the spring, when it's lambing time, the total sheep population might reach 100 million. We remember driving from Queenstown to Te Anau once and losing count of the number of being-born and just-born lambs in paddocks we passed.

It seemed like every sheep in New Zealand was pregnant. That's when we found out that sheep are born with long tails, which are cropped when they are babies. Being city folk, we never knew that. But then a week or two in New Zealand will teach you all sorts of things about sheep.

Like for instance most ewes have multiple births; two are usual, but quads or even quints are not unusual. If a ewe only gives birth to one lamb at a time, she's soon off to the knackers—the abattoir. Among the many breeds, you see mostly **merinos** (the sheep that made Australia) and **Romneys.** It will not be uncommon to see a sea of sheep moving up and down the hills being pushed and prodded by one or two sheepdogs, a marvelous sight. One term you're likely to run into is "hogget," which is a one-year-old sheep, which the Kiwis prefer eating to spring lamb.

When the United Kingdom joined the European Economic Community in the early 1970s, one of New Zealand's major meat markets was severely restricted. As much as half of all New Zealand's exports were going to Great Britain—within a decade, it was down to just over 10 percent. *New Zealand and the EEC continue to be the world's major dairy product producers.* Much of the country's mutton and sheep output is now going to the Near East, and to a certain degree, North America. The first sheep in New Zealand were introduced by—who else—James Cook on one of his stops at Queen Charlotte Sound.

The Kiwi sheep business even has a folk hero, a Robin Hoodish type named **James McKenzie**. A devious Scot, McKenzie and his sheepdog, Friday, stole sheep from the rich farmers around the Canterbury District and snuck them back into the mountains. When they finally caught him in 1855, he had more than 1,000 purloined sheep. He was tried, convicted and sentenced to five years, but pardoned after one. Friday, his faithful dog, wasn't so lucky—he was tried as a witch and hanged.

If you want to see the sheep business up close, try one of the farm stay properties; nine out of 10 will likely be raising some sheep. And if you're on the North Island the first week in March, head for Masterson, a small farming community 100 kilometers northeast of Wellington, where you will find the annual Golden Shears contest, which decides the best shearer in the country. Contestants are each given 20 sheep, which they shear at the rate of about one a minute (which is light speed), but are also judged on the quality of their cutting.

OH, GIVE ME A HOME

So there you are, driving along through the clean, green, nuclear free farmlands of New Zealand, admiring the view, admiring the clean air, admiring the farm animals. Sheep, of course. Cows, hogs. Horses, almost every one with a protective blanket. Sheepdogs. **Deer**. *Deer? Yes, indeed, one of the country's most lucrative farm animals, deer.* More than 5,000 New Zealand farmers are now involved in rasing deer in one form or another, and at the moment, there are in excess of 1.5 million deer behind fences in New Zealand.

The hope is that farm-raised deer meat—venison—will become a staple in the red meat markets of the world. Venison, they tell you, is designer red meat, with less fat than chicken breasts, fewer calories than broiled salmon and the same amount of cholesterol as broiled bass. Also, they will tell you, farm-raised venison does not have the gamy taste of deer killed in the wild. And because it's being raised in mostly pollution-free New Zealand on mostly grass and no chemicals, it's about as pure as meat can get. *The major market for New Zealand venison is Germany,* which imported about 4 million pounds in 1990. (Germany usually imports a total of more than 10 million pounds of venison from various sources—they definitely like their jaegerschnitzel in the German Republic.) New Zealand meat is also shipped to Japan, Switzerland, Australia and Sweden. The total import of New Zealand deer meat to the United States in 1990 was about 1.2 million pounds. Industry estimates are that about *85 percent of all venison served in American restaurants comes from New Zealand.*

The deer business is particularly important to New Zealand these days because many deer operations were set up in hopes of adding supplemental income to farmers dependent on the usually volatile international wool and mutton/lamb markets. The country is having hard economic times, and there's a lot riding on the success of the deer industry. One of the things that makes deer farming so attractive is that after capital costs (fence, barns, buying the stock), it costs something like $10 a year per animal to raise a deer. "Just stick them in a field and give 'em some grass," one farmer said. Growers say deer require less land per pound of meat than other animals, and are up to three times as profitable as raising cattle or sheep. Raising deer in New Zealand these days is fairly pastoral. But it wasn't always so. Ironically, the industry began as a conservation measure. Starting in the late 1850s, colonial settlers in New Zealand imported red deer from England for sporting purposes. Red deer—actually a species of elk—are hardy, adaptable animals. That, coupled with the fact that there are no natural predators in New Zealand, meant that by the 1930s, red deer were a plague all over the country, destroying their own environment and causing problems for farmers.

The government finally allowed hunting to begin in the early 1970s, and hunters soon discovered there was a market for deer meat, and more importantly, for deer velvet, the soft new antler growth produced every year by male deer. The Asian market for velvet (and other deer parts) as a medicinal aid—especially in South Korea—is enormous and highly profitable. Not too long ago, velvet was selling for as much as $US200 a kilogram (it's now down to around $US60 a kilo.) To harvest the velvet, stags are tranquilized and the soft horn removed with a bone saw; a good stag can produce excellent velvet for 10 or 15 years.

THE HELICOPTER WARS

The market for New Zealand deer—alive or dead—became so attractive that what came to be called "the Helicopter Wars" began. At first, there were few attempts to capture deer live; rather they were shot from helicopters. Then, some far-sighted farmers figured it would be cheaper—and more profitable—to start their own herds and began capturing the animals. *The traditional capture method was for some crazy Kiwi to ride the skids outside a chopper, then jump onto the back of a deer. This was not only dangerous, but very inefficient.* But many New Zealand farmers got started in the deer business that way. (Later, they started using nets, sometimes with success, sometimes not). At times, the competition got very nasty—helicopters were sabotaged by putting sugar in gas tanks, pilots were shot at. Some years, 50 or so helicopters were involved in the killing/capturing business. It is estimated that some choppers made 12,000 kills a year, and that sometimes as many as 100,000 carcasses were sent through abattoirs annually. In the process, 130 helicopters crashed, and 25 pilots or crew were killed in accidents.

Today, the majority of venison exported from New Zealand is farm raised, although there are still a few hunters in business, and quite a few hunters from around the world come down to pursue red deer in the wild. *Most of the deer raised in New Zealand are red deer, but some farmers are raising wapiti-North American elk, virtually the same species as the red deer.* The vast wild red deer herds have been reduced to a manageable level. And in the process, the New Zealand deer industry has become very sophisticated and very successful, a far, far cry from the days of the helicopter wars.

THE PERFECT VACATION

Shotover Jet Boat

In New Zealand, it's not what to do, it's how to narrow down the choices. Given the size of the country (easy to get around), and the varied climate, New Zealand is Vacationland out of Central Casting—you want it, you can do it. Every taste, every pocketbook.

But the emphasis in Kiwi Kountry is definitely on outdoor recreation, especially hiking (they call it tramping), skiing, fishing and hunting. Oh, yes, and that most insane of all New Zealand inventions, bungee jumping. We'll try to explain.

BUNGEE JUMPING

You find a highway bridge, or a trestle or a hot-air balloon or actually any place really stupid, as long as it's high and dangerous. Then you get a big rubber band maybe 200 feet long (the bungee itself), and you attach it to the bridge. Then you wrap the other end around your ankles. Then you jump. Now, most observers of the passing scene would have you believe that New Zealanders are sedate and calm compared to their earthier, louder cousins, the Australians. But beneath that Kiwi kalm, there must be a vein of total idiocy, and bungee jumping might just be the tip of the iceberg.

Bungee jumping

If you want to join the thousands of other crazed folks who have taken a dive, two of the best spots are near Queenstown on the South Island: the historic suspension bridge over the **Kawarau River gorge** on Highway 6 northeast of town, and the **Skipper's Canyon bridge** over the Shotover River north of town. The Kawarau jump is 143 feet; Shotover, 229 feet. It'll cost between NZ$90 and NZ$200 to do a jump. One outfit in Queenstown that does bungee jumps is run by A.J. Hackett, who took a dive off the Eiffel Tower and is generally regarded as the daddy of the bungee jumping business. The motto of his company: "Jump with the professionals—you'd be crazy not to." Right. Find his place at the corner of Shotover and Camp streets in Queenstown; ☎ (03) 442-1177.

For the saner members of our audience, try these diversions:

TAKE A HIKE

Kiwis like to walk so much that in 1975, Parliament passed legislation setting up a national system of trails intended to run from the north tip of the North Island to the south tip of the South Island. The system isn't completed yet, but there are hundreds of trails around the country, from gentle urban walkways to serious wilderness tracks that are only for the very fit. Many of the tracks are old Maori trails. You can go walkabout by yourself or on a guided tour; you can go for an hour or for a week. Many of the best hikes are in the country's system of national parks and nature preserves.

HIKING THE SOUTH ISLAND

Some of the finest trails in the country are in the south, either in the Alpine country or amongst the fjords on the southwest coast. Indeed, *the most famous of all New Zealand's trails is in the fjords, the world-renowned Milford Track. The track runs from Lake Te Anau to Milford Sound, a distance of about 30 miles.*

Because the Kiwis are so keen about hiking, they have made it relatively easy—and comfortable—to keep your body dry and warm out in the boonies. *There are something like 1,000 back-country huts, from the basics to some owned by private companies that have everything but a butler.* There are no fees to walk around national parks or reserves, but there is a charge for using most of the huts.

The huts basically come in three categories:

Category One huts are fully serviced, with cooking equipment, sleeping platforms with mattresses, toilets, washing facilities and water. They are usually heated and lighted and often have a hut warden on duty. These run about NZ$12 a night.

Category Two huts have sleeping platforms with mattresses, toilet and washing facilities and water. Some have cooking equipment, some do not. They are about NZ$8 a night.

Category Three huts are basic, with bunks or sleeping platforms, toilet and water. They are about NZ$4 a night. There is an annual pass for NZ$60 for the huts, or you can buy tickets—a category One hut would require three tickets, for example. The tickets are available from Department of Conservation offices, visitor centers and some businesses which display a hut ticket sign

A word about guided hikes in general: most include day packs, meals, rain gear, accommodations in lodges or hiking huts and the guides themselves. They can be booked from North America through travel agents. Or you can book them in New Zealand, realizing that if it's summer, many parties will already be filled, and if it's winter, some trails are closed. The guided tours can be for single tracks or a series of trails, and can be hard or soft. For example, one tour company, Alpine Recreation Canterbury Ltd. headquartered in Lake Tekapo (northwest of Timaru), offers a series of outings, using minibuses to get you to places to take day-hikes throughout the South Island. The 13-day small-group tour, including meals, rental equipment, accommodations, guides and boat cruises run about NZ$2500 per person (discount for groups).

Split Apple Rock, Abel Tasman National Park

There are literally dozens of companies offering guided tours all over New Zealand. *Generally, these guided tramps will start around NZ$100 a day per person.* Many are combined with other activities, such as river rafting, helicopter trips, jet boating or camping. *One of the most popular trekking areas is Abel Tasman National Park northwest of Nelson.* The best trail is probably the coastal track, with great views of Tasman Bay. The trek up the coast will take a couple of days, the stretch down the interior of the park a bit longer. *Be prepared for sand flies. It's usually crowded in the summer and the huts might be full; take a bag.*

HIKING THE NORTH ISLAND

While not as well known, there are several tracks on the North Island worth a visit, especially around Tongariro National Park, Lake Taupo and Urewera National Park. The Tongariro trails get you right in amongst the volcanic activity; probably the most interesting of the North Island excursions.

A final note. *In addition to the most powerful bug dope you can find, be sure to take along some water purification equipment* (or boil the drinking water.) The once-pristine rivers, lakes and streams of New Zealand are now subject to giardia, a very nasty little bug that can cause major internal distress. A transplanted American living near Nelson, Alan Riegelman, has a company that offers two- and three-week tours for day hikers and backpackers. Day hikers are given modest accommodations in private homes, farm stays or an occasional motel; backpackers do the campground number. Riegelman and his staff do 90 percent of the cooking to save money. The three-week tours, which include air fare from Los Angeles to Christchurch, run about *NZ$5500* per person; two week tours are around *NZ$3100* for backpackers and *NZ$3300* for day trippers. Informtion on the tours is available from his company, ★ ★ ★ **New Zealand Travelers Inc.**, P.O. Box 605, Shelburne, Vermont 05482; ☎ (802) 985-8865, or his New Zealand operation at Tealcot, Teal Valley RD1, Nelson, New Zealand; ☎ 545-1141.

MOUNTAIN CLIMBING

The next step up from serious hiking is, of course, mountain climbing. Does the name Edmond Hillary ring a bell? The man who, with sherpa Tensing Norkay, became the first human to climb Mt. Everest was born in New Zealand. He did a lot of his pre-Himalayan training in the Darren and Humboldt mountains between Queenstown and Milford Sound. The series of 10,000-foot-plus peaks in the Southern Alps offer climbing challenges from easy to advanced, from rock-face to ice fields. The government has placed mountaineering huts at strategic spots, or you can put your tent where you decide to stop. In addition to specialized companies, there are also local climbing clubs, and information is also available from national parks. Two good sources of information about mountain climbing possibilities are the **New Zealand Mountain Guides Association,** P.O. Box 20, Mt. Cook, or the New Zealand Mountain Safety Council, P.O. Box 6207, Wellington.

FISHING

New Zealanders are justifiably proud of their streams, filled with salmon, steelhead and trout, as well they should be. They get a little carried away now and then, proclaiming it to be the best in the world, but they might be close to right. What New Zealand offers that you don't often find in other great fishing spots is solitude. A tour bus driver on the way to Milford Sound said some of the streams we were passing were full of rainbow trout. "You see maybe two fishermen a year along here," he said, whereupon some of us collapsed into a mumbling heap, remembering the elbow-to-elbow crowds on the Au Sable in Michigan and the San Joaquin up by Mammoth Lakes in California. What this lack of fishing pressure means is large average catches. Eight-pound browns are not uncommon, for example.

Trout fishing on the Mohaka River

And the other beauty of fishing in New Zealand, aside from the silence, is the fact that there are great streams all over, some private, many public. *As we noted in the accommodations section, it's possible to spend a bundle and stay at one of the upscale fishing lodges on both islands. Or you can find a motel near a stream and have at it, as well.* Many lodges have their own private streams. The North Island, especially around the Bay of Islands, prides itself on great salt water fishing, but the South Island ain't far behind, with some fine opportunities for marlin and shark. New Zealand is surrounded by water, remember, meaning that surf casting is everywhere. And, to cap everything off, the Kiwis make it fairly cheap to cast a line. They do like it when you catch and release, which is the only civilized way to fish, anyway. A one-week license goes for about NZ$10, or a month for about NZ$30. Guides are also inexpensive, compared to some other places (Alaska comes to mind). Look for stream and lake trout guides to run from around NZ$200 to NZ$500 a day. There is **trout fishing** all year. Some speciality outfits will put you on a helicopter and drop you right next to a virgin mountain stream—this is where old trouters go to die. You can fish any style you want, but *most Kiwi trout fishers stick to fly fishing.*

Hiking to a secluded fishing hole in the Wairinaki Forest

Salmon fishing is found along the east coast of the South Island where a series of glacier and snow melt rivers flow to the sea. The country is majestic, the salmon fishing quite literally some of the best in the world. If you haven't tried it, fly fishing for salmon is one of the great challenges in life, right up there with throwing a fly at a bonefish or tarpon. One of the more popular east coast rivers is the Rakaia River, only 35 miles southwest of Christchurch.

DEEP SEA FISHING

For serious deep-sea activity, the waters around New Zealand, especially the east coast of the North Island, have some of the most active and least known sport around. **Striped marlin** average 200 to 300 pounds off New Zealand, with larger fish weighing in at 400 pounds or so. But there are also **blue marlin** up to 500 pounds and even an occasional **Pacific black marlin** that can go over 600 pounds.

As a for instance, there are about two dozen charter boats in the Paihia/Russell area of the Bay of Islands. The charter boats go from US$350 to US$600 per day and up. The fees normally include food, accommodations and tackle. Close in, for light tackle types, there are kingfish, cod, flounder and snapper, among others. No license is required for ocean fishing.

One good bet for a fishing tour is through **The Best of New Zealand Fly Fishing,** an outfit located in Los Angeles. It represents a number of fishing lodges in New Zealand, and has a variety of packages available. For example, a two-week, three-lodge tour of the South Island runs about US$4600 which includes air fare from Los Angeles, a rental car, accommodations, meals, fishing guides and helicopter fly-ins. A week at one lodge, including all the goodies and guides, runs around US$3500. Contact Mike McClelland at the company, 11872 La Grange Ave., Los Angeles CA 90025; ☎ (310) 826-9105, or ☎ (800)528-6129.

Another group well worth talking to is **Shoreline International**, based in San Jose, CA. The company, owned by New Zealanders, has worked out arrangements with most of the major fishing lodges in the country, and offers a wide range of fishing trips from stream fly fishing on both islands to game fishing off both coasts. You must provide your own transportation to New Zealand, and then internal transport to your fishing area. Once there, you are put up in a variety of accommodations, ranging from motel to such lush digs as the Huka Falls Lodge and the Moose Lodge. Professional guides and equipment, if needed, will be provided. Information: **Shoreline International,** 1004 Willow St., San Jose, Ca. 95125; ☎ (800) 932-5055, or ☎ (408) 294-2160. In New Zealand, the company address is RD1 Taupo Bay, Mangonui, Northland, New Zealand; ☎ (09) 406-0951. East Coast fishers might also want to contact **Frontiers,** a Pennsylvania-based company also organizing fishing/ hunting trips. Information: P.O. Box 959, Pearce Mill Road, Wexford, Pa. 15090; ☎ (800) 245-1950. In Pennsylvania, ☎ (412) 935-1577. Another possible is Pathways International, P.O. Box 3276, Spartanburg, S.C. 29304; ☎ (800) 628-5060 or ☎ (803) 583-7234.

As noted, many of the fishing lodges are also hunting lodges, with game ranging from rabbits to elk. In addition to open range hunting, there are a number of private herds of game animals that can be hunted for a per-trophy charge.

DIVING

There are several good diving areas in New Zealand, several of which are protected in marine reserves. The **Poor Knights Marine Reserve**, for example, is situated in the islands of the same name near Whangarei north of Auckland. The volcanic islands are filled with caves and lava tubes, and home to a wide variety of tropical fish and other marine animals. In the **Cavalli Islands**, off the east coast of the North Island near Whangaroa Harbour, *lie the remains of the Rainbow Warrior, the Greenpeace ship bombed in Auckland by the French Secret Service.* The ship was scuttled here to make an artificial reef and is an excellent diving spot. In the south, fjord diving offers a look at some of *the only black coral in the world growing less than 20 feet underwater*—layers of silty fresh water close off light, allowing the coral to grow. Underneath the fresh water is salt water with good visibility. The fjords and inlets of the South Island are also home to schools of friendly porpoises. There are dive shops throughout the country; to get air, you have to have a card certifying that you're a qualified diver.

RAFTING

The **Shotover River** *near Queenstown is famous as a whitewater challenge, with some rapids up to Grade 5 and long stretches of narrow canyons and walls of water six feet high.*

One of the rapids is called "Mother." It is. There is also a little beauty called **"The Toilet."** Not far behind is another Queenstown river, the Kawarau. The **Kawarau** has one quarter-mile stretch called the **Chinese Dogleg** which is about as hairy as it gets. On the North Island, there are several rivers worth a try, including the **Rangiaiki**, the **Wairoa** and the **Tongariro**, all of which can be as nasty as the southern streams.

There are literally dozens of companies offering trips, many of which combine accommodations, meals and helicopter trips as part of the package. You can do the rivers in short legs or days-long trips. In Queenstown, check with **Danes Shotover Rafts Ltd.,** which does the Shotover, the Kawawrau and the hard-to-get-to Landsborough River. It also does the **Wiatoto River**, which is almost all Grade 4-5 rapids. On the North Island, try **Huka Jets** in Taupo; ☎ (07) 374-8572.

Equipment check on the Mohaka River

JET BOATING

Jet boating is also a popular sport in New Zealand, and no surprise, the major rafting rivers are also the main targets for the jet boats. In the Queenstown area, it's the **Shotover** and **Kawarau** again, and on the North Island, the **Rangitaiki** and the **Waikato** are popular. Many of the jet boats are run in combination with helicopter trips and rafting excursions. For a jet boat trip only, expect to pay around NZ$40 to NZ$50. Combination trips run between NZ$100 and NZ$500. A good bet in Queenstown is **Shotover Jet**, which can be booked through any of the many tourist offices or by calling ☎ (03) 442-8570. On the North Island, try **Huka Jet** in Taupo, ☎ (07)374-8572.

The Shotover River

Also popular in New Zealand is **kayaking**, both in streams and in the ocean. Popular ocean areas include the Marlborough Sounds and also the fjords of the southwest coast. Rivers offer top kayaking with many chances at Grade 5 rapids. You can rent kayaks and canoes or take escorted tours. Kayak rentals run about NZ$30 a day, canoes NZ$20 a day or so.

GOLF

We have some friends who would probably trade in their first-born for a chance to play a good 18 holes any Saturday, any place, so it was no surprise a couple of years ago when they spotted one of the periodic good deals for air/drive trips to New Zealand and took off for a 10-day golfing spree. Part of their package included an RV, and they hit the ground putting, stopping wherever they could find a course. *They didn't have much trouble finding a course, either, what with more than 400 scattered around the country.* They are still raving about it. The Kiwis would have us believe that you can't drive 30 miles in any direction without hitting a golf course, and we'll take their word for it, since the whole country looks like a golf course to begin with.

Our golfing friends were also blown away by the prices and the lack of crowds. Some of the courses they play around Northern California can charge as much as US$200 green fees for 18 holes. Top courses in New Zealand might charge US$25, and the courses are almost always in excellent condition. *Many courses do not have golf carts; some, in fact, don't even allow pull-carts.* They have this silly idea that golf is supposed to be exercise. At the clubs which do offer electric carts, expect to pay about NZ$20 for a cart per round.

Most clubs welcome visitors, but note that some courses will be crowded in the summer. *Most of the private courses offer reciprocal memberships to members of North American clubs—just bring a letter of introduction from the club secretary.* The New Zealanders, who mostly disregard reality when it comes to weather, claim you can play golf all year, and thus off-season is dandy for overseas visitors because nobody's on the course. But there's a down side, too. We saw the course at Greymouth one spring day when the wind was blowing a full gale, and the rain was so heavy, a golf ball wouldn't have rolled three inches on a green.

Millbrook

At any rate, you'll find special tour offers from time to time, such as one not long ago for a nine-day golfing tour for about US$1600 per person, which included air fare from Los Angeles, green fees, accommodations, all internal travel, two meals a day, sightseeing and other special activities.

You can do what our friends did—toss your clubs on the plane and just take pot luck—or book a full tour in advance. Your best bet for information or tour bookings is **New Zealand Golf Excursions Ltd.**, 2041 Rosecrans Ave., No. 103, El Segundo, CA 90245; ☎ (800) 622-6606. General information in advance is available from Executive Director, **New Zealand Golf Association,** P.O. Box 11-842, Wellington. N.Z.

SAILING

Once upon a time, gazing out over the 30-below-zero snowbanks in our front yard in Minneapolis, we said, "This sucks," and decided, with some other demented friends, to build a boat and sail away from it all. Which, five years later, we did. It was a 38-footer, and we took it all the way down the Mississippi to the Bahamas. Paradise turned out to be a tad boring, so eventually we sold the boat and went back to work—in Minnesota. But the bug had definitely bitten.

Due to pecuniary problems and logistics, we haven't had a boat since, but that hasn't stopped the sailing. That first trip qualified us to the point that we can lease a bareboat yacht almost anywhere in the world, which, from time to time, we do. It is probably the most perfect of all vacations. It's not for everybody, of course, but if you are like us, or know somebody qualified to run a 30- to 40-foot boat, *New Zealand offers some of the finest—and safest—sailing waters in the South Pacific.*

Opua Harbour, Bay of Islands

And just to compound the problem, some of the deals available from time to time are downright criminal—for sailing vacations, that is. Like around US$4000 a couple, which includes round trip international air, a one-week charter of a 32-foot Beneteau (sure, they're beamy, but they're also very safe), an additional week's rental of a car and all accommodations, plus transfers. If you're a little unsure of your sailing skills, for an additional US$210, a professional, licensed sailing instructor will spend the first three days aboard showing you the ropes. As these things go, this is a very nice deal.

A lot of the sailing packages base you in the Bay of Islands, which is relatively mild because of the many anchorages and the fact that you're almost never out of sight of land. It's very much like sailing in some of the smaller Greek island groups. If sailboats aren't your thing, there are also cruisers for rent—a group of six aboard a 36-footer runs about US$1,500. There are a number of companies offering bareboat or crewed boats. One that seems to consistently have good deals is **Rainbow Yacht Charters**, which works with Air New Zealand and Mount Cook Line. In North America, contact Rainbow at ☎ (800) 446-5494.

We'd be deficient in our duties if we didn't mention our favorite rent-a-skipper in the whole world, Ron Palmer, who has probably the best job in the South Pacific. He owns a gorgeous, 55-foot, Australian-built, metal-hull ketch named the **Koloa**, and splits his time between New Zealand and the Kingdom of Tonga. He has day-sails, week-sails, or if you have the money, honey, he'll take you about anywhere in the South Pacific you want to go. We haven't sailed with him in New Zealand, but the parties and good times we shared in Tonga are the stuff of legend. He's based in Wellington or Vava'u in Tonga. He's the best. For information, contact him at **Koloa Yacht Charters**, P.O. Box 40-228, Wellington, ☎ (04) 277-856. Tell him we said howdy and ask about Flamenco.

SKIING

Some folks, not content with just looking at those gorgeous mountains, just have to ski them. No doubt about it, the chance to ski down a glacier or through absolutely virgin snow accessible only by helicopter is highly tempting to gung ho skiers. Most of the country's ski areas are in the South Island, within easy access of either Christchurch or Queenstown, the ski capital of New Zealand. In all there are about a dozen commercial ski areas and a dozen private club ski areas. Many of the private areas offer ski packages through tour agents. These areas tend to be a bit less sophisticated than the commercial areas, but many offer great skiing. There are also plenty of cross-country trails available. In addition, there are several companies which offer heli-skiing.

Packages are almost always available. Mount Cook Line and Air New Zealand usually offer winter packages (June-August) for maybe US$1,400 per person, which includes air travel to New Zealand, interior flights, first-class accommodations and ski lift tickets for **Coronet Peak** or the **Remarkables**, two of the best ski areas in the country. Check with Mount Cook Line in North America, ☎ (800) 345-3504.

Depending on location, the ski season can start as early as June and last through November. Generally it starts earlier on the South Island and lasts longer on the North Island. More than half of the commercial resorts have snow-making equipment. Most commercial areas charge about NZ$50 a day for lift tickets. In addition, just to make you grind your teeth, many commercial areas also have a road toll. Private roads, you see, and maintenance costs...still, it's a bit cheeky.

As an example of what you might expect from private club areas that do allow non-members to come and play is the **Mount Olympus** area, about 130 kilometers from Christchurch. There are four rope tows, accommodations in heated dormitory style huts (NZ$25 with three meals) and lift tickets for non-members going for NZ$22. *The North Island's two commercial ski areas are on either side of 9,174-foot Mount Ruapehu, an active, often smoldering volcano and the tallest mountain on the North Island* (9,173 feet). Both areas are inside **Tongariro National Park**, about 350 kilometers equidistant from Wellington and Auckland. The two areas are:

Whakapapa—It has 43 trails on **3,322** acres of terrain, with a total vertical drop of 615 meters (**2,018** feet). Among the lifts available are two quad chairs, five doubles and six T-bars. It has about a dozen advanced trails, some very hairy. It has three cafes and a restaurant. No accommodations.

Turoa—The drop here is 720 meters (**2,362** feet), with about 900 acres of skiable terrain. It has one quad, two triples and three T-bars plus other lifts. Like Whakapapa, it's possible to ski down to the bubbling lake in the mountain's crater. It has three cafes and a restaurant; no accommodations.

South Island commercial slopes include:

Mount Lyford—Lyford is new and at the moment not much to write home about. It has a vertical drop of **1,000** meters (**3,281** feet) and only four rope tows. The lift tickets are about half the other developed areas, however. It's about 140 kilometers north of Christchurch. It has a cafe, no accommodations. Plans are underway to expand its total area and facilities.

Rainbow Valley—The farthest north of the commercial areas on the South Island, with much better slopes than Lyford. *It has some short but nasty advanced slopes* (Dick's Drop comes to mind), but a lot of intermediate territory. It has a vertical drop of 280 meters (about **920** feet). It's about 140 kilometers southwest of Nelson. It has a cafe, no accommodations. Road toll.

Porter Heights—This is the closest ski area to Christchurch (90 kilometers), and has what many Kiwi skiers rate as *two of the best advanced runs in the country:* Big Mama and Bluff Face (we're talking damned near vertical drops). The owners have installed a new snow board run. The Heights also has the honor of being one of the few ski areas that has on-site accommodation - a 40-bed bunkhouse-style facility with meal service. The area has a vertical drop of 670 meters (about **2,200** feet), three T-bars and other lifts. Road toll.

Mount Hutt—*This is the prestige ski area in New Zealand, host to the first-ever World Cup ski races held in New Zealand, in 1990.* It sits in a huge bowl at the top of the mountain, with virgin powder fields at the top accessible only by helicopter. In addition, it has about 740 acres of skiable terrain, with 10 lifts including a quad, a triple and three T-bars. It has an advanced snowmaking system, which means it opens in May, closes in November. It has a restaurant, cafe and snack shop. It's about 100 kilometers from Christchurch. Road toll. There are no accommodations, but the resort village of Methven, about 25 kilometers away, has almost 30 lodges and motels.

Mount Dobson—As yet a small operation, Mount Dobson sits in a nice range of peaks near Lake Tekapo about 100 kilometers northwest of Timaru. With only a 415 meter drop (**1,360** feet), it's not the longest of areas, but *there are some short and tricky advanced runs* and huge areas of challenging intermediate stuff. It has only one T-bar and several other tows. It has a cafe.

Ohau—This area claims the longest T-bar in New Zealand, 1,033 meters (**3,390** feet) and has a very nice and very reasonable lodge on site (which is noted for some of the biggest ski parties in New Zealand). A double is about $90NZ, which includes lift tickets and meals—try to find that in Colorado. The area has a vertical drop of about **1,300** feet, and overlooks Lake Oahu where the lodge is situated. It's about 150 kilometers from Oamaru.

The five Queenstown-area commercial areas are:

The Remarkables—Named after the mountains that overlook the city, this area is about 20 kilometers north of town on the Invercargill highway. If you go all the way up the Shadow Basin chairlift, you get an incredible view of Lake Wakatipu and Queenstown. *It has a 325 meter vertical drop (about* **1,070** *feet), two quads and a double*. It has a cafe and restaurant; road toll. Like all the Queenstown-area facilities, buses run from town to the ski area and back. Note: none of the buses are free; expect to pay around NZ$20 for a round trip; the good news is that most of them will pick you up at your hotel. Combination lift tickets are available that let you also ski nearby Coronet Peak.

Coronet Peak—This is the oldest area around Queenstown, and while quite popular and well-admired for some of its runs, is *subject to chancy snow conditions because of its relatively low top altitude* (although snow-making equipment has now been installed). It has a 428 meter drop (about **1,400** feet), with one triple, a double and two T-bars. It has two cafes and a restaurant; no road fee.

Cardrona—Fully 75 percent of this sprawling area is set aside for beginner and intermediate, and was the site of the 1991 national snowboard championships. *It has two quads and a double.* There are two cafes and a restaurant; road fee. It's about 60 kilometers from Queenstown, which is easily spotted on a clear day from the top of the Captain's Quad.

Treble Cone—*This is where the experts come to play,* with 40 percent of the slopes devoted to advanced trails. The vertical drop is 660 meters (about **2,165** feet). There are several nice beginners' slopes as well as some aggressive intermediate. *There is also an excellent snowboard run.* The best advanced run is named—what else—Top Gun. It has one double and two T- bars. It's about 100 kilometers from Queenstown.

Waioru Nordic area—This is the South Island's premier cross-country facility, opened in 1989. *It is the only nordic-only area in the country,* offering about 25 kilometers of groomed trails—about 10k of which are beginners' trails. There is a ski rental shop, cafeteria and huts for overnight ski treks. The area is near Cardrona, about 50 kilometers from Queenstown. Fees are NZ$20 for adults; equipment rental about NZ$10. The season is July-September.

HELI-SKIING

Heli-skiing is popular all over the Southern Alps, including what some folks think is the greatest experience of all, skiing down the Tasman Glacier. The company to talk to about getting off the beaten path is Harris Mountains, a heli-ski outfit based in Queenstown and Wanaka.

First, they recommend that in order to try heli-skiing, you should be able to ski at least intermediate level. Normally, they will take you in a group of five or six similarly experienced skiers. The company offers 280 runs on 140 peaks on six separate mountain ranges, with runs varying between *2,000-* and *4,000-*foot vertical drops. The company builds its trips around the total vertical feet you can ski. For instance, you could shoot for the 100,000-foot vertical drop total, taking 12 days and 13 nights, for around NZ$8,000, including accommodations, meals, guides and the helicopter lifts. One-shots, on the other hand, start at around NZ$80 for a one-way ride.

Ski-planes on the Tasman Glacier

On the other side of the mountains, **Alpine Guides** also runs heli-skiing trips, including the ride up to the Tasman and Fox glaciers, plus runs on Mount Cook for advanced skiers. These trips cost about NZ$450, which seems to be the normal fee charged by most heli-skiing companies. Further information is included in a free ski guide available from the New Zealand Tourism Board in Santa Monica.

CYCLING

The lack of traffic and scenic views along New Zealand's highways make for almost ideal cycling tours of the country. On the South Island, especially, there are challenges for the experienced biker or easy riding for novices—or lazy types. And New Zealanders, unlike folks in some parts of the world, don't go out of their way to force cyclists into ditches or off cliffs.

There are bike rental agencies in most major cities and tourist centers. Or, you can book them ahead from North America. One company worth a try is **Pedaltours of New Zealand**, which has an office in Seattle. Tours can be road cycling or mountain biking or a combination of both, lasting from a week to 20 days or so, with routes on both North and South Islands. Prices, depending on itineraries and duration, run from about NZ$1,500 to NZ$4,000, which includes accommodations, meals and transfers; air fares extra. Information and brochures are available by calling ☎ (800) 788-6685 or writing to the company at 224 W. Galer, Suite B, Seattle, Wash. 98119.

THE ESSENTIAL
NEW ZEALAND

Milford Sound

HELPFUL HINTS & INSIDE TIPS

WHEN TO GO

The weather in New Zealand, being Down Under, is upside down compared to North America. Seasons below the equator are reversed; thus summer in New Zealand is December-February; fall is March-May; winter is June-August and spring is September-November. Generally, the North Island is warmer than the South Island, although, as noted, it snows in parts of the North Island, sometimes enough to block major highways and cause all sorts of horrid driving conditions. *And the hottest temperatures in the nation are likely to hit on the northeastern end of the South Island.* In the winter, you are almost guaranteed lousy traveling conditions on the west coast of the South Island as storms roar in across the Tasman and drop gallons of water or stiffer precipitation. Even in the shoulder seasons, spring and fall, it's not uncommon to run into week-long periods of rain and fog. Many a visitor has been disappointed driving down the highway expecting to see grand views of the Alps, but because of low clouds and rain, never catching sight of towering Mount Cook or the glaciers. Aside from the west coast of the South Island, *the heaviest rainfall totals are found around the Bay of Plenty on the North Island, which gets something like 65 inches a year.*

Wellington—Windy Wellington, sitting on the Cook Strait—also rains at the drop of the hat, averaging about 50 inches a year. Sometimes down south, it seems the storms are definitely anti-Yank. They hit the west coast and sometimes start going counter-clockwise, and if you're driving the same way, say from Greymouth to Invercargill and up to Christchurch, the deluges follow right along. After three days of seeing nothing but windshield wipers and wet sheep, you will wonder why you have come. But another group of tourists, just a few days behind you, will have nothing but bright sunlight all the way. Note also that it's not unusual to have a nasty storm roar in during the summer, chilling the air and dampening the party. It can get plumb hot too, especially the Canterbury Plains where Christchurch sits. ChCh has been known to get well above 100 degrees. Still, in spite of the sometimes iffy weather, we think the best times to see New Zealand are in the off-seasons. Air fares tend to be lower, all the Kiwi kids are in school, the hot tourist spots are nearly vacant and you can drive around for hours, particularly on the South Island, and see maybe two cars an hour. In the summertime, by contrast, especially during the Christmas holidays, it's almost impossible to get your RV aboard the Cook Strait ferries because they've been booked for sometimes a year ahead. And given a complete choice, *we'd opt for February-April, when things tend to be just a bit more settled.*

The only way to approach New Zealand weather is with a leery eye. It's no joke that some days, you get all four seasons in an hour, and the chance of rain is almost a universal given. It's a good idea to take an umbrella and rain gear. And a periscope. Wait till you get there to buy a sweater, however.

HOW TO GET THERE

New Zealand is about 6,500 miles southwest of San Francisco, 4,600 miles from Honolulu, 1,300 miles from Australia—in any direction, a long haul.

BY PLANE

While cruise ships do call in from time to time, flying is the obvious way to get there. The cheapest fares will be from the West Coast, and folks living Back East will have to add the time—and the money—needed to get to Los Angeles, San Francisco or Honolulu onto their travel plans. In some instances, as we have noted, a trip to New Zealand is part of a package which includes Australia. Often these itineraries begin in Australia, then fly from Sydney to either Wellington or Auckland. The major international airport in New Zealand is in Auckland, where most West Coast-originated flights will land. The airport, about 14 miles outside town, is new and modern and split into two parts, domestic and international, about a quarter-mile apart. A taxi from the airport to town costs about NZ$35; an air-porter bus which hits the main hotels, is about NZ$10. There are also international airports at Wellington and Christchurch. A number of North American carriers serve New Zealand. U.S. companies include United and Continental Airlines. Canadian Pacific flies from Vancouver and Toronto. These flights are all one-stops, usually in Hawaii. Major foreign airlines are Air New Zealand (the national carrier), Qantas (the Australian national carrier) and UTA (part of Air France). Polynesian Airlines (Western Samoa) has service to Auckland from Los Angeles through Samoa. Fares from the West Coast depend on when you go. In the off-seasons, expect to pay about US$1,000 per person for a round trip ticket. In high season (Kiwi summer), fares will run around US$1,400. New Zealand needs tourist dollars, and it seems there are always some very attractive packages to lure us down, many offering free or reduced rates on cars or campers or accommodations. For instance, a year or so ago, one Southern California agency was offering to sell one high season round- trip ticket on Air New Zealand for US$1,300—and a second companion ticket for US$250. Plus, the price included a free car for a week—and accommodations. Or another deal, this one from a leading New Zealand tourist company, offered a 15-day coach tour of the country for US$2,249 per person including air and accommodations; the same company sold a round trip ticket for about US$1,250 and threw in a camper for a dollar. To check on what current deals are available, contact the airlines, the New Zealand Tourism Board, your local newspaper or your travel agent.

NOTE: *New Zealand charges an airport departure tax that must be paid at the airport in New Zealand currency.* However, major credit cards may be used in lieu of Kiwi dollars. Some domestic airports are also pondering a departure tax—keep some cash handy.

FORMALITIES

Passports are required for U.S. and Canadian citizens. They must be valid for at least three months after the passenger's arrival in New Zealand. Entry permits will be issued at the airport on arrival and are good for three months. New Zealand, like Australia, is free of many diseases prevalent in other parts of the world—such as rabies—and wants to keep it that way. So, all planes bound for the country are by law sprayed to kill bugs and smaller pests that might have hopped aboard. You sit in your seat, they pass by spraying into the air. On one trip, we were sprayed before take-off in Hawaii, on another we were sprayed on arrival in Auckland. Whatever, you will be sprayed before you leave the plane; they claim it's safe. You will also have to fill out a declaration form listing what foods, plants or animal materials you are carrying. *Fishers note: you can bring rod, reel and lures, but no flies made from chicken feathers* (if in doubt, leave the flies at home). There is no limit on the amount of currency, foreign or New Zealand, that can be brought into the country. There are **currency exchange** offices at the Auckland airport and at most banks in towns and cities. Visitors can bring in these amounts of taxable goods: 200 cigarettes, or 250 grams of tobacco, or 50 cigars or a mixture of all three weighing not more than 250 grams (about 8 ounces); 4.5 liters of wine (six regular-sized bottles of wine, 750 milliliters) and a quart bottle of booze (not to exceed 1,125 milliliters).

MEDICINE

New Zealand's liberal medical services are not extended free to visitors. The Kiwi government strongly recommends that you have health insurance that covers personal problems overseas. Some American HMOs and **health insurance** companies do have overseas coverage. Check with your company, or insurance agent, before leaving. **Trip insurance,** which can cover everything from lost luggage to major medical emergencies, is available from travel agents. A policy we looked at, for example, offered a US$50,000 policy for about US$200. It included death and dismemberment coverage, as well as lost luggage and trip cancellation insurance. It also included enough money to ship your body home if you died overseas. We raise this only because a couple from California was killed in New Zealand, and the family did not have enough money to ship the bodies home. The United States government will not pay for such services, nor will the governments of most foreign nations. *Visitors are covered, however, for accidents. Under New Zealand law, you are entitled to benefits as the result of an accident, regardless of blame.* Benefits normally include hospitalization and medical treatment. New Zealand, because of its isolation, has no dangerous reptiles or other nasties—except for one very rare, semi-dangerous spider; see Animals.

MONEY, WEIGHTS & MEASURES

The Kiwis, like the Americans, Canadians, Australians and a bunch of others, call their currency the dollar, which we are told probably came from the German word *taler.* It always causes confusion in prices to have all those different dollars running around. *All prices in this book, unless otherwise noted, are in New Zealand dollars* because of the fluctuations in the exchange rates between our dollars and theirs. The mid-1990s exchange rate is somewhere around 50 to 60 cents U.S. to the New Zealand dollar. Kiwi banknotes come in 1, 2, 5, 10, 20, 50 and 100 dollar denominations. Coins come in 1, 2, 5, 10, 20 and 50 cent pieces. Banks are normally open from 9:30 a.m.–4:30 p.m., Monday–Friday, but some also have currency exchange windows open on Saturdays and some holidays. Major credit cards are accepted everywhere—especially MasterCard and Visa. Foreign currency traveler's checks are accepted by large hotels, banks and resorts. *Note that most smaller stores will not accept foreign currency travelers checks.* Everybody seems to take New Zealand traveler's checks—you might think about changing your Yankee checks into Kiwi ones to save bank time. Gas stations and dairies (the corner market) are usually open seven days. *Weights and measures are officially metric, although you'll find many folks still hanging in with the old English measures.* It wouldn't be uncommon to hear somebody measuring a board say it was "two meters and about a quarter-inch." And in some parts of the country, they still figure beer in ounces and vow to never give in to the metric system. Canadians, who have already gone metric, will supposedly have no problems. For Americans, all you need to know is that gasoline comes in liters, distances are posted in kilometers, temperatures are in Celsius and things are weighed in kilograms. It's not that tough. If you're in a rental car, the speedometer is in kilometers, so if the limit is 60, just drive 60 and forget miles. (If you absolutely have to know, multiply the number of kilometers by .62 and you'll get the miles.) For temperatures, just remember water freezes at 0, 20 is mild, 30 is damned hot and if it's 40, you're probably in the Canterbury Plain area and need a cold beer immediately. A kilogram is about 2.2 pounds. If you forget all this, don't worry, just ask somebody. After all, they've only been at this metric business a few years themselves.

ELECTRICITY

New Zealand current is 230 volts, 50 hertz. Just to be difficult, the usual European two-round-prong plug is not used. Instead, they use a three-pronged flat plug that looks like a smaller version of the plugs Americans use on electric clothes driers. Norelco's international travel kits have a plug that will work in New Zealand and Australia (two, rather than three prongs, but ok) and converter plugs can be found in some department stores and camping outlets in New Zealand. The Norelco kit is a good idea, anyway, because it contains a 50-watt and 1,600-watt transformer in case you're carrying appliances that won't convert to 220. If you're going upscale, forget all the electricity differences, because *most high-grade hotels in the country have 110-volt outlets in the bathrooms,* or if not, loaner transformers that will do the job. (Many of the 110-outlets will not safely handle hair driers and other high-wattage appliances, however.)

PHONES

Phone service is efficient and relatively expensive. Local calls are NZ20 cents a minute. Overseas calls from pay phones are high, in the neighborhood of NZ$3 a minute to North America. *Many pay phones will not accept coins. Instead, they take plastic cards with magnetized strips* that come in various denominations from NZ$5 to NZ$50. Just stick the card in the phone, dial your number, and the fee is automatically deducted from the card. A display on the phone tells you how much money is left on the card. The cards, which can be bought in many local stores displaying a Telecom PhoneCard sign, are quite colorful, showing various scenes from New Zealand life. *The phone numbers we list in this book are subject to change.* Currently, New Zealand numbers, like those in Australia, are not standardized. Some places have seven digits, some five or six. The New Zealand government phone service, Telecom, is trying to standardize numbers. So if a number we listed turns out to be completely wrong, we apologize. It probably wasn't our fault. *The emergency number in most localities to summon police or fire is 111—no coin or card required.* You get the operator by dialling 010; for directory information, 100. If you do much calling in New Zealand, you'll soon run into the Kiwi habit of doubling and tripling numbers when they talk. For instance, an American would read this phone number—544-1117—as "five-four-four, one-one-one-seven." But the Kiwis would say "five-double four, triple one-seven," which, when spoken rapidly and with a New Zealand accent, can be most confusing. They also double and triple street addresses.

TIME

New Zealand is just the other side of the International Date Line from North America, so it's always ahead of us. Like Tonga, it's close enough to the dateline for New Zealanders to claim that they live where time begins. (Auckland sits at about 175 degrees east latitude.) Anyway, New Zealand is 12 hours ahead of Greenwich Mean Time. That means it's 20 hours ahead of Los Angeles. And that means when it's noon in Wellington, it's 4 p.m. the day before in Los Angeles. So you want to call home? One way to make it a little easier is just forget the 20-hour bit and figure that Wellington is 4 hours behind Los Angeles, but a day ahead. Make sense? If it's 10 a.m. Monday in Wellington, then it's 4 hours later in San Francisco, or 2 p.m., but a day earlier, or Sunday. The country goes on daylight savings time from October to March. The easy way around the whole thing is to buy a watch with room for two times zones, or not to call home.

GETTING AROUND

Many of the special packages offered by New Zealand or North American agencies combine air travel with either a rental car or RV. There are also many fly/car-drive packages that include accommodations. We discuss motoring vacations in the drive section later in this chapter. *For those who simply can't afford to drive, or because of one thing and another will not drive in New Zealand, there are still many options that will let you get out and around to see the country.* In fact, we know of no other country that makes it so easy to see it all, whether you're a backpacker or a stock broker.

LEAVE THE DRIVING

At the top of the list are dozens and dozens of bus tours, which is a very good way to see the country—New Zealand has an excellent group of tour operators who can tailor a guided vacation to your special needs or desires. You can stay in New Zealand private homes, farms, B&Bs, motels, top hotels, hostels. Or you can do your own bus tour on your own time at your own pace. A bus in New Zealand, by the way, is called a "coach." **Guided bus tours** come in all sizes, all shapes, all itineraries. Generally, a tour of sights and attractions on both islands is set on a 12-day schedule, although there are a number of tours that go longer. Prices also vary widely, depending on style of accommodation, destination, meal policy and tour length. We saw one trip advertised for 16 days around both islands for about US$2,300 per person, not including international air and including two meals a day. But another company was offering a 14-day tour of both islands for US$2,000 per person, including round trip air from the U.S., accommodations and breakfasts. So you have to shop around. In addition to the grand tours, it is also possible to take short bus tours around interesting spots. For instance, one Kiwi company was offering a three-day tour from Auckland to Rotorua for about NZ$430 per person, double occupancy. The price included most meals, guided tours and superior accommodations. There is also an hour and a half tour of Auckland for NZ$18, or take a coach tour of the city followed by dinner on a sailing yacht for about NZ$80—endless possibilities. Many of these bus tours can be booked from North America; or if you choose, you can wait until you get to New Zealand.

Reservations are probably a good thought in the summer for some of the more popular tours, such as Queenstown or Te Anau to the Milford Sound. But, you say, you hate tour groups, wouldn't be caught dead on a tour bus, want to do it your way or no way at all. Not to worry. New Zealand has an extensive **public transportation** system. The major bus line is *InterCity,* which also operates the nation's passenger train service, both of which connect to the Inter-islander vehicle and passenger ferry service between the two islands.

BUSES

The buses go to more than 1,000 communities and all major tourist spots. This means *with a travel pass from InterCity, you can see the whole country without buying additional tickets.* The **InterCity Travelpass** comes in three types: 8 days of travel in a 14-day period for about NZ$380; 15 day's travel in a 22-day period, about NZ$470, and 22 days in a 31-day period, about NZ$620. The passes can be purchased in North America from travel agents, or in New Zealand. InterCity also has a special pass for backpackers, good for 30 days. It combines the InterCity buses, the Interislander ferries and most trains with a special backpacker's bus, the Kiwi Experience. The bus (actually several buses) runs from Auckland to Wellington and back, and from Picton to Queenstown to Christchurch to Picton. You can get on and off the buses at will as long as you confirm your seat. Using the Kiwi Experience and the other buses and trains, you can pretty much go where you want, when you want.

Presently, the backpacker passes are not available in North America, but can be purchased at InterCity offices or travel agencies in New Zealand. The passes are actually a packet of vouchers. Two vouchers are used for a train trip, for example, or one for each InterCity bus trip. The prices are 10 vouchers, about NZ$315; 15 vouchers, NZ$420, and 20 vouchers, about NZ$525. InterCity also has a **Youth Hostel Association** pass. The pass gives you 50 percent off on all InterCity services except sightseeing buses. The 14-day card is about NZ$80 or 28-day for about NZ$110. Another choice in the South Island is Mount Cook Landline, which serves most of the major southern cities. The company offers the **Kiwi Coach Pass**, which is used in conjunction with other bus companies to provide service to the whole country. The pass, depending on what season you travel, starts at 7 days during an 11-day period for about NZ$330 to 33 days in a 45-day period starting at about NZ$700. Passes are available both in New Zealand or from travel agents at home. A North Island alternative is **Newmans Coach Lines**, which also uses other bus lines for additional service. The Newmans passes are good either for one island or both. Two-island, 7-day passes are about NZ$$260, 30-day about NZ$550. The one-island passes are about NZ$220 for seven days, about NZ$500 for a 30-day pass. The passes can be purchased before or after arrival in New Zealand.

AIR TRAVEL

There are three major domestic airlines in New Zealand: **Air New Zealand, Ansett New Zealand** and **Mount Cook Airlines.** All three have travel passes. Air New Zealand offers the Visit New Zealand Pass, which is good for four or six sectors; four for about NZ$400, six for about NZ$500. The pass must be purchased outside New Zealand. The airline also has **Thrifty Fares**, which also must be purchased before arrival, which allow 40 percent discounts on domestic flights subject to availability. Other discounts are also available. Ansett has the See New Zealand Fares, which represents a saving of about 30 percent on internal travel. The pass can be purchased either inside or outside New Zealand. Note, however, that tickets purchased before arrival are not subject to the current 12.5 percent goods and services tax. Mount Cook's reductions are covered by its **Kiwi Air Pass,** which also allows discounts on the airlines' flightseeing trips to the glaciers and other destinations. The pass can be purchased before or after arrival. The cost is about NZ$900. The domestic airlines use a combination of modern short-haul aircraft, including 737s, BAE Whisperjets and Dash 8s. If you're not on an air pass, some sample one-way fares might be: Auckland-Christchurch,NZ$320; Auckland-Queenstown, NZ$540; Auckland-Wellington, NZ$240; Wellington-Christchurch, NZ$200.

BY TRAIN

Modern, fairly fast, efficient, comfortable—if train trips are to your liking, several routes in New Zealand are right up your tracks. They're less expensive than air travel and a bit smoother than buses. The main cities are routinely served, as are several scenic routes. *As noted, the InterCity passes are also good for rail travel.* Most trains are non-smoking. We have heard very few complaints about Kiwi trains. They do tend to keep them a bit overheated in the winter, the legroom and seats are a tad small and the overhead storage is a bit undersized. The main trains are: **The Silver Fern** is the daytime commuter special between Auckland and Wellington. The trip, about 430 miles, takes about 10 hours, and leaves both ways Monday-Saturday at around 8:30 a.m. Morning and afternoon snacks, as well as lunch are served; bar service is available. The cost is about NZ$100 one way. Overnight, non-sleeper service between the two cities is available on the **Northerner**, which leaves both ways around 8 p.m. and arrives around 6:40 a.m. Light meals are for sale, as are tickets to a lounge where videos are screened. The cost is about NZ$75. **The Coastal Pacific** runs from Christchurch to Picton daily along the east coast of the South Island, often offering some very nice scenery. (Sit on the right side going north.) The daily service leaves ChCh at 8:10 a.m. and arrives in time to catch the 2:20 p.m. ferry to Wellington— the ferry doesn't sail until the train arrives. Southbound, the train leaves at 2 p.m. and arrives in Christchurch at 7:25 p.m. It's a non-smoking car and has food and beverage service. The cost is about NZ$50 one way. One of the more popular trips is on the daily **Tranz-Alpine Express,** which runs from Christchurch up over Arthur's Pass to Greymouth. The trip over to Greymouth and back can be done in a long day. The express leaves ChCh at 7:40 a.m., arriving in Greymouth at 12:25 p.m. You can take a bus tour of Greymouth during the hour or so you're there, which is no big deal. The return trip starts at 1:40 p.m. and you return to Christchurch around 6:30 p.m. The scenery is marvelous, and you'll marvel at the engineering, including about 20 tunnels, one of which is about 5 miles long. Food and bar service available. Round-trip cost for the trip is about NZ$80. **The Southerner** is the main South Island route, and runs from Christchurch down the east coast to Invercargill, Monday–Friday. It leaves ChCh about 8:40 a.m., arrives in Dunedin around 2:30 p.m., then Invercargill around 6:10. The same service leaves Invercargill at 9:20 a.m., arriving in Christchurch around 7 p.m. Buffet car and bar service are available. One way is about NZ$70. In addition to these express trains, there is other service on slower, less-scheduled timetables between major cities, as well as service to smaller communities and resort areas.

White water river thrills in Queenstown

ACROSS THE STRAIT

It was the last crossing of the day, leaving Picton about 7:45 p.m., and it was one of those nights—windy, spitting rain, cold. Behind the ticket agent in the Picton Interislander Ferry office is a big wheel with an arrow on it to tell passengers at a glance what the sea conditions are like. While we watched, he moved it from bad to worst: high seas, lousy visibility, a nightmare for anybody who gets even remotely seasick. It was an interesting crossing, seas running very high, big car ferry heeling over and over until the decks seemed to almost touch the water. They closed the bars and only a few people were wandering around. Three hours of either hell or fascination, depending on your inner ear. We raise this only to point out that *the Cook Strait separating the North and South Islands can be very wicked*—so bad that on rare occasions the crossings are cancelled.

BY FERRY

It's the only break in a 900-mile stretch of mountains, and the Roaring Forties are funneled through the strait with a vengeance. Winds of up to 150 miles an hour have been recorded at Wellington. But it's not always a tempest—on other trips we've taken, it's been almost like glass. *That's the way it goes in New Zealand—if you don't like the weather, wait a minute.* New Zealand is fairly rare, as countries go, because it is divided in two by water. Maybe some day in the distant future, they'll build a bridge over the strait (about 15 miles across at the narrowest point), but in the meantime, if you want to go north or south you either fly or take the ferry.

For North Americans, it's amazing to discover there are a number of New Zealanders who have never visited one island or the other. Take the trip in the daytime, at least one crossing. *The scenery is wonderful, particularly coming out of Picton, up Queen Charlotte Sound and into the strait.* It reminded us of the trip between Helsinki and Stockholm, fir trees and islands and fjord-like waters. Coming into Wellington, you are greeted by hundreds of sea birds, especially large Dominican and red-billed gulls. *The Interislander line makes the crossing quite comfortable on its two modern passenger/vehicle ferries, the Arahura and Aratika*, plus the freight ship, Arahanga, which has limited vehicle space. Both the passenger ships are equipped for handicapped travel (elevators, special toilets), and come with all the amenities you'd expect on a small cruise ship—cafeterias, restaurants, fast-food outlets, movie theaters, bars, observation lounges, souvenir shops, arcade games, kiddy play areas, television. The crossing, depending on the weather gods, takes about 3 hours. The food is good, not great. But the beer is cold.

The normal schedule calls for three or four sailings each way all week, with the first around 8 a.m. from Wellington or 5:30 a.m. from Picton, and the last crossing at 6:40 p.m. from Wellington, 7:40 from Picton. The fare schedule depends on the time of year, and is divided into standard and bargain fare seasons. The fare periods are fairly complicated and subject to change, and should be checked before leaving for New Zealand. Rental agencies, for reasons best left for them to explain, will not let you take a car between islands, but rental RVs are OK. A number of discounted fares are available. Some approximate sample fares: During bargain periods, passengers on foot, one way are about NZ$30 per person. But if all you want to do is ride the ferry as an outing, a one-day excursion fare for a round trip is also NZ$30; the excursion tickets must be purchased a week in advance. During standard periods, add about NZ$10 to these fares. Kids under four travel free. Two passengers plus a small RV would be about NZ$120 in the bargain periods, and about NZ$150 in the standard periods. Good deals are available if you travel on any weekend except the period between early December and mid-February. This is holiday time in New Zealand, and spaces are often reserved a year in advance, especially vehicle spaces. Under New Zealand law, the ships must undergo safety and maintenance surveys once a year, so there will be periods when only two of the three will be in service. It's important to make reservations during these times.

If you're making the crossing in fall or spring you probably won't have a problem getting aboard without reservations, but calling ahead is always a smart play. If you are hoofing it, note that the Picton dock is within walking distance of the train station, and free buses are provided in Wellington to get you from the dock to the trains—except for the one crossing a week that leaves Picton around 10:30 p.m.

INFORMATION

Your first best look at New Zealand will be from the **"New Zealand Book,"** a magazine-style publication available free from the country's tourism offices in North America. In addition to basic information, it also contains advertisements from many of the major companies that offer services in New Zealand. It splits the country up into regions with information about accommodations and transportation. The tourism offices also have a number of special interest publications available on such things as fishing, farm stays and adventure travel. The North American offices of the New Zealand Tourism Department are located at 501 Santa Monica Blvd., No. 300, Santa Monica, Calif. 90401, ☎ (800) 388-5494; and at the New Zealand consulate at Suite 1200, 888 Dunsmuir St., Vancouver, B.C. V6C 3K4; ☎ (800) 888-5494. Once in New Zealand, you'll find that every community of any size has a visitor information office where you can check on local attractions, as well as get information on accommodations and food. There are also a number of regional tourism offices available.

For informational purposes, New Zealand is broken up into six regions by the New Zealand Tourism Department in Wellington, which are in turn divided into sub-regions.

Region I

also known as Northland, is all of the country north of Auckland.

Region II

takes in Auckland, the Bay of Plenty, Coromandel Peninsula, East Cape, Hawke's Bay, Rotorua and the Lake Taupo area.

Region III

is the south half of the North Island, including the area around lovely Mt. Egmont and south to Wellington.

Region IV

is basically the west coast and north end of the South Island, including Franz Josef and the Fox glaciers.

Region V

is the Canterbury area on the east coast of the South Island, including Christchurch, Mount Cook National Park, Akaroa and Lake Tekapo.

Region VI

is the fjord country of the southwest coast, the Otago Peninsula and Dunedin, Stewart Island and the famous Milford Track. Among the many local tourist offices available are: for **Region I,** the Whangarei Visitors Bureau, Tarewa Park, Otaika Road, ☎ 0800 657-474, or (09) 438-1079; open from 8:30 a.m.–5 p.m.

For Region II, Auckland International Airport Visitor Centre, open 24 hours at the International Terminal, ☎ (09) 275-6467. **Region III,** Wellington City Information Centre, Wakefield Street, Old Town Hall Building, ☎ (04) 735- 063, open 9-5. **Region IV,** Nelson Visitor Centre, Trafalgar and Halifax streets, ☎ (03) 548-2304, open 8-5. **Region V,** in Christchurch, the Canterbury Information Centre, Worcester Street and Oxford Terrace, ☎ 799-629. **Region VI**, Queenstown, New Zealand Tourist and Publicity (NZTP) office, 49 Shotover Street, ☎ (03) 442-8238.

HOLIDAYS

The major national holiday, the equivalent of the Fourth of July, is **Waitangi Day** on the 6th of February, which commemorates the signing of the Treaty of Waitangi in 1840. Despite mixed feelings in the Maori community, Waitangi Day usually sees a fair share of traditional Maori festivals throughout the country, especially at the spot near Russell where the pact was signed. Other national holidays include: Jan. 1—**New Year's Day, Good Friday, Easter Monday** and **Anzac Day**—commemorating the landing of Australian and New Zealand troops at Gallipoli in 1915, April 25. **Queen's Birthday**—First Monday in June. **Labour Day**—Fourth Monday in October. **Christmas Day**—Dec. 25. **Boxing Day**—normally Dec. 26.

In addition to the national holidays, there are many local observances throughout the year, which might find you facing closed banks and stores. Always check ahead with a local tourist office and with the New Zealand tourism offices in North America. **School holidays** usually mean families are out and about, meaning crowds. The actual dates vary from year to year, but generally expect these school holiday periods: **May holidays**, for both primary and secondary, second to fourth weeks in May; **Mid-term break**, primary and secondary, first two weeks in July; **August holidays**, primary, first two weeks of September; and secondary, last week of August, first two weeks of September; **Christmas holidays**—primary, last two weeks of December, all of January; secondary, last three weeks of December, all of January.

HOURS

Normal shopping hours in New Zealand are Monday-Thursday, 9 a.m.–5:30 p.m., Fridays 9 a.m.–9:30 p.m. and Saturdays 10 a.m.–1 p.m. Some stores in tourist areas might be open on Sundays.

Banks, as noted, are generally open from 9:30 a.m.–4:30 p.m. Monday–Friday. Post offices are open from 8:30 a.m.–5 p.m. Monday-Thursday and until 8 p.m. Fridays.

EMBASSIES

In case of trouble, both the United States and Canada have embassies in Wellington. U.S. citizens should note that American embassies and their consular sections are limited in the amount and type of help they can offer. They are not travel agencies, they are not banks, they are not welfare agencies. They will not, for example, pay hospital costs or pay for airplane tickets to get you home if you become stranded or critically ill. They can help you by contacting relatives back home and are able to replace passports if they have been lost or stolen. The U.S. embassy is at 29 Fitzherbert Terrace, Thorndon, ☎ 722-068. The Canadian High Commission is in the ICI House, Molesworth Street, ☎ 739-577.

WHERE TO STAY

One of the real joys of a visit to New Zealand is the huge variety of places to hang your hat, everything from farm stays to 5-star hotels, trout-fishing lodges to thermal spas, youth hostels to motel chains. And, being New Zealanders, they go out of their way to make it easy to pick your choice. As we have mentioned, government travel agencies, national airlines and North America-based wholesalers and travel agencies are zealously trying to lure travelers Down Under, and there always seem to be some excellent package deals available, almost all of which include accommodations. And in most cases, the choice of accommodations is up to you. One of the very best ways to get up close to New Zealand and its friendly folks is to stay in their homes. There are literally hundreds of home stay places around the country, or if you want to get close to the national animal—the sheep—scads of farms ready to roll out the red carpet. These sorts of accommodations are available to independent travelers on their own in bus, car or train and are also part of escorted tours.

HOME & FARM STAYS

There are several nation-wide organizations which among them represent nearly all home and farm stay places in the country. Using North American wholesalers and travel agencies, you can book and prepay a whole series of stays allowing you to tour one or both islands. Some samples: **Rural Holidays New Zealand Limited** offers

South Island farm stays, complete with three meals, for about NZ$80 per person a night; kids between NZ$30 and NZ$45 depending on age. These rates are without tax.

A farmstary in Hawkes Bay

A typical farm might have sheep and deer, maybe some horses, often a private trout stream, perhaps a tennis court, swimming pool, and lots of "tramping" trails. Some are large, most small, and all are willing to show you how the rural life is practiced in Kiwiland. They'll even let you milk the sheep, if you've a mind. If you like set itineraries, New Zealand Farm Holidays Limited has self-drive or coach/rail packages covering both islands.

For instance, a week-long tour of the South Island, including an unlimited kilometerage, manual rental car, accommodations, meals and insurance, will run about NZ$1,800 for a couple. If you have your own rental car, you may purchase accommodations/meal vouchers for around NZ$80 per person per day. There is also a 7-day rail/coach tour for about NZ$1,300, per person, which includes transfers from public transportation centers to the farms. Or a four-day, self-drive trip around the North Island goes for about NZ$700 per couple. Another good bet is the **Farmhouse and Country Home Holidays** group, which also has self-drive or rail coach packages. Prices are comparable to the others; a week self-drive around the North Island will run about NZ$1,400. A free bed and breakfast brochure is available from the New Zealand Tourism Board in Santa Monica.

OVERNIGHT IN A PUB?

One interesting group, which we tried several times with great success, is Pub Beds. Yes, indeed, they put you up in—or usually over—a friendly Kiwi pub in cities and towns all over the country. The pubs run from historic and quaint to new and modern. Some are hotels with pubs attached, some are pubs with rooms attached. And most are economy priced and the rooms, while not fancy, are clean. One of our favorites is the **Law Courts in Dunedin**, complete with family restaurant and two very comfy bars for about NZ$55 for a double with private bath.

Another is the venerable **Mountaineer Hotel** in the heart of Queenstown, NZ$60 double with private bath. Note: reservations to the member pubs must be made directly, not through a travel agent. Your host at a member pub will, however, make reservations ahead for you at no cost. For information, contact **Pub Beds**, Box 21, Auckland; ☎ (09) 274-2600.

If you're in Auckland, check with the folks at the **Albion Hotel** at the corner of Wellesley and Hobson streets for information about the group. In Wellington, try the **St. George Hotel**, corner of Willis and Boulcott streets. Members of the group have brochures which entitle you to discounts. There are several motel chains in New Zealand, and in all, there are some 1,400 motels and motor inns around the country. Most of the chains have discount passes for tourists. Prices for a good unit will run you between NZ$70 and NZ$100 or so. Many, such as the motels in the Golden Chain group, have kitchen facilities. *Also, New Zealand, like Australia, has the very civilized practice of including an electric kettle and tea/coffee makings in motel rooms.* Most motels can be booked ahead from North America or at member motels in the country after arrival.

RV PARKS

Another cost-saving alternative is to stay at a caravan park—what we'd call an **RV park**. Many parks have permanent tourist units for rent, either in cabins, small motel-style units or in camper vans. Prices vary, but on-site camper vans will run about NZ$40 per unit, which usually includes cooking gear. Bedding is usually available for rent. Cabins without cooking facilities or hot and cold water will run around NZ$30 per couple; cabins with cooking facilities and water about NZ$40 per couple, and "en suite," or cabins with private bath but no cooking facilities, about NZ$40. The full shot—a tourist flat, complete with private bath and cooking facilities—will run around NZ$50 per couple. *New Zealand, as we have said, is a backpacker's paradise, one of the easiest places we've seen to do the hostel scene.*

YOUTH HOSTELS

Any tourist office in the country will have a bunch of brochures on local hostels, as well as hostel groups with units around the country. The hostels are generally first-class and are found in big cities, as well as in popular tourist areas. Remember that many will be fully booked during prime vacation times. Most hostels rent bedding, but it's a wise idea to carry a sleeping bag. Most also have laundries, cooking facilities and often amenities, such as a swimming pool. Many hostels are open to all, first come, first served basis. To stay at a facility which is associated with the International Youth Hostel Association, you must be a member.

Remember, however, that membership is open to all, regardless of age. You can join by contacting any **YHA hostel** in North America or at YHA centers in New Zealand. *Or just show up at a Kiwi hostel and join on the spot.* New Zealand adult memberships run about NZ$40 per person. Kids under 15 have free membership. A guide to all 5,300 hostels around the world is available from YHA offices for a small cost. Hostel rates will run in the NZ$10 to NZ$20 per person range. Information: **YHA offices**—Christchurch, corner of Gloucester and Manchester streets, ☎ (03) 799-970; Auckland, corner of Customs and Gore streets, ☎ (09) 794-224. **Budget Backpackers**—Taupo, **Rainbow Lodge**, 99 Titiraupenga St., ☎ (074) 85-754; Christchurch, **Foley Towers,** 208 Kilmore St.,☎ (03) 669-720; **Picton Street Backpackers**, 34 Picton Street, Freeman's Bay, Auckland; ☎(09) 789-966; **Pavlova Backpackers** (South Island only), offices in Franz Josef, Queenstown, Greymouth, Christchurch and others cities. In ChCh, it's **Pavlova Backpackers**, 50 Cathedral Square, ☎ (03) 665-158. In addition, tourist information offices usually have several free newspapers printed especially for backpackers, full of tips, information, discounts and advertisements —invaluable stuff for the backpacking crowd.

UPSCALE DIGS

You can spend as much as you want on a bed in New Zealand, which has a number of very upscale lodges and resorts scattered about. Such places as the **Huka Lodge** in Taupo, the **Puka Park Lodge** on the

Coromandel Peninsula or the **Kimberley Lodge** in Russell offer refined stays with top cuisine, excellent service and lush surroundings. The **Moose Lodge** near Rotorua, for example, sits on a gorgeous lake and has its own private thermal pool. Many of the lodges and resorts are "sporting lodges," which specialize in hunting and fishing and have guide services. The rates for these places are in the NZ$200 to NZ$1,000 a night per couple range. The rates almost always include meals. Travel agents have lists of some of the better lodges, or you can get information from New Zealand tourism offices in North America.

DRIVING DOWN UNDER

To our minds, the best way to see a place is to rent a car or RV and just take off. We're too lazy to take a bike, too spoiled to hitchhike, too independent most of the time to take tour buses. One of our favorite methods of getting around, especially when we're doing research, is to get a small camper. It's a trade-off, of course. You sacrifice the speed and ease of driving you get with a car, but on the other hand, you save bucks on accommodation costs.

The Arthur's Pass Highway at Bealey

A driving vacation in New Zealand is especially attractive because the country is small and easy to move around in, and also there are scads of very attractive fly/drive vacation packages available all the time. These trips are among the most popular ways to see New Zealand. We fully understand that driving in a strange country isn't for everyone, but still, if you can work it out, *it's probably the single best way to get a full taste of what's going on.*

We got our basic training for driving on the wrong side of the road in England and Australia. The English drive fast and recklessly on narrow roads, and the Aussies aren't much better. New Zealanders, we are happy to report, drive on the wrong side of the street, too, but at much more intelligent pace. Aside from a few freeways around the major cities, Kiwi highways are two-lane and, in the off-seasons, particularly on the South Island, relatively deserted. There are a few things to ponder, however. We have driven all over New Zealand, from the twisty, foggy stretches over Arthur's Pass to the barren, mystic Desert Highway north of Wellington, to the straight stretches through the sheep-laden farms of the Canterbury Plains and the narrow precipitous lanes of the Banks Peninsula on the road to Akaroa. And seeing that we highly recommend that anybody serious about seeing New Zealand rent a car or camper, it's only fair that we try to fill you in on some of the subtler forms of fun and games you can run into tooling around Down Under.

THE RIGHT WAY TO DRIVE ON THE LEFT SIDE OF THE ROAD

The basic problem is, of course, the fact that we drive on the right and the New Zealanders drive on the left. Depending on your coordination and reaction times and common sense, this can be a very large deal, indeed, or no big thing. The most common mistake North Americans and continental European drivers make is looking the wrong way at the wrong time, usually at cross streets. The basic rule is the same that you see painted at every pedestrian crosswalk in London (where they lose an American at least once a day): LOOK RIGHT. This tendency to look the wrong way cuts both ways, of course. No less a personage than Winston Churchill was hospitalized in 1931 after being knocked on his poopdeck by a New York City taxicab while he was trying to walk across Fifth Avenue. (He forgot to look left.)

A sense of direction is particularly important Down Under when approaching that devilish English invention, **the roundabout**. We'd call it a traffic circle. *Just remember to look right, because anybody coming that direction has the right of way.* Once on the roundabout, remember, clockwise, go clockwise. Once on the circle, you supposedly have the right of way, but we observe the California Freeway

Right-of-Way Rule: if they want it, let 'em have it. When turning left onto a street, the traffic coming from the right has the right of way.

You'll also notice that if you've rented a camper or car with a manual transmission, you have to shift left handed (the foot controls are the same). This is no problem, and allows you to get a driver's tan on your right arm for once in your life. The bottom line is probably this: if you're a good driver in Fresno or Vancouver, with a little thought and concentration, you'll be a good driver in New Zealand.

A FEW MORE TIPS ON DRIVING DOWN UNDER

Kiwi highways are every bit as good as North American ones, perhaps just a tad narrower. They are well marked (make sure you're up on your international traffic signs) and well maintained. There are few unpaved roads in the country, and some of them are off-limits to RVs anyway.

Basic speed limits are about what you'd expect—50 kilometers an hour in built-up areas (or slower) and **100k** on open highways. Don't try to work that out in miles per hour—the speedometer is in kph, so just look at the gauge. One note: Americans by now are used to turning right after stopping at a red light. This is a no-no in New Zealand. There's also one sign you'll come across that is a bit perplexing: **LSZ**. It stands for "limited speed zone" and means slow down and be careful.

One other little peculiarity you'll run into, especially on the South Island, is the **one-lane bridge**. They always seem to be situated just as you come around a curve. The New Zealanders have tried to make these equitable by placing right-of-way signs at both ends of the bridge. The signs will have two arrows, one large, one small, pointing different directions. If the large arrow is pointing toward the bridge, it means you have the right of way; if the small arrow is going your direction, you must yield. Often, you'll come to a bridge where you have the right of way but a car is already on the bridge heading your way—just wait until the other car passes. The bridges also have pull-over spots at either end so cars can get out of the way to let traffic pass. Basically, it's just a matter of common sense and good manners.

One further twist. In a few places, the one-way bridge is also a **railroad bridge**—yes, indeed, cars and trains both share the same road. There's only one rule here: the train wins. *If you meet a train on a* *oneway bridge, you may have to back off to let it pass.* If you want to see one of these beauties, turn north at Kumara Junction (intersection of the Arthur's Pass highway and Highway 6) and go a couple of miles toward Greymouth. It's an eye-opener.

RENTAL & INSURANCE

New Zealand has an **Automobile Association**, which is the same as the AAA and the CAA. If you're a North American member, you have reciprocal membership privileges in New Zealand, which gives you free maps and trip planning services, as well as towing and accommodations guides. There are AA offices in all major cities. *Make sure you take your card.* Most of the major international car rental companies are doing business in New Zealand—Hertz, Avis, Budget, etc., and you can get almost any size car you want. It's easy to rent a car or camper in New Zealand. Canadians and Americans just need their normal state or provincial driver's license. *Buying New Zealand vehicle insurance is usually mandatory.* As we mentioned earlier, visitors to New Zealand are entitled to medical care if they are involved in an accident, regardless of fault. There is usually a 3-day minimum to get discount rental rates. We rented a small Hertz car in Wellington for the one-day drive to Auckland and it ran about NZ$200, including insurance. Average rental rates for a bottom-line car (small compact) will run around NZ$500–NZ$700 a week, unlimited kilometerage. But there's always a special going on. One we saw not long ago was through Avis, and offered a 10-day vacation for about US$1,200, which included a car and round trip air fare. Many of the farm stay, B&B vacations or fishing and hunting packages also throw in a free car. From time to time the airlines serving New Zealand will also offer special fly/drive packages. In addition, Budget has a fleet of rental cars adapted for handicapped drivers. All cars, as well as camper vans, can be booked in advance from North America, either through the car companies themselves or through a travel agent. Or they can be hired in New Zealand.

Economy 4WD Rental Company in Christchurch will rent camping equipment to go with its four-wheel-drive rental vehicles. Camp kits, for two people or more, are NZ$15 per person a day, and include a tent, sleeping bags, cots, towels, gas stove, cooking equipment, dishes, table and chair and tools. The vehicles themselves, for a minimum of 6 days with unlimited kilometers, insurance and taxes, start at NZ$115 and go up to NZ$175. North America Information:

So/Pac Travel Marketing, ☎ (800) 551-2012. Gasoline (they call it petrol) is expensive in New Zealand. Last time out, we were paying between 90 cents and NZ$1 a liter, which translates out to about US$2.30 a gallon. *Diesel, for those driving the larger RVs, is a tad cheaper.* One of the things you can do to keep the co-pilot occupied while you're driving is converting kilometers-per-liter to miles-per-gallon, then figuring out your cost per gallon. Or you can just forget it and drive.

THE CAMPER SCENE

RV travel is one of the favorite ways Kiwis get out and around their country on vacations, as the large number of RV parks will attest. In New Zealand, like Australia, these are called **Caravan Parks**, and they range from one-lung Mom and Pop joints up to spiffy modern parks with swimming pools and tennis courts. Most RV parks will have an electric kitchen with sinks, a coin-operated laundry, TV/recreation room and what the Kiwis call "an amenities block," meaning showers and toilets. Many camps also have tent spaces, cabins and on-site RVs for rent. (See the Accommodations section.) Many also have bars and restaurants.

Lake Wanaka in Central Otago

In addition to independent parks, there are several groups that are dotted all over the country. Our favorite is the **Top 10 Group,** which has about 40 parks on the islands, almost all of which are well-equipped and have a good standard of amenities and cleanliness. Top 10 parks, like most Kiwi RV camps, will run you some-where between NZ$10 and NZ$20 a night for a powered site. Another group of parks worth a nod is **Kiwi Camps** of New Zealand with about 50 parks. Many parks in both groups are also members of the Camp & Cabin Association of New Zealand. *Brochures and guides to caravan parks are usually found in tourist information offices, or will be given to you when you rent your RV.* One of the best guides is **Jason's Budget Accommodation**, which sells for about NZ$5 but is usually provided free. In addition to RV parks, it also lists hostels, B&Bs, farm stays, country pubs and other low-cost accommodations. And, as mentioned, AA offices also have RV and other accommodations guides.

It's simple to rent an RV from North America, and the deals are always coming, it seems. The first time we went to New Zealand, it was because Air New Zealand was offering round trip air from the West Coast for under US$1,000 per person—and threw in a free camper for 10 days. We bit like sharks. You'll find the New Zealanders especially anxious to deal in winter, when all their kids are in school and the fleets of RVs are just sitting there.

For instance, Maui **Campas**, the largest camper rental agency in the country, not too long ago was offering a two-berth RV for about US$350 a week and threw in free stays at any Top 10 park in the deal. The big boys—six-berth deluxe RVs—were going for under US$600 a week. Another deal, this one from Mount Cook Line, offered an Air New Zealand package for about US$1,200 per person and threw in a week's RV rental for a dollar more per person.

RV RENTAL COSTS

For normal, no-deal rentals, expect to pay between US$600 and US$1,000 a week for a two-berth unit, between US$850 and US$1,400 for a six-berth, the prices depending on the time of year. Most RV rentals, specials included, are for unlimited kilometerage; in some cases, minimum rental periods are required. *Insurance, which is mandatory, is usually offered two ways. The first method is a charge put on your credit card, usually around NZ$500,* which covers damage to the vehicle. At the end of the trip—providing you haven't had an accident—they tear up the credit card charge. The problem is, the insurance is NZ$500 deductible. Which means if you get a rock through the windshield (about NZ$350 to replace), it comes out of that NZ$500 deposit. This is the cheapest way to go, if you figure you either won't have an accident or can afford to part with the money.

The second method—and the one we always take—is a flat, daily charge of around NZ$20. No refund at the end of the trip—lost money. But no deductible and it covers everything: busted lights, cracked windshields, crushed bumpers. We've never had an accident in New Zealand but have traveled more comfortably knowing everything was covered.

Well, almost everything. *No insurance covers damage to the top of the vehicle.* This rule makes you conscious of low bridges and the low roofs in some gas stations. Also there are a few roads around the islands off limit to RVs—drive on them, have an accident, and the whole thing is your responsibility.

One of the major wholesale companies providing camper rentals to travel agents is Leisure Port, which has Maui Campas, Newman's Motorhomes, Budget Motorhomes, Mount Cook Motorhomes and Horizon Holidays. **Leisure Port** has large facilities at the airports in Auckland and Christchurch. After you clear customs, you wait for one of the company's free vans, which takes you to the rental office. Give them your voucher, sign this and that, and usually within an hour, you're in your RV heading for wherever—if you're smart, the nearest RV park to get over jet lag. Very fast, very efficient.

TIPS ON RV TRAVEL

Don't expect super mileage from a camper. Depending on terrain and how fast you drive, you're looking at around 17 to 20 miles a gallon, less with larger vehicles. And it probably goes without saying that in the smaller, two-berth units, you'd better be on good terms with your bunkie. Space is tight, you're always misplacing stuff and there is no way you'll ever keep the floor clean. All that aside, it's a great way to travel and a good opportunity to meet a lot of similarly minded New Zealanders. (Although in the winter, the chances are the folks in the camper next door are probably from Cleveland.)

The fleets of RV vehicles available in New Zealand are new and modern, and come equipped with most of the necessities of life, including bedding, dishes and cooking equipment, interior lights, brooms, dishwashing stuff and—this is a necessity—heaters. Some are now being equipped with microwave ovens, the camper's best friend. Some even have TV sets, basically useless on the South Island where

TV signals are few and far between. The only complaint we have is with the can openers—never met one yet that worked right. We take our heavy-duty opener from home. Saves primal screaming trying to open a can of beans. If you really get serious, you might also bring along a small cutting board, or buy it when you arrive.

FOOD & DRINK

There's a lot more to New Zealand cuisine than mutton and lamb chops. New Zealand produces world class wines, beers and cheeses, and remember, it's an island nation, and that means the supply and variety of seafoods and fish are superb. Especially marinated mussels. Huge, maybe two inches across, sweet, saucy. You can buy them in almost any market, and they come in a variety of sauces, from plain marinade to honey or hot. They are highly addictive and one thing we will always miss when we're not in New Zealand.

As for lamb. Well, if you've never had **Kiwi lamb**, you've never had lamb. It's so good it's sinful, the best in the world, and the New Zealanders, not surprisingly, know how to prepare it properly. They also do good work with beef and venison.

THE GOOD AND THE BAD

On the other side of the coin, you can also find some really vile stuff, particularly some of their fast foods. A packet of fish and chips from a Mom and Pop joint comes to mind, probably the greasiest and worst chunk of lunch we've ever had. The Kiwis, like the Australians, are also big fans of pies—meaning **meat pies**. Done correctly, these can be quite good. Done badly—and many times they are—it's instant heartburn. Fast food coffee should be avoided at all costs—it's truly abominable. Like the Aussies, the Kiwis sometimes eat spaghetti for breakfast, sometimes on toast. Pork and beans should be avoided, also. Actually, almost anything they put tomato sauce in—canned or fresh—is quite strange, many of the canned offerings tasting something like a stew made from vienna sausage and ketchup. Another Kiwi delicacy we can live without is **Muttonbird**, a Maori favorite. It's basically an oily, salty baby seagull, preferably smoked. Yecch. But generally, you'll find that Kiwi Cuisine is quite acceptable, and you'll never starve.

If you have a Yankee attack, rest easy—the major cities are full of American fast food chains—McDonald's, the Colonel, Pizza Hut. There are also scads of ethnic places, especially for lunch. Chinese take-outs are popular and often will be the only thing open late at night. Many restaurants, even in major cities, operate on limited hours, so always check before venturing out.

Fruits are high on New Zealanders' lists, and the many orchards and groves around the country supply excellent fare. You'll find stalls near most orchards where the local crop is on sale in season. Californians already know about two of New Zealand's better exports, **Granny Smith apples** and **Kiwi fruit**.

KIWI FRUIT

Kiwi fruit, long associated with New Zealand, is actually the Chinese gooseberry, which originated in the Yangtze Valley. They were introduced into New Zealand around the turn of the century and went commercial in the 1930s on the North Island. *They were named kiwi fruit in the 1950s, partly because the brown fuzzy skins resemble the bird,* partly as a marketing gimmick. In addition to having a wonderful taste, kiwi fruit are also higher in Vitamin C than apples, and contain all sorts of good minerals, plus being low in sodium and cholesterol. They are also rich in enzymes—the juice is used to marinate squid. A major center of the kiwi industry is at Kerikeri near the Bay of Islands on the North Island. During the harvest season—May to July—you can buy enough kiwi fruit to feed an army for a few dollars, more than you'll ever be able to eat.

FRESH FROM THE FARM

In addition to the excellent Granny Smith apples, orchards also produce Red Delicious, Golden, Sturmer and Gala types. *The two major apple-growing areas are Hawke's Bay on the North Island and the Marlborough and Nelson areas of the South Island.* Picking season is March to November. The Nelson area also produces berries—**loganberries, elderberries, strawberries, blackberries**. Other fruits you'll run into are **pepino melons, passionfruit, kiwona melons and the nashi, a sort of apple-pear**. The Kiwis tell us that Queen Elizabeth's favorite honey comes from the pohutukawa (Christmas tree), which produces a white honey and can even be bought by us commoners.

New Zealand honey, coming as it does from some exotic New Zealand plants, has some remarkable flavors, and is widely used in candy and candles. It's also used to make mead, the Druidic potable that makes you sweet and swacked at the same time. If you've a thirst, try

Havill's Mazek Mead Company in Christchurch, which uses honey produced from Canterbury clover. And for more honey products than you thought existed, check out Honey Village outside Taupo.

Driving down a road near the Coromandel Peninsula, we were amused to see signs saying: "Swedes for sale." No, not the white slave trade, but the **New Zealand rutabaga.** Other farm produce you'll find are **courgettes (zucchini), capsicum (bell peppers), aubergine (eggplant) and silverbeet (Swiss chard).** Being a Polynesian culture as well, New Zealand also has taro (used in place of potatoes), yams and kumara. **Kumara,** which originated in South America, is a sweet potato, brought to New Zealand with the first Maori settlers 1,000 years ago. The Kiwis also are fond of **beetroot** (red beets), but haven't gone insane like the Australians, who put it on everything, including, yuk, hamburgers. **Cheese** country is to the southwest of the North Island in the Mt. Egmont area. The city of Eltham, particularly, is a good place to explore Kiwi cheeses. Try the **Galaxy Cheese Factory** on High Street, which has a cheese bar and will mail cheese back home. For those who like excitement in their cheeses, we recommend **Ferndale's Blue de Bresse**, a superior blue-vein product. *The traditional cheese in New Zealand was a mix of Gouda and white cheddar,* but now the industry has branched out and produces **gruyere, mozzerella, brie, camembert, feta, romano** and many other varieties. The Kiwis pride themselves on the purest cheese on earth—the old "clean, green and nuclear free" thing again.

SHEEP AND OTHER ANIMALS

Lamb. Well, it gets tough after a while, driving around in the spring and seeing all those wee sheep being born or romping around the paddocks, to keep eating lamb, but there's no doubt it is superb.

A **lamb roast** is the usual Sunday dinner in many Kiwi homes —eaten, we might add, without that awful mint jelly. They also eat a lot of mutton, which is not strong and gamy. And rather than spring lamb, many New Zealanders prefer **"hogget,"** a Scottish word for a year-old sheep, which they claim has more flavor. Lamb and mutton are cheap in local supermarkets, and come in a variety of cuts, often pre-breaded. Sometimes, however, the lamb on sale is from Australia, which floods the market from time to time. Many New Zealanders think Aussie lamb is inferior. It's not a battle we choose to get into.

Lambs on Rainbow Farm, Rotorua

While not especially known for **beef**, New Zealand does raise excellent meat, tender, flavorful, fairly low-fat. *They have a tendency to overcook it, however, so make sure if you like it a bit rare you tell the waiter exactly what you want.*

As for **venison**, raised in prodigious quantities, you'll probably have to go to an upscale restaurant to find it. (See the section on deer.) If you do find some in a market, one thing to remember about Kiwi venison if you cook it without liquids (broiling, frying)—*it must be cooked quickly and never well done because of its low fat content.* In restaurants, it often comes in a stew form or roasted with a marinade. Breakfast meats offer a mixed bag. There are basically two kinds of **bacon**, middle and shoulder, both of which are quite lean like Canadian bacon. **Sausages** tend to be English-style bangers, made with a cereal/meat mix, very bland, virtually tasteless to somebody used to Jimmy Dean-style sausage. You can also find lamb sausage (also fairly bland) and venison sausage, which has a nice flavor—just don't overcook it.

On the South Island, we spotted what we thought were North American-style wild turkeys—which turned out to be North American-style **wild turkeys**. Farmers look on them as pests because they eat grains and grasses used to feed sheep and cattle. There are enough of them flying around, however, that come Christmas, they are hunted down, and served up with all the trimmings (the traditional Kiwi Yuletide feast.) This method keeps the turkey population under control. The farmers, we were told, wouldn't touch a turkey with a 3-meter pole, preferring, perhaps, a lamb roast at Christmas.

SEAFOOD

Seafood, seafood. No menu is without it, from **crayfish to cod, oysters to smoked marlin**. Fish by the ton, including **John Dory, sole, eels, albacore tuna, trevally, flounder, salmon, snapper, monkfish, shark** (also used in fish and chips). Bivalves, including the aforementioned *mussels* (arguably the best in the world marinated, steamed or broiled), **scallops, clams, paua (abalone)**. **Rock lobster, squid.** *But no trout. It's against the law to sell trout commercially. If you catch one at a farm or lodge, they'll be glad to cook it up for you, however.*

AND FOR DESSERT...

Kiwis do like their desserts—rich and fattening. Like **"Lamingtons,"** pieces of sponge cake dipped in chocolate or fruit syrup, then sprinkled with shaved coconut. Or **Pavlovas**, a baked meringue with fruit and whipped cream. Or **trifle**, sponge cake soaked in brandy or sherry and topped with custard or canned fruit. Or **cream buns**, a jellyroll stuffed with sweet cream paste. In restaurants, they roll out the dessert trolley, stacked with an assortment of goodies to drive anybody on a diet to drink. They encourage you to try several selections, then send for a block and tackle to get you out of the chair.

No place in New Zealand is without a **teahouse**, where you get **Devonshire Tea**—tea and scones (pronounced skawns) served with whipped cream. And markets sell dairy custard, a sweetened milk and egg mix that comes in small milk cartons and is used to make a quick dessert with fruits.

Because of some language differences, you're likely to run into some things in markets and on menus that might seem strange. While it's not a complete dictionary, we offer a few:

THE NEW ZEALAND FOOD DIRECTORY	
Green ginger	unpeeled, fresh ginger root
Punnet	a half pint dry measure, for example, the way berries are often packaged
Castor sugar	confectioner's sugar
Gingernuts	gingersnaps
Golden syrup	Honey-colored light molasses

THE NEW ZEALAND FOOD DIRECTORY

Rice Bubbles	Snap, crackle and pop
Wheetbix	A sort of granola bar
Hokey pokey	Butterscotch ice cream
Bickies or biscuits	cookies
Chips	French fries
Chook	Chicken
Cuppa	Tea or coffee
Dairy	The neighborhood market, selling everything from newspapers to ice cream cones, usually open late
Junket	A dessert, sort of like a thin pudding
Marmite or vegemite	A salty yeast product that we think tastes like piano polish but which is worshipped in New Zealand and Australia
Milk bar	A shop selling dairy foods and hot fast foods
Mince pie	Ground meat pies in a pastry shell, hot or cold
Pudding	Generic name for any dessert
Take away	Fast food
Supper	A snack before going to bed; the evening meal is often referred to as tea
After	Dessert, as in after a meal
Griller	A broiler chicken
Tomato sauce	ketchup
Trolley	Grocery cart
Hangi	The Maori luau, cooked in an underground pit
Scroggin	Gorp or trail mix designed for hikers
Tamarillo	The tree tomato, often used in preparing sauces. It's shiny and egg-shaped

We should mention in passing that at least one famous chef owes his inspiration to New Zealand—Graham Kerr, the Galloping Gourmet. Originally from the UK, Kerr spent seven years in New Zealand, a period which he says was "the most important stop in my life." He wrote his first cookbook in New Zealand, then went on to be a TV celeb in the United States in the late 1960s. The book, "Graham Kerr—the Galloping Gourmet" uses recipes based on New Zealand foods, and is worth checking out of your local library before heading off to New Zealand.

An additional resource found, as far as we know, only in New Zealand, is Michael Guy's Eating Out, a guide to Kiwi food specialties and restaurants around the country. It's sold in bookstores.

WHAT TO WEAR

Some rules. New Zealanders, while essentially laid back and pretty informal, do tend to dress for dinner. Jackets are a good idea, and in fancy spots, you might need a tie. In the summer, men can wear sports coats, walking shorts and long socks (buy them there). For women, a skirt and blouse, perhaps a floral-print dress. Pants suits and slacks are proper in resort areas.

TIPPING

Tipping is generally not done, but on special occasions or in very fancy places with very fancy service, it's not a total tabu. You'll also notice that most restaurants do not add service charges to the tab. Menu prices might or might not include the 12 percent goods and services tax, so check.

DRINKING

Liquor licenses in New Zealand, like Australia, are hard to obtain, so many restaurants and cafes are BYOB—Bring Your Own Bottle. You stop off at a bottle shop and pick up some wine, and the restaurant will decork and serve it for you. Often, there is a corking fee, sometimes not much, sometimes outrageous. (We paid NZ$5 to uncork an NZ$8 bottle of wine once.) Some BYOBs have beer, wine and liqueurs, but not hard booze.

ON-SITE RESTAURANTS

Many motels and small hotels have a restaurant on site, which is often cafeteria-style. The usual procedure is to pick up your salads and cold foods, order your hot food, and find a place to sit. They'll either call you for the order or deliver it to the table. The food is often basic—stews, macaroni and cheese, curries. But note well, they tend to think everybody who eats is a farmhand, and the servings can be prodigious. In pubs that serve counter meals, you normally must order and pay for beer or wine separately from the food.

Finally, as a general guide when eating out, look for a place that has a yellow and white emblem with "KiwiHost" on it. This means the establishment has personnel specially trained in the gentle art of pleasing tourists. The program is administered by the New Zealand Tourism Department.

A paraglider is another great way to see the land

WINE PRODUCING REGIONS

Californians, at least Californians from our neck of the woods, tend to be fairly sophisticated about wine. It's not that we go out and study enology from dawn to dusk, or that we take classes on how to be really snotty when it comes to picking wines. It's basically because, like France, California has a lot of wine-growing areas and a professional group of vintners producing world-class wines, and your level of expectations in this sort of situation is always bound to be high.

Hotel Du Vin, South of Auckland

Which is why it's such a delight finding that our southern cousins are producing wine every bit the equal of Europe or California.

Big-league wine growing and appreciation in New Zealand is a recent development, although the first wine was produced near the **Bay of Islands** around 1835. Prior to 1960, there was a small industry, with virtually no exports at all. But by 1980, things were beginning to expand rapidly, and by 1990, almost 400 growers were producing wine. The total vine area is estimated at around 15,000 acres or so, at the moment, with an annual production of more than 11 million gallons. By contrast, California's Napa Valley has more than 170 wineries—and one of the largest, St. Helena-based Sutter Home, produces something like 34 million (almost 9 million gallons) liters of wine a year by itself.

Although the bulk of New Zealand wines are white, the reputation of its cabernet sauvignons is gaining world status. Among the whites, New Zealand sauvignon blancs already are on a par with any in the world, and some critics put them at the top.

About 75 percent of the country's wine is produced along the east coast of the North Island between the Hastings/Napier area and Gisborne—basically the areas behind Hawke's Bay and Poverty Bay. Another important region is the Marlborough district on the northeast coast of the South Island near Blenheim and Nelson. But such is the growing popularity of interior consumption, as well as exports, that there are vineyards almost tip of coast to tip of coast on both islands.

Like California, many wineries welcome tasters, and in many cases, with normal Kiwi hospitality, they offer local cheeses to go along with the samples. Also like California, many winery showrooms are also galleries and many wineries conduct tours to educate first-time sippers.

The success of the Kiwi wineries is such that almost every wine-growing region has at least one company that specializes in wine tours. Or, if you have wheels, you can do what we Californians do of a weekend—go winery hopping. This spoils us, of course, but makes us all the more eager to sample the pressings of other countries when we have the chance. We won't try to list all the New Zealand wineries. You can get a more complete listing when you visit major cities close to the vineyards.

WHERE TO SAMPLE NEW ZEALAND'S WINES

WEST AUCKLAND

Near Auckland is the winegrowing area of West Auckland. The vines are about a half-hour from downtown, in the Henderson area to the west of the city. The most common variety in the region is cabernet sauvignon, with substantial plantings of merlot and pinot noir. Among the 15 or so wineries are:

Babich—Babich Road, Henderson. Chardonnay, fume vert, Muller-Thurgau, pinot noir, cabernet sauvignon. Sales and tasting 8–5:30, Monday-Saturday. ☎ (09) 833- 8909.

Collard Bros.—303 Lincoln Rd., Henderson. Chardonnay, chenin blanc, Rhine riesling and Merlot. Sales and tasting 9–5:30 p.m., Monday-Saturday. ☎ 836- 8341.

Corban's—426 Great North Road, Henderson. One of the country's oldest and largest wine companies. Also distributes under the Cooks, Stoneleigh and Longridge labels. Grapes from all over New Zealand are used. Chardonnay, fume blanc and sauvignon/merlot. Sales and tasting 9–6, Monday-Saturday. ☎ 836-6189.

Delegat's—Hepburn Road, Henderson. Primarily Hawke's Bay grapes. Chardonnay, cabernet sauvignon, fume blanc. Sales and tasting 9–5, Monday-Friday, 10–6, Saturday. ☎ 836-0129.

Matua Valley Wines—Waikoukou Valley Road, Waimauku. Given credit for introducing sauvignon blanc to New Zealand. Sales and tasting 9–5, Monday-Saturday. ☎ 411-8301.

Selaks—Old North Road and Highway 16, Kumeu. Award-winning sauvignon blanc, as well as Methode Champenoise wines. Sales and tasting 9–5:30, Monday-Saturday. ☎ 412-9609.

THE GISBORNE AREA

Some observers feel that the Gisborne area has declined as a major wine area because it generally produces sweeter, flusher wines in an era when the direction seems to be going toward drys. Several of the major wine companies still have vast vineyards growing in the area, shipping the grapes to Auckland facilities for processing and bottling. Some wineries:

Matawhero Wines—Riverpoint Road, Matawhero, Gisborne. Gewurztraminer, chenin blanc, cabernet merlot, chardonnay. Sales and tasting 9–5, Monday-Saturday. ☎ (079) 88-366.

Milton Vineyard—Papatu Road, Manutuke, Gisborne. Muller-Thurgau, riesling, sauvignon blanc/semillion, chenin blanc. Sales and tasting 9–6, Monday-Saturday, October-June. ☎ 28-680.

Revington—State Highway 2, Manutuke, Gisborne. Chardonnay, Muller-Thurgau, pinot noir blush, gewurztraminer. Sales and tasting 9–5, Monday-Saturday.

HAWKE'S BAY

It's pretty hot around the bay, and the result is some truly world-class red wines, especially cabernet sauvignon, merlot and pinot noir. Hawke's Bay wines are noted for their fullness, aging well and deep flavor. But the area is also producing some very good chardonnays. Some wineries:

Brook Fields Vineyards—Brookfields Road, Meeanee. Cabernet sauvignon, cabernet merlot, pinot gris. Sales and tastings 9–5, Monday-Saturday. ☎ (070) 834-4615.

C.J. Pask—Omahu Road, Hastings. Cabernet sauvignon, sauvignon blanc, chardonnay, pinot noir. Sales and tastings, 10–6, Monday-Saturday. ☎ 879- 7906.

Crab Farm—125 Main Road North, Bayview—A small winery with a good location (right on the highway). Muller-Thurgau, sauvignon blanc, cabernet sauvignon. Sales and tasting 9–5, Monday–Saturday. ☎ 826-6678.

Esk Valley Estate—Main Road, Bayview. Chenin blanc, cabernet merlot, sauvignon blanc, cabernet sauvignon. Sales and tasting 9:30–5, Monday-Saturday. ☎ 826-6411.

Lombardi—Te Mata Road, Havelock North. Specializes in fortified wines, vermouth and wine liqueurs. Marsala, ruby port, dry vermouth. Sales and tasting 9–5, Monday-Saturday. ☎ 877-7985.

McDonald Winery—200 Church Rd., Taradale. Now part of the Montana empire, which produced its first vintage here in 1990. Cabernet sauvignon a specialty. Sales, tasting and tours 9–5 Monday-Saturday. ☎ 844- 2053.

Ngatarawa—Bridge Pa, Hastings. Housed in elegant old stables, specializing in dry wines. Sauvignon blanc, chardonnay, Stables red. Sales and tasting 10–5, Monday- Saturday. ☎ 877-5356.

Bay Tours in Napier offers a winery tour, which includes visits to several wineries, tastings, tours, talks with winemakers and several tourist stops. The fare, not including lunch, is about NZ$35, Tours depart at 10:15, return at 2:15 p.m. Monday-Friday; from 1:15-5:30 p.m., Saturdays. Information: ☎ (06) 843-6953.

MARLBOROUGH

This section of the South Island is Montana Country. When the company decided to plant here, it increased the national vineyard supply by 30 percent. This is mainly a sauvignon blanc area, but chardonnay and rieslings are also coming of age. A few:

Cellier Le Brun—Terrace Road, Renwick. Sparkling wines a la champagne are the specialty here. Bruts, roses, blanc de blancs and non-sparkling chardonnay. Sales and tasting 9–5, Monday-Saturday. ☎ (057) 28-859.

Corbans Marlborough Cellars—Jackson's Road, Blenheim. This is a joint venture with Australia's giant wine company, Wolf Blass. Riesling and sauvignon blanc plus chardonnay. Sales and tasting 9–6, Monday-Saturday. ☎ 28-198.

Hunter's—Raupara Road, Blenheim—Late harvest chardonnay a speciality. Garden setting with restaurant. Pinot noir, Rhine riesling, sauvignon blanc. Sales and tasting 9–5, Monday-Saturday. ☎ 28- 489.

Montana Riverlands—State Highway 1, Blenheim. This is the largest winery in the country, plus the New Zealand base for a French champagne company working with Montana. Sauvignon blanc and Rhine riesling are some of the best in the country. Sales and tasting 9–5, Monday-Saturday.

NELSON

This is probably the most French-like grape area in the country, a beautiful stretch of forests and low mountains, with loamy soils and cool nights. The climate is often compared to Burgundy. The main wines are sauvignon blanc, chardonnay and Rhine riesling. A few:

Ranzau—Patons Road, Richmond. Muller-Thurgau, gewurztraminer, gamay beaujolais, cabernet sauvignon. Sales and tasting. 10–6, Monday-Saturday, December-February. ☎ (054) 23-868.

Weingut Seifried—Main Road, Upper Moutere. Rhine riesling and gewurztraminer. Sales and tasting 9–6, Monday- Saturday. ☎ 21-795.

Neudorf—Neudorf Road, Upper Moutere. Dry chardonnays, beaujolais, merlot, cabernet sauvignon. Sales and tasting Monday–Saturday, December-February. ☎ 21-643.

Korepo—Korepo Road, Upper Moutere. Gamay beaujolais, cabernet sauvignon, sauvignon blanc, pinot noir. Sales and tasting 9–6, Monday-Saturday, November-early March. ☎ 22-825.

CANTERBURY

The wine area to the north and south of Christchurch along the coast started developing in the 1970s, but wine has been produced here since the French settled Akaroa in the early 1800s. The normally dry climate produces reds of good quality. A few:

St. Helena—Coutts Island Road, Belfast. The first commercial vineyard in Canterbury, planted in 1978. The 1982 pinot noir was an international award-winner. Sales and tasting 10–5,Monday-Saturday. ☎ 323-8202.

Amberley Estates—Reserve Road, Amberley. Dry riesling, chardonnay, gewurztraminer, pinot noir. Hours 11–5,Tuesday-Saturday. ☎ 314-8409.

QUEENSTOWN

Only three we know of at present:

Gibbston Valley Wines—Located not far from the bungee jumping bridge at the Kawarau Gorge about 25 kilometers from town. The owners claim it's the southernmost winery in the world. Included are pinot noir, pinot gris, gewurztraminer and Muller-Thurgau. Hours 10 a.m.–6 p.m., Monday-Saturday; noon–6 p.m., Sunday. ☎ 442-6910.

Taramea—Speargrass Flat Road. Specializes in gewurztraminer and riesling.

Chard Farm—Perched above the same bungee river 8 kilometers from town. Chardonnay, pinot noir, gewurzt. Hours 10 a.m.–5 p.m., daily.

THE SOUTH ISLAND

Contemplation, Southland

We admit it, we're biased—if forced to pick only one locale in New Zealand to visit, it would just have to be the mountains, fjords and rugged country of the South Island. Hopefully, you'll have enough time to do both islands, but if not, we strongly suggest you concentrate on the south. Most tour groups do both, and in some cases, the delights of New Zealand flash by in a blur. We realize that, for some, this will be the only chance to see the country, and after spending all that time and money, you'll want to see it all. But there's just something about going slowly, seeing Mount Cook, hiking one of the alpine tracks or driving over a pass through the Southern Alps that makes the delights of the North Island pale a bit. If you are doing

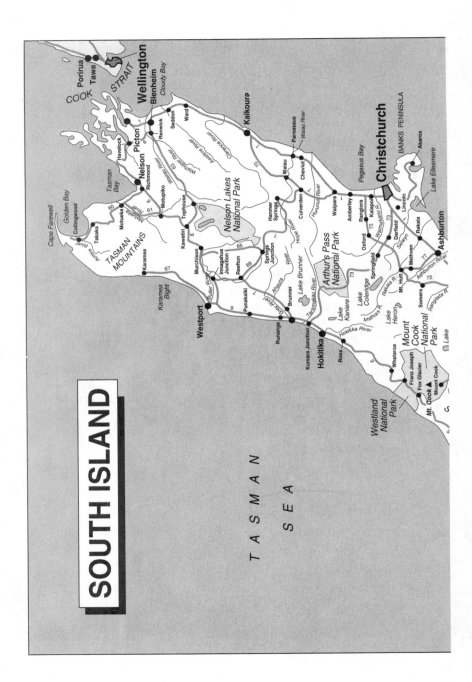

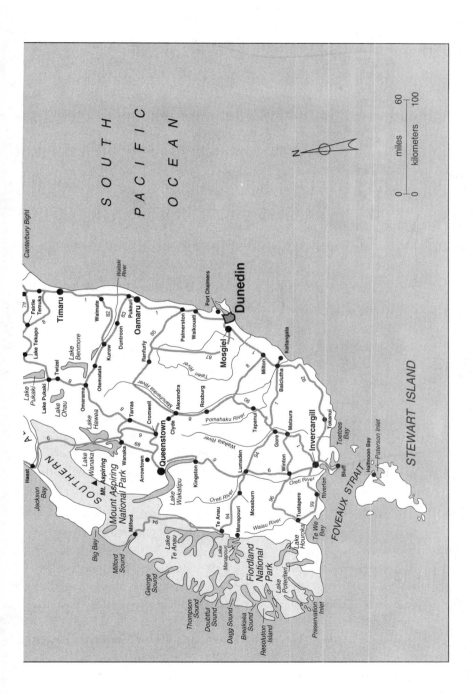

both islands, it's probably better to start in the north; going north after being on the South Island is a bit of an anti-climax.

The major draw for the **South Island**, in addition to its diverse and wonderful scenery, is the lack of population. Christchurch, the biggest city in the south, is tidy and manageable, and traffic on the southland's highways tends to be light. The male member of this party, being a Coloradoan by birth, is drawn to mountains like a moth to a bug zapper, and standing on top of a mile-high glacier in the Southern Alps is an experience right up there with marinated mussels and beer.

The road system in the south is good, and you can go all the way around the island with little difficulty. Most people make their way from the Picton ferry dock to Christchurch, either driving themselves or taking the coast train. From Christchurch, you can either go south or west to reach the mountains and fjords.

THE FASTEST WAY TO THE ALPS

Our suggested route, and the fastest way to the Alps and the glaciers, is to take Highway 73 west over Arthur's Pass, then south on Highway 6 to Fox Glacier and Franz Josef. From Fox Glacier, you

go over the lovely Haast Pass highway to Queenstown, the center of activity in the mountain country. From Queenstown, you can go to the fjords, south to Invercargill and Stewart Island, or east to Dunedin and the coast. Christchurch to Franz Josef is about 400 kilometers (240 miles or so), and Franz Josef to Queenstown is about 215 miles. The highways in the south are mostly well-paved, a bit narrow and filled with one-lane bridges. (See the Driving section). Some highways are subject to closure in the winter.

In the beginnings of Maori colonization—and later in the European era—the South Island was the population and economic center of the country. This century, however, the North Island began to dominate, until now, only about a third of the total population lives in the south. *The Maoris probably got their name for New Zealand—Aotearoa, the Land of the Long White Cloud—from* the clouds that often obscure the Southern Alps. The mountains split the island into two distinct climatic areas. On the west, or seaward side, is a narrow belt of heavy precipitation and lush rain forests. To the east, the land is drier and has been built up into huge plains by deposits washed down from the mountains. Because of the divide, the climate in the south is at once the coldest and the hottest of both islands, as well as the wettest and driest. Most of the country's national parks are on the South Island, including Fiordland, the largest. The plants of the south are both sub-tropical and sub-antarctic, and there are large populations of seals and the only on-land rookery for the royal albatross. Starting in the early 1860s, there was a series of gold rushes on the South Island, greatly swelling the country's population, a fate shared by both Australia and California. There are still a few important deposits of minerals on the island, but mostly what the land is good for is grass—and the animals that feed upon it. And, of course, tourism.

CHRISTCHURCH

ChCh, as you'll see it referred to in headlines, is often described as a very English city, what with the River Avon and Anglican cathedrals and large expanses of lawn, a statue of Good Queen Vickie in the central park.

Antartctic Centre, Christchurch

Perhaps. But to our minds, the comparison is a bit stretched Christchurch is a very pretty, very green city, but it's too Down Under to really be English. It's like saying downtown Boston is English, which it is, sort of. What Christchurch is, is a city easy to get around in, a city with lots of arts and theater going on, a city with some very nice restaurants and some exceeding fine hotels. The pace is much closer to town than city. Green? It's estimated that more than 10 percent of the city is parks or preserves. Whatever, it's our favorite city in New Zealand. The streets will give you away as a Yank, of course: Worcester is pronounced Wooster; Gloucester is Glawster—you get the idea.

THE CANTERBURY REGION

Christchurch is the focal point of what is called the Canterbury Region, which is that portion of the South Island that generally lies east of the Southern Alps, and from just south of Kaikoura to just north of Oamaru along the coast. The city's population is a manageable 300,000 or so—the third largest in the country—and dates from around 1850. The city sits just to the north of the Banks Peninsula, with Pegasus Bay and the city's harbor, Lyttelton, to the east. It began life as a Church of England settlement (hence the name) and was supposed to be a haven for landed gentry and good Christian souls of lesser caste. Utopia in the Antipodes, perhaps. But economic reality reared its ugly head, and soon, to make ends meet the fledgling community was forced to let in riff and raff, including —and here's where the downfall truly started—Australians fed up with conditions across the Tasman. As a church community, it was probably doomed from the start—there were so many clerics in town in the early years, there were church wars with bishops of all sorts stumbling around cheek by jowl trying to take control of minds and souls. Critics also suggested that the caliber of clergy being sent to the community was not the highest—mostly parsons who couldn't make it in the real world and had to settle for an island in the middle of the South Pacific.

The city was laid out in grids with the Avon meandering through the heart of town. (The river was named after a Scottish brook, by the way, not Will Shakespeare's famous creek). Because of its wanderings, there are many bridges in the city, one of the most poignant being the Bridge of Remembrance, built in 1923 to commemorate the casualties of World War I—plaques to honor other war dead were added later. It's on Cashel Street.

ON TO ANTARCTICA

Christchurch has a special connection to Antarctica. It was from here that the Englishman Robert Falcon Scott first set out to explore the frozen continent, and from here in 1910 he left on his misguided and doomed attempt to beat Roald Amundsen to the South Pole.

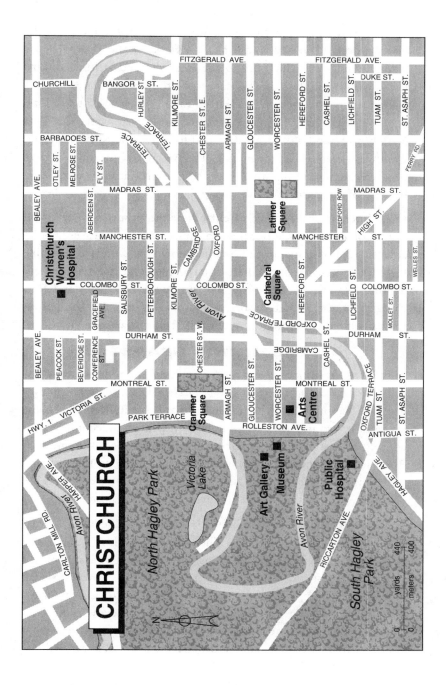

There is a statue of Scott, standing in winter gear, on Oxford Terrace next to the Avon. At Victoria Square, there's also a statue of Capt. Cook, another explorer who sailed from New Zealand to explore the polar regions. The city is also headquarters for the United States Antarctic mission, which, given the New Zealand attitude toward the environment and the abysmal record the United States has had of fouling its own nest in Antarctica, might not last. Not too long ago, the U.S. used explosives to blow up a toxic waste dump at McMurdo Sound, not an act designed to amuse the Kiwis. Maybe it wasn't us—blame it on the French. The Americans, meanwhile, have been threatening to pull their polar operations out of New Zealand because of the country's anti-nuke policies.

The International Antarctic Centre near the airport has a splendid display of icy exhibits about the Frozen Continent: ice caves, a polar aquarium, photos and an audio-visual show. It was built to resemble large ice formations and is part of a complex that provides services for the Antarctic research programs run by the U.S., Italy and New Zealand. It also includes a bar, gift shop and cafe. It's located on Orchard Road about five minutes' walk from the airport.

THE GOTHIC HEAPS

One of the striking things about Christchurch, in addition to its feeling of genteel comfort, is the stash of lovely old Gothic heaps left over from the Victorian Era. The wallahs in charge of publicity for the city say right up front that Christchurch has the finest collection of such edifices in Australasia—a statement which might be taken amiss by Australians looking down Macquarie Street in Sydney. Still, there are some dandies in Christchurch, and many of the best examples are churches, just what you'd expect given the city's genealogy.

The premier building is probably the **Anglican Cathedral**, begun in the 1860s and finished in 1881. The church tower is 215 feet above the square, and gives a commanding view of the central downtown area. Of interest inside is a panel with the Lord's Prayer in Maori. Outside is a statue of Robert Godley, the father of Christchurch. Tuesdays and Wednesdays at 5:15 p.m. the cathedral choir does evensong. You can climb the 133 steps up to the tower 9 a.m.- 4 p.m., weekdays and Saturdays, 1-4 p.m., Sundays. Admission is about NZ$2 for adults. The Cathedral is the centerpiece of Cathedral Square, a pedestrian area flanked by the church and several other old lovelies, including the **Press Building** (1909), housing the city's oldest newspaper; the **Regent Theatre** (1905), and the former **Central Post Office** building (1879). The square (public toilets available) is the Hyde Park of Christchurch, with speakers odd, sincere or both taking voice during the lunch hour. The most famous of these is the Wizard, who wears a wizard suit, stands on a ladder and is generally given credit for establishing the right to have a Speaker's Corner in the square to begin with. He's a Brit, and judged to be a bit daft by many. He's very photogenic, however, and normally works the crowds at 1 p.m., weekdays, but takes the winter (June-July) off. According to the free local tourist paper, the Wiz has been classified as a "living work of art." Some people think he's a sexist and a bit of a racist. You judge.

Many architectural judges think the best Victorian Gothic structures in the country are the **Provincial Council Buildings**, a gaggle of structures of both wood and stone built between the 1850s and 1860s. Particularly impressive is the 1865 Council Chamber with its high tower, vaulted ceilings and stained glass windows. The complex is located near the corner of Armagh and Durham streets, southwest of Victoria Square. It's open weekdays from 9 a.m.-5 p.m. and guided tours are offered at 2 and 2:30 p.m., Sundays. Information: ☎ 351-6776 or 332-6184.

Some other buildings worth a look are the **Theatre Royal** (1908) on Gloucester Street; the **Roman Catholic Cathedral of the Blessed Sacrament** (1905) on Barbadoes Street; the **McKenzie and Willis** buildings (1878) on Tuam Street and the **Canterbury Club** (1874) on Cambridge Terrace.

CANTERBURY UNIVERSITY

While Cathedral Square has its allures, we prefer to go walkabout near the city's **Botanic Gardens**, which lie west of the river—from Cathedral Square, just walk down Worcester Street and keep going. Just before arriving at the Botanic Gardens, you'll come to the impressive former campus of **Canterbury University**, with a series of Gothic stone buildings begun in 1876. In one of the buildings is the den used by New Zealand's most famous scientist, Ernest Rutherford, who received the Nobel Prize for chemistry in 1908 for work involving the atomic nucleus. It's open for visits. The campus and its buildings are now the home of the **Christchurch Arts Centre**, which is home to a ballet troupe, a theatre company, a school of music, several small galleries and artisans and a couple of movie theaters. Musical performances are given in what is probably the most impressive of the old buildings, the Great Hall, built in 1882. In addition to the crafts shops (which include hand spinning and weaving, stringed instrument manufacture and Maori arts) there are a couple of restaurants and offices of the Nuclear Free Society and an animal rights group. The centre is open daily, and on weekends is home to arts fairs where local artisans display their wares. For information, ☎ (03) 660-989.

A bit further on, where Worcester meets Rolleston Avenue, you'll find the **Canterbury Museum**, housed in some 1870 buildings. The highlight of the museum, which has displays of Maori culture and early colonial life, is the **Hall of Antarctic Discovery**, a first-rate presentation about the men who explored the last continent. The museum has a snack bar; it's open daily, 9 a.m.-4:30 p.m. Admission is free, but donations are welcomed. Information: ☎ 668-379.

Behind the museum is the **McDougall Art Gallery**, which has some fine Maori portraits and a couple of Rodin statues. It also houses a striking display of paintings and other objects relating to the two World Wars. Same hours as the museum; admission free. Information: ☎ 650- 914.

Also behind the museum is the main entrance to the **Botanic Gardens** (gate closes at 6 p.m.). The gardens (1863) are actually part of 450-acre **Hagley Park**, situated on a loop of the Avon. The oldest sports building in the country is here—the Hagley Oval, home to Kiwi cricket—and the gardens themselves are full of native and imported trees and flower beds. You can walk or, in the summertime, catch the electric-powered "Toast Rack," a trolley which takes visitors around. In the center of things is **Victoria Lake**, a favorite for radio-control boat fans. You can pick up lunch at the **Gardens Restaurant**, not far from the lake, which has a daily noon-time smorgasbord.

Another favorite stroll is to start at Victoria Square, itself a nice urban park with a statue of Queen Victoria herself, and walk down the Avon to the Montreal Street bridge. Here you'll find the **Antigua Boatsheds**, built in 1882 for the all-male Christchurch Boating Club but now willing to rent paddle boats and canoes to all comers for around NZ$10 an hour. Or if you feel like being pampered, you can be punted down the Avon for about NZ$15 per person for a 45-minute trip. Punts in this case are not what you do on fourth down, but rather the English gentry's equivalent of the Venetian gondola. Punts leave from the Canterbury Information Centre, the Town Hall restaurant and the Thomas Edmonds restaurant. Bookings can be made at the information centre. Punts operate from 10 a.m. until dusk.

The folks who live in Christchurch have always loved their flowers, and for the last 10 years or so, the Christchurch Beautifying Association has planted something in excess of 20,000 daffodil bulbs along Park Terrace on the banks of the Avon next to North Hagley Park. Unfortunately, the project might not continue because thieves keep stealing the bulbs. At one point, it was estimated that almost 90 percent of the plants had been taken.

Some other spots in and around Christchurch for a visit:

AROUND CHRISTCHURCH

Air Force Museum For war and/or airplane freaks, a great place, full of displays, aircraft and memorabilia about the Royal New Zealand Air Force from World War I on. If you've never seen a Spitfire or P-51 up close, here's your chance. It's open from 10 a.m.-4 p.m. Monday-Saturday and 1-4 p.m. Sunday. Admission is about NZ$10. The museum is located at Wigram Aerodrome, a few miles west of town on Highway 1 (the Main South Road). If you're afoot, take a No. 8 or No. 25 bus from Cathedral Square. It's open Monday-Saturday 10a.m.-4 p.m., Sunday, 1-4 p.m. Information: ☎ (03) 343-9532.

Mona Vale This turn-of-the-century mansion shows you how the swells used to live in Christchurch. The huge house was built in 1900 and bought in 1905 by Annie Townend, the millionaire daughter of a wealthy sheep rancher. It's located on the Avon, a couple of kilometers from town. There are morning and afternoon teas and smorgasbord lunches daily except Saturday. The grounds themselves are open from 8 a.m. to 6:30 p.m in the summer. Punting at Mona Vale is also available for about NZ$10 a half-hour per person. Tickets are available at Mona Vale or at the ChCh information centre. The mansion is entered from Fendalton Road. Information: ☎ 489-660.

Orana Park Wildlife Trust OK, animal fans, here's your chance to see two of the biggies in the New Zealand fauna world in one shot—the kiwi and the tuatara (see Animals). In addition to native New Zealand animals, the reserve also has 400 species of exotics, including lions, zebra, rhinos and giraffes. The park is located on McLean's Island Road, northwest of the international airport. Admission is about NZ$10 for adults. It's open daily from 10 a.m.-5 p.m. Information (including feeding times): ☎ 597-109.

Ferrymead Historic Park This is sort of a 20th century Down Under Williamsburg. The theme is a busy little town from the turn of the century, with a working printer's shop, bakery and artisans shops. It's a self-contained village with the emphasis on vintage technology—cars, railroad engines, airplanes and agricultural equipment. Included in the displays are a working railroad and a tram line. It's located off Ferry Road on the Heathcote River, southeast of the city. It's open daily 10 a.m.-4:30 p.m. Adult tickets are about NZ$10. Information: ☎ 841-708.

Queen Elizabeth II Park and Leisure Centre—If you want to go for a swim—or relieve a teen-ager who's climbing the walls, this is the place for you. The centerpieces of the complex, built for the 1974 Commonwealth Games, are its four indoor heated pools, squash courts and running track. It also has bumper cars, miniature golf, two waterslides, a maze, a poolside cafe and an outdoor snack stand. The amusements are open daily from 10 a.m. to dusk; pool hours vary. The facility is located in New Brighton, on the coast north of Christchurch. There's a good beach nearby, as well. Information: ☎ 834-313.

THE ESSENTIAL CHCH
CLIMATE

The city sits next to the ocean on the Canterbury Plains, so it gets climatic influences from mountains, plains and sea—meaning the weather is changeable. Look for summer highs to be around 20-25 degrees Celsius (70 to 80 degrees F, 50s at night) and winter lows in the 4-6 range (40s) with highs in the 50s. Rainfall is heaviest in the summer. It might snow once in a while.

INFORMATION

Your best source of city and regional information is the Canterbury Information Centre at the corner of Worcester Street and Oxford Terrace. In addition to written information, maps and brochures, the centre is also where a number of local services, such as city tours, rental cars and accommodations can be booked. During the week it's open from 8:30 a.m.-5 p.m.; weekends and holidays from 9 a.m. to 4p.m.; ☎ 799-629. Information is also available at the airport and at the government (NZTP) office at Cathedral Square.

The city also has a special information service for handicapped travelers. Located at 314 Worcester St., the office has information about equipment, facilities and access. ☎ 666-189. Active types should call the Outdoor Recreation Centre, ☎ 799-395.

BANKS

Normal banking hours are weekdays from 9 a.m.-4:30 p.m. (Tuesdays, open from 9:30 a.m.) Hours for bureaux de change at the airport and at downtown locations vary; some are open Saturday mornings. We found most of the banks clustered near Victoria Square; some did not charge for changing travelers checks, but Thos. Cook did.

PHONES

The area code for Christchurch is (03). The emergency number (police, fire, ambulance) is 111. For police non-emergency; ☎ 793-999. The number for the U.S. consulate is ☎ 790-040.

GETTING THERE

By Air—Christchurch is served internally by Ansett and Air New Zealand from the North Island and other cities on the South Island, and by Mount Cook from the resort areas on the South Island. Daily service from Auckland to Christchurch is about NZ$320 per person, one way. Daily service from Wellington is about NZ$200. South Island fares to Christchurch from various cities include Dunedin, NZ$190; Invercargill, NZ$230; Nelson, NZ$170; Queenstown, NZ$260, and Mount Cook, NZ$220. These fares include the goods and services tax but are lower using one of the many air passes available. Continental and United, which fly from Australia, have offices in Christchurch; United: ☎ 661-736; Continental: ☎ 652-971.

By Bus—The fare from the ferry dock at Picton to Christchurch is about NZ$60 per person, one way. Other fares into the city include: from Fox Glacier, NZ$70; Mount Cook, NZ$60; Queenstown, NZ$90; Invercargill, NZ$90, and Dunedin, NZ$50. These fares include tax but are lower with passes. There is also a coast-to-coast service from Christchurch to Greymouth and back with stops at Arthur's Pass. The service, called Coast to Coast Shuttle, picks up passengers at any YHA, or backpackers hotel or at the Pavlova Backpackers at 50 Cathedral Square. The buses will take bikes, luggage or skis at no extra charge— and no, you don't have to be a backpacker to ride the bus. Christchurch to Arthur's Pass is NZ$25; ChCh to Greymouth, NZ$35; round-trip ChCh- Greymouth-ChCh, NZ$60 (must be used within three days). Buses leave the city around 7:30 a.m., and return around 5:30 p.m. The company recommends reservations; for information, call toll free at ☎ (0800) 800-847.

By Rail—From Picton, the daily Coastal Express fare, one way, is about NZ$50. Other rail fares on the South Island to Christchurch (which may mean some bus segments) include: Nelson, NZ$70; Te Anau, NZ$105; Greymouth, NZ$60; Dunedin, NZ$55; Fox Glacier, NZ$80, and Franz Josef, NZ$80. The bus and train terminal in Christchurch is on Moorhouse Avenue; information ☎ 799- 020.

HOW TO GET AROUND

By taxi—They don't cruise in Christchurch, so find a cab rank (or a hotel) or call them. Try Blue Star Taxis, which has vans and also wheelchair taxis available, ☎ 799- 799.

By bus—There's an extensive bus system around the Christchurch metro area. Fares are per zone; the normal fare around town and to close-on environs is about NZ$1.60. The city also runs hourly buses from the airport to Cathedral Square for about NZ$3; takes about a half hour. Carrington's also runs a shuttle for about double the price and will pick you up at your hotel; ☎ 352- 6369. For information about city bus service, check with the Canterbury Information Centre.

By bike—ChCh is a flat city, ideal for bikers who can remember to stay on the proper side of the road. There are several bike rental shops in town. Try Cyclone Cycles at 245 Colombo Street, ☎ 332-9573; both mountain bikes and touring bikes available. Or try Christchurch Leisure Sports, 94 Gloucester Street, ☎ 772-827; they have bikes, mopeds (no special license needed), mountain bikes, twin bikes —almost any kind of sports equipment is available for rent. Or try Christchurch Rent-a-Bike, 82 Worcester Street, ☎ 64-409. Depending on type of bike, insurance rates and the individual outlet, expect to pay around NZ$10 to NZ$15 a day, or around NZ$60 to NZ$100 a week. The Canterbury Information Centre has biking maps for the city and nearby countryside; it also has maps of city walks and hikes in the area.

RENTAL CARS/RVs

All the major multinationals have offices in Christchurch: Budget, Hertz, National, Thrifty, Avis—plus a bunch of locals. For rental costs for automobiles and camper vans, see the driving section. Among the locals worth checking with are Newmans and Maui, both national companies. Maui is especially recommended for RVs. There are also some cut-rate local agencies which we haven't used who offer pretty good deals. Hey, it's New Zealand—they have to be honest, right? The Automobile Association office downtown is at 210 Hereford Street, next to the Occidental Hotel, ☎ 791-280.

TOURS

The major attractions downtown are within fairly easy walking distance—remember the city is flat—but for those who choose to ride, there are a number of tour companies that offer scenic drives around the city, the environs or day trips, and longer, to attractions in the Canterbury district. Most of the tours can be booked through your hotel, through the tourist offices, travel agents or by calling direct. Among the best:

CTB Coachlines—The historic three-hour Christchurch tour does all the necessary spots, and runs about NZ$20 for adults. The company also has tours to Akaroa (one-day) about NZ$30; a trip to Orana Park and a salmon farm (half-day), about NZ$25; a trip to Milford Sound and Queenstown (one long day), about NZ$120. Local tours leave from the CTB kiosk at Cathedral Square. Local and tour passengers will be picked up at hotels prior to departure if requested in advance; the tour prices do not include meals. The Queenstown/ Milford Sound trip leaves from the Vacation Inn on Colombo Street. Information: ☎ (03) 794-268; after hours, ☎ (03) 661- 999. The Queenstown office is at 37 Shotover St., ☎ (03) 442-7028.

Canterbury Scenic Tours—City tour (half-day), about NZ$25, which includes snacks and hotel/motel pickup; leaves at 9 a.m. and 1:30 p.m. Information: ☎ 366-9660.

Canterbury Scenic Tours, P.O. Box 32113, Linwood, Christchurch; ☎ 669-660 (24 hours). The company will arrange other itineraries on request.

Gray Line New Zealand—Always a good bet, the Gray Line operation in New Zealand is no exception. There are two city tours, one in the morning, one in the afternoon, for about NZ$20 for adults. The price includes free motel/hotel pickup and snacks (there is an optional airport drop-off on request). Tours depart from the Canterbury Information Centre.

Gray Line, in cooperation with Mount Cook Landline, also runs a tour to Kaikoura, about 2-1/2 hours north of the city on the coast where you can pick up a boat to go searching for whales, dolphins, seals and seabirds—or you can take a glass-bottom boat trip. The round-trip to Kaikoura is about NZ$45. The best time to see the 70-foot sperm whales along the coast is in the winter. The whale-watching trips leave about two hours after arrival, and return just before the bus heads back. The cost is about NZ$80 per person. The glass-bottom boat trips run about four hours and include lunch; price is about NZ$50 per person. You can stay over in Kaikoura and catch another return bus. For current whale-watching prices (or to book without a bus tour), ☎ (0800) 655-121.

There is also a tour from ChCh to Queenstown with a stop at Mt. Cook—you can return from Mt. Cook or stay over in Queenstown. The ChCh-Mt. Cook-ChCh fare is about NZ$80, no meals; the trip to Queenstown is about NZ$60, no meals. City tours depart from the Canterbury Information Centre; regional tours depart from the Mt. Cook Landline depot at 40 Lichfield St. Hotel/motel pickups available on request. Information in Christchurch, ☎ (03) 790-690; throughout the country, ☎ (0800) 800-737. Newmans Coaches also has service to Kaikoura; ☎ 795-641. Or if you want to splurge, Air

Charter Christchurch will whip you to the whales for NZ$150 per person. The pilots will also fly you to Mount Cook and the glaciers (NZ$250 per person) or down to Queenstown for the day (NZ$500 per person).

During the summer holiday months (December-February), the Christchurch City Council runs a London double-decker around town, leaving from Cathedral Square. An adult ticket is about NZ$5 and the tours leave starting at noon. For information on this bus, call the Christchurch Transport Kiosk (which also has information on regular city buses) at ☎ 794-260.

SPORTS

Skiing—Christchurch is within a few hours of a bunch of ski areas, including Mt. Hutt and Mt. Dobson, and many people actually base in the city to bus or drive down to ski near Queenstown. Thus the town has a number of companies offering ski packages from Christchurch to almost any ski resort of your choice. For further information, see our section on Skiing.

Golf—There are four courses in Christchurch. Serious golfers will want the 18-hole Waitakari championship course at Burwood; information ☎ 383-0729. Or another 18-holer, the Coringa Country Club course, information ☎ 359-7172. Green fees will be in the NZ$10-NZ$20 range, and club rentals are available.

Tennis—You might get invited to a private club, or else try Tourist Tennis, which has 10 lighted courts and equipment rentals; information ☎ 351-6826.

Squash—When in Rome... There are a number of public squash courts, including those at the Queen Elizabeth II Park, information ☎ 383-4313.

Beaches—The Christchurch beaches are on the coast, east and northeast of the city, most within 10 kilometers or so. Local word is that sharks are few and far between but that there are often nasty undercurrents. Many areas of the beaches are patrolled. There are also swimming areas in Lyttleton Harbour and on the Banks Peninsula southeast of the city.

There are lots more things available—bowling, horseback riding, go-carts, fishing, dancing—you name it. Check either with the Canterbury Information Centre or with the Outdoor Recreation Centre, ☎ 799- 395.

SHOPPING

Normal weekday shopping hours in the central city are from 9:30 a.m. to 5 p.m., Friday night to 9 p.m. Many of the stores in the malls and in the suburbs also stay open weekends; hours vary. Credit cards are widely accepted.

There are several shopping complexes in the city, including the dozens of stores that sit around the pedestrian-only mall running along Cashel Street, then down High Street to Hereford (they say Haira-furd). Many of the stores and cafes in Christchurch, by the way, are totally smoke free. Two new suburban shopping centers are the

Riccarton Mall on the road of the same name, a bit over a kilometer west of Hagley Park, and the

Linwood City Shopping Centre at the corner of Linwood Avenue and Buckleys Road, which is a couple of miles east of the city centre. Both are open Thursday and Friday nights.

The aforementioned

City Arts Centre in the old Canterbury University campus has a number of crafts shops and galleries, normally open seven days a week. One we recommend taking a peek at is **Riki Rangi**, a Maori arts studio that specializes in carvings of native wood, bone, stone and shells. Adjacent to the workshop is a gallery where the finished products are on sale. It has some of the best greenstone jewelry around. Hours are 9-5, week-days and 10-4, weekends. Information: ☎ 664-943. The outdoor **Arts Centre Market** on Worcester Street, next to the campus, is open weekends, 10-4.

Christchurch being part of New Zealand, it's no surprise the town is up to its fetlocks in

Sheep stores, one of which is the **Sheep Station** at the corner of Colombo and Gloucester streets. Lots of lambskin clothing, suedes, leathers, rugs. Another good store is the **Skin Pool** at 76 Moorhouse Ave. Also try **Woolpak** at 30 Battersea St., which has a large assortment of rugs and car seat covers. Or the **Rusa Leather Co.** factory at 174 St. Asaph St. **The Tannery**, on Worcester Street next to Noah's Hotel, has deerskin and mohair goods. For some flashy knitwares and designer scarves, try **Nature's Choice** at 755 Colombo St. Most stores will ship stuff home if it's too bulky to pack or carry on the plane.

You'll also see stores all over selling

Canterbury clothing. The Canterbury line of jerseys is world famous and is worn by many of the world's soccer and rugby teams. You can pick up a version of the All-Blacks rig almost anywhere. Canterbury stuff ain't cheap, but it's exceptional quality and well worth the money. One place with a large assortment is the **Canterbury of New Zealand** store in the Riccarton Mall.

WHERE TO STAY

Parkroyal—This is our favorite of the biggies downtown, situated at the corner of Kilmore and Durham, streets next to the new Town Hall and overlooking Victoria Square. The centerpiece of the eight-floor building is a glass atrium, a nice place to be on a sunny day. The 300-room hotel, built in the shape of a truncated pyramid, has a laundry room plus 24-hour laundry service, a business center, a gym, a sauna, baby-sitting service, TV and coffee/tea. Traditional Japanese food is served in the Yamagen Restaurant, and the Victoria Street Cafe in the atrium has a good salad bar and light lunches. The Canterbury Tales restaurant serves up-scale meals; look for the wall tapestries depicting scenes from Chaucer's classic. Rumpole's Bar is popular with the local barristers, not because of the name but because of the hotel's proximity to the Town Hall courts, and the First Edition Bar has live music and meals until late. Standard singles and doubles are about NZ$260 plus GST; there are also luxury suites. ☎ 657-799.

Noah's—Corner of Worcester and Oxford Terrace. Another popular hotel, it looks sort of like a giant, bowed computer chip, but lots of business types use it for their ChCh base. It has 208 rooms, with main dining in the Waitangi Restaurant and the Brogues Brasserie for meals at all hours. There are three bars, including the very nice Worcester Bar. Standard single/double rooms are about NZ$215; deluxe are NZ$230; suites start at NZ$515, and the royal suite is NZ$875. ☎ 794-700.

Vacation Inn—Another hotel overlooking Victoria Square, the Vacation (formerly the Hyatt Kingsgate) has about 90 rooms, most refurbished, with a nice second floor restaurant, the Terrace, overlooking the square. There is a ground-floor coffee shop. Doubles are about NZ$160. ☎ 795-880.

Christchurch Airport Travelodge—On Memorial Avenue and Orchard Street in Harewood, close to the airport. Motelish. Pool, courtesy van to the airport, restaurant with nightly Maori entertainment, nice bar. Standard doubles are about $145; suites available. ☎ 583-139.

Quality Inn Chateau—On Dean's Avenue near the west side of Hagley Park. It has handicapped access, TV, coffee/tea and the Camelot Restaurant, all darkly medieval with an excellent wine list (Tuesday-Saturdays) and the Lamplighter Restaurant, open seven days. Standard doubles are NZ$185. ☎ 488-999.

Cotswold Inn—88-90 Papanui Rd., Edgeware (15 minutes from the airport, five minutes from downtown). If you don't mind being away from central downtown, this is a dandy. About 70 rooms including 11 studios and a pair of royal suites. The exterior is Norman half-timbered, all bunched around a central courtyard. It has a pool, spa, some kitchen units, baby-sitting service and an airport courtesy van. The Earl of Essex bar is quite nice, as is Crofter's Restaurant. Singles start around NZ$155, doubles around NZ$165. ☎ 355-3535.

The George—50 Park Terrace. One of those pastel and earth-tones places, lots of glass, lots of marble. It has a very nice location, right on the Avon, across from Hagley Park. It has baby-sitting and a courtesy airport van. The Pescatore offers up-scale Kiwi food, specializing in seafood and venison; live entertainment, Friday-Monday. The Piano Bar, with fireplace, is a cozy spot in the winter; there's a brasserie for casual dining. Standard doubles start at about NZ$195. ☎ 794- 560.

Quality Inn Durham Street—Corner of Durham and Kilmore streets, northeast of Cathedral Square. About what you'd expect; boxy, centrally located, quite serviceable. Spa, tea/coffee, sauna, handicapped access, fridge, mini-bar, baby-sitting, gym; bar and Sarah's Brasserie, with light snacks or five-course meals. Standard doubles are about NZ$170. ☎ 654-699.

Moderate

If all else fails in Christchurch, just drive down Papanui Street—it's lined with small motels and B&Bs. Actually, the town is full of places. A few of the better motels:

Abel Tasman Motor Lodge—110 Sherborne St., 15 minutes from the airport. All kitchen units, some family, some suites, studios. Spa available, laundry room, baby- sitting, breakfast available. Rates NZ$76-130, depending on unit. ☎ 699-085.

Airport Lodge Motel, 105 Roydvale Ave. Kitchen units, laundry, close to golf course, courtesy airport van. Singles, NZ$80; doubles, NZ$90. ☎ 585-119.

Akron Hotel—87 Bealey Ave. A Golden Chain unit, all kitchens, studios and two-bedroom units. Laundry, tea/coffee, baby-sitting, bike available, bus stop at the gate. Doubles, NZ$80-85. ☎ 661-633.

Avon Hotel—356 Oxford Terrace, on the Avon River, northeast of the city center. Pool, sauna, spa, gym, fridge, tea/coffee, restaurant. Doubles, NZ$100. ☎ 791-180.

Canterbury Court Motel—140 Lincoln Road near Hagley Park. Kitchens, laundry, spa available, close to supermarket and bus stop. Doubles, NZ$80. ☎ 388- 8351.

Carlton Mill Lodge—19 Bealey Ave., opposite north Hagley Park. Some kitchens, some suites, laundry room, minibars, baby-sitting, courtesy coach, bar and restaurant. Standard doubles are NZ$110. ☎ 661-083 or 068.

Latimer Motor Lodge—30 Latimer St., heart of downtown, off Worcester Street. Some kitchens, tea/coffee, fridge, minibars, baby-sitting, restaurant, bar. Doubles, around NZ$140. ☎ 796-760.

Pacific Park—263 Bealey St., 15 minutes from the beach areas. Fridge, minibar, tea/coffee, laundry room, bar and Aggie's Restaurant, a New Zealand Lamb Board gold medal winner. One to three persons, NZ$110. ☎ 798- 660.

Budget

These next three are for backpackers or budget-minded travelers planning on catching a bus or train at the Moorhouse Avenue station. Both are within several blocks of the station.

Ambassador's Hotel—19 Manchester St. Pretty basic, with shared and private facilities and backpackers rooms. TV lounge, laundry room. Courtesy van to the station. NZ$70, double, B&B. ☎ 667-808.

Coker Hotel—Century old hulk further down, at 52 Manchester. Three bars, a restaurant, live music. Private and shared facilites, most rooms refurbished. Doubles, NZ$70-80. ☎ 798-580.

Excelsior Hotel—Corner of Lichfield, Manchester and High streets. House lounge, bar, bottle shop. Breakfasts available. Double with shared bath, NZ$45; private double, NZ$55. ☎ 669-489.

Others

Colombo Travelodge—965 Colombo St. Discount for AA members, coffee/tea, fridge, electric frypans, breakfast available. NZ$60-70, double. ☎ 663-029.

Windsor Hotel—52 Armagh St. Colonial-style B&B. Coffee/tea, laundry. Double, NZ$80. ☎ 366-1503.

Shirley Lodge Holiday Village—108 Marshland Rd., Shirley. Seven acres of parks, one- and two-room units. Fridge, pool, restaurant, bar, laundry, game room, bus stop. Motel units with kitchens, NZ$60, double; tourist flats, NZ$56 double. ☎ 385-3132.

Meadow Park Holiday Park—A Top 10 facility, with pool, spa, laundry, TV lounge, BBQ facilities. Supermarket and dairy a few blocks away; bus stop. Cottages, NZ$50-60, double; cabins, NZ$50; smaller cabins, NZ$35. ☎ 352-9176.

Hostels

YMCA—12 Hereford St. New, 100 rooms, bunks, apartments, motel units; game room, 24-hour check-in, TV lounge, laundry, gym, coffee/tea. Basic, NZ$40 per person; motel units, NZ$90, double. ☎ 660-689.

Pavlova Backpackers—50 Cathedral Square, heart of town. Rates around NZ$15 a night. ☎ 665-158.

YHA Rolleston House—5 Worcester St. TV and family room, kitchen. Members, NZ$18; non-members, NZ$22. ☎ 666-564.

WHERE TO EAT

More than a dozen restaurants in Christchurch, including many of the top spots, do not allow smoking. Many more have no-smoking sections. It's a growing trend in ChCh to have smoke-free environments in stores and restaurants.

Some of the best lamb we ever had in New Zealand was in an unlikely place, the **Lone Star**. We must report that despite the decor (drugstore cowboy) and some of the main courses (Tex-Mex stuff named after John Wayne and other stars), the Lone Star manages to put out excellent food in a very lively atmosphere. The service is fast and efficient and it's so popular if you're not in the place by 6 you might have an hour's wait. What a lot of folks do is sign up for a table, then go spend the hour waiting at the nearby **Loaded Hog** brew pub, which serves up some very tasty beer. The Lone Star serves a grilled lamb with mint salsa that'll knock your socks off. It's at 26 Manchester St., down from the train station, across from the Ambassadors Hotel. Open for dinner from 6-11 p.m. Moderate prices. Yes, it does have Lone Star beer. ☎ 657-086.

Dizzy Lizzy's is a comfy old 1860s cottage with a blackboard menu and tasty lamb specialties. It's one of the non-smokers. Moderate prices. It's open for dinner from 6:30 p.m. to midnight. BYO. It's at 471 Ferry Rd. ☎ 896-529.

If you're in the area of the Arts Centre, **Dux De Lux** proves that vegetarian food can be prepared so even dedicated carnivores won't scream. It's set in a Tudor building with garden seating in warmer months. There's live local music and a brew pub next door with tapas. Mushrooms stuffed with capers are a specialty at the Dux. It's open from 10 a.m. to midnight, dinner starting at 5:30. Very popular. Located at the corner of Hereford and Montreal streets. ☎ 666-919.

Double D's Bar and Grill is in the Art Centre complex, and does very good pit barbecues and Kiwi meat platters. It's cafe style, nothing pretentious, moderately priced. It's open seven days for lunch from 11 a.m., dinner, 5 p.m.-midnight. ☎ 650-566.

Cheers Cafe, at 196 Hereford, serves up what is almost California cuisine —fish in dill sauce, salmon and eggs, that sort of stuff. It has a blackboard menu, a pleasing atmosphere, good prices. It's BYOB, open for breakfast and lunch weekdays, 7 a.m.-3 p.m. ☎ 663- 431.

We throw in the unpretentious **Cafe Bleu** as a representative of the small specialty cafes you'll find scattered around the city. This one, in the Cashell Street mall, serves up huge portions of pub-style food. Try their potato hunks with salsa and cheese—a meal by themselves. Lunch and a couple of beers, for under NZ$20. The Bleu also has live jazz at night on the weekends.

The Gardens Restaurant is the place to haul into if you're doing the tour of the Botanic Gardens and Hagley Park. It serves a decent smorgasbord lunch for around NZ$15 per person and also morning and afternoon teas. The smorgasbord, which fills up rapidly, is open from noon to 2 p.m.; teas are at 10 a.m. and 4 p.m. It's fully licensed. ☎ 665-076.

Where, you ask, do oysters go to heaven?

Pedro's, probably, an eatery run by an Iberian who takes Las Ostras and grills them, then puts them inside a corn shell with ham, celery and cheese. Or mussels with garlic and lemon, any seafood with a zap of Spanish flavor. Pedro's, located at 143 Worcester St., near Cathedral Square, is very popular and his portions are huge. BYOB, moderate prices. Open Tuesday-Saturday, 6-10 p.m. ☎ 797-688.

The Town Hall Restaurant, at the corner of Kilmore and Victoria streets, overlooks Victoria Square and is another smorgasbord-for-lunch place made for famished tourists doing the tour bit. There's a very nice view with a fountain, and on weekends, the menu goes a la carte; live entertainment comes in Friday and Saturday nights. The smorgasbord is open weekdays from noon to 2 p.m. Weekend dinner service runs 5:30-8:30 p.m. Moderate prices. ☎ 666-651.

Good pub food is to be had at the

Excelsior Hotel at the corner of High, Manchester and Lichfield streets, close to the shopping malls. It's open seven days for all meals. Very reasonable.

Nice views of the Avon are available from the outdoor tables at

The Oxford Restaurant at the corner of Colombo Street and Oxford Terrace. Salad bar, blackboard menu, traditional Kiwi meat dishes. Very reasonable. Open 11 a.m.-9 p.m., Sunday-Thursday; 11 a.m.-10 p.m., Friday and Saturday. ☎ 797-148.

The Imperial Swan is a good-enough Chinese restaurant with low prices, fast service. It's at 150 Armagh St. BYOB. ☎ 793-226.

Out of town, but always listed among Christchurch's best, is

The Sign of the Takahe in Casmere Hills on the Summit Road over the Banks Peninsula. The Takahe is one of several "Sign" roadhouses built along the highway (Sign of the Kiwi, Sign of the Bellbird) but is definitely the most ornate and best preserved. It's a baronial-style castle with views of the city and, on a clear day, the Southern Alps. The emphasis here is on silver service and candlelight. The specialties are crayfish, venison, game birds and lamb. Expensive but worth it. Or go for a Devonshire tea if the purse is a little strained. Lunch and teas from noon to 2 p.m.; dinner, 7-11:30 p.m.

CLUBS AND ENTERTAINMENT

The Great Hall at the Arts Centre is one of the better venues in Christchurch for a wide variety of music from madrigals to jazz, flamenco guitar to African dancing. Hours of concerts vary. The best place for information is the information center at the arts centre.

Irish music is on tap most nights at two bars at

Warners Hotel at 50 Cathedral Square. Imported beer, Guinness on tap. Lunches available; music starts around 8 p.m. ☎ 665-159.

Disco and a laser show are the offering at the

Paladium on Gloucester Street, opposite the public library. The music is live Wednesday through Saturday. Open seven days. ☎ 790-572.

Jazz and rock bands hang out at

Caeser's Night Spot at the corner of Gloucester Street and Chancery Lane. The Spot is part of the Chancery Tavern and Restaurant. Open seven days, 7 p.m.-3 a.m. ☎ 794-317.

Vesuvio's, 182 Oxford Terrace, is European in style, with Le Jazz Hot and cabaret-style motif. Open 10 a.m.- midnight, music around 8 p.m. Good cafe food. ☎ 662- 666.

Yellow-eyed penguin poses on the Otago Penninsula

AROUND CANTERBURY

LYTTELTON

Lyttelton Harbour, Christchurch's port, is the collapsed and flooded crater of an ancient volcano, one of two that formed the Banks Peninsula and blew apart, creating the harbors at **Lyttelton** and **Akaroa.** Modern Lyttelton still shows signs of the colonial past, despite the intrusion of heavy ship traffic moving in and out of the container and bulk terminals.

A number of Victorian buildings still stand, including several from the 1860s, such as the remains of a jail and the **Most Holy Trinity Anglican church**. You can tour the harbor by boat, and there is regular service to two historic islands in the harbour, **Ripapa** and **Quail**. It was at this harbor that the original settlers of Christchurch landed in 1850. The Banks Peninsula District Council is currently spending money to beef up London Street in the city center with a central square and other improvements.

AKAROA

The choicest piece of land near Christchurch, to our minds, is the almost-but-not-quite-Irish country of the Banks Peninsula with its chief tourist attraction, Akaroa. It's some of the most attractive real estate in the whole country, well worth a drive or a tour. The highway—Summit Road—gets narrow and twisty here and there, but *the scenery is great with valleys and meadows covered with sheep and deer.* It's about 90 kilometers from Christchurch to Akaroa, much shorter as the crow flies. Akaroa was founded by the French in the 1840s and one of the reasons His Majesty's Government was so anxious to take control of New Zealand. The village is—well—quaint and a popular tourist spot. There are remnants of the French settlers—one house dates to the original colonists—and there are French names here and there. The main drag is Rue Lavaud, and a sign down the street advertises, we are sad to report, "Le Mini Golf." The **Bank of New Zealand** is worth a photo stop. How many lavender and violet banks have you seen?

There's a **harbor cruise** to take aboard the **Canterbury Cat** (dolphins, penguins, a volcanic sea cave). The tour begins at 1:30 p.m.

daily; November to March there's also a sailing at 11 a.m. Cost is about NZ$30. There are several hotels or **B&Bs** around the Akaroa harbor area, one of which is the **Grand Hotel,** an old queen of a place, a tad seedy but still popular with the locals. It serves a good lunch and has a pair of resident cockatoos (name of Crackers and James) to watch while you sip a brew. The **Grand**, at 6 Rue Lavaud, charges NZ$22.50 per person a night. More modern and more expensive is the **Akaroa Village Inn** with doubles starting around NZ$90, suites for about NZ$160. There are also places to stay at other spots along the Summit Road, such as the **Des Pecheurs Hotel** in Duvauchelle with rooms for about NZ$80. Check out the excellent **Relais Rochefort** restaurant in Duvauchelle, fairly expensive but very good.

Included among restaurants worth a try in Akaroa are the **LaRue Restaurant**, specializing in French cuisine and lobster, on the Rue Lavaud; **Montarsha Restaurant**, mixed menu, located on the main road in Akaroa (Beach Road and Rue Lavaud are the same), and the **Akaroa Bakery**, the best place for breakfast, fresh pastries. For fast food or sit-downs, try the **Pier Cafe**, located on the pier where the *Canterbury Cat* ties up. Information on dining, accommodations and activities in Akaroa and the Banks Peninsula is available from the Canterbury Information Centre in Christchurch; from the Akaroa County Council in Duvauchelle or from the information center at the Akaroa Museum, corner of Rue Lavaud and Rue Balgueri; ☎ 304-7614.

Hikers note: there's a great track that circles the peninsula in about four days with some often interesting cliffs and spectacular coastline. Accommodation is in huts; food and lodging runs about NZ$20 a day. Registration is necessary because the route passes private land and the number of hikers per day is restricted. For information, call the Outdoor Recreation Information Centre; transportation from ChCh to the track start can be arranged.

KAIKOURA

This is whale-watching central, a bit of irony because this was a major whaling area in the 1840s and through this century. Indeed, the last sperm whale was harpooned off the coast here in 1964. Fittingly, whales are important to the economy here once again, but now it's tourists and not whale oil that are bringing in the bucks. There are at present two companies taking tourists out to the whales, a business that sees about 20,000 people a year come for a look and which generates something in excess of NZ$1 million. Whale-watching seems so lucrative, in fact, that several companies have put in bids to start boat tours. The end result will probably be limits on the number of boats allowed to operate in the whaling waters, much the same as the controls on gray whale excursions off the coast of Northern California.

Seal colony

Many whale-watching tours originate in Christchurch (see prices in the ChCh section). But there's more to see than whales—including rare **Hector's dolphins, blue penguins, fur seals** *and flocks of sea birds, including* **albatross** *and* **petrels.**

The town sits about halfway between Christchurch and Picton on the main road (Highway 1) and is also on the Coastal Pacific train route (it's about 200 kilometers northeast of ChCh). The population of the town is about 3,000, and it sits along a curved harbor with the main road, the Esplanade, running along the ocean to the tip of the peninsula where the town was built. *There are some very nice trails from the end of the road back up the peninsula,* including a walk along the ocean which can be dangerous if the seas are rough.

There is a nice little museum in town, full of Maori information (there is evidence suggesting Maori presence here a millenium ago). There are also displays from the early whaling days. The museum, just up from the town center, is usually open on weekends. The town's information center is in Memorial Hall on the Esplanade;

☎ :(03) 319-5641. There are three hostels: the **YHA** is ☎ (03) 319-5931; the **White House** is ☎ 319-3916, and **Pavlova Backpackers** is ☎ 319-6699.

Because of its growth as a tourism center, Kaikoura has a number of motels and a couple of old hotels. The motels (**Alpine View, Blue Seas, Sierra Beachfront**, to name a few) have doubles in the NZ$70 a night range. Try the **Caves Restaurant** near the Maori Leap Cave for decent food. Ask about crayfish. The cave, by the way, is a sea-created limestone cavern. You can take a tour for cheap. It's about 3 kilometers south of town on the main road.

Kaikoura Tours is one of the two whale-watching companies in Kaikoura. The office is located in the train station; ☎ (03) 319-5045. Reservations are a must during whale season. The cost is about NZ$80 per person. A trip aboard a glass-bottom boat will run about 4 hours and includes lunch; price is about NZ$50 per person. For current whale-watching prices (or to book), ☎ (0800) 655-121.

ARTHUR'S PASS

One of the best drives in New Zealand is the trip on Highway 73 from Christchurch to the west coast of the South Island, up and through the Southern Alps. You get to see most of the ecosystems prevalent in the south, from the wide, grassy Canterbury Plains to the sub-alpine and alpine country around Arthur's Pass National Park, to the wind-swept, damp rain forests of the coast. And about two-thirds of the way along is the hamlet of **Arthur's Pass**, a most excellent place to haul in for a couple of days to eat, hike or just enjoy the scenery. It's also a stop (or a stay-over) for passengers on the Tranz-Alpine Express, which runs from Christchurch to Greymouth.

In the winter, it's a popular place for skiers (Temple Basin, Porter Heights and several other areas are close by), and in the summer it's popular with hikers and campers. The road can be a true test in foul weather with gale-force winds, fog and snow, all on top of some very curvy stretches. But when it's clear, the scenery is great, particularly going through the **Otira Gorge** on the Greymouth side of the pass. The South Island's continental divide is nearby, and the top of the pass itself is about 3,000 feet above sea level not high by North American standards but still exposed to the full force of the Roaring Forties. The pass was originally used by the Maoris from the west coast to trade greenstone with their neighbors on the east side. The road was pushed through by Christchurch merchants wanting to cash in on the 1860s gold rush and was built mostly by pick and shovel. The road was opened in 1866; the railroad followed in 1923. The national park is about 390 square miles of 7,500-foot peaks, gorges, rivers and glaciers—the most northerly glaciers on the South Island.

The park is a hiker's paradise with a number of serious tramps plus some just leisurely strolls. There are also some excellent mountaineering opportunities. The park is full of huts—about 90 huts and shelters are scattered about. Information about the park, the trails, the huts and park wildlife (red deer and chamois abound) is available from the information centre and national park headquarters in Arthur's Pass. Information: Park Headquarters, Box 8, Arthur's Pass; ☎ (0516) 89-211. Just behind the park headquarters is the beginning of a trail that goes almost straight up along a series of waterfalls to the top of the low mountains back of the village. Not technically difficult, great scenery. Note the keas wandering around—don't feed them or the rangers will get rancorous.

The range of accommodations is not extensive on purpose. Growth of the village, indeed the whole area, is rigorously restricted; most of the permanent population of under 100 are railway workers. The village has a school, post office, tea rooms, one licensed restaurant and a chapel.

WHERE TO STAY

The best place in town to stay is probably the Chalet, which also has the best food.

The Chalet has 8 rooms, some with in-room facilities, with TV and continental breakfasts. The decor (as with many things in the village) is Alpine, in this case, Swiss. There is a coin laundry. This place is a favorite with us. Doubles are NZ$75, shared facilities, $85, private bath. Information: ☎ (0516) 89-236.

More standard is

Alpine Motels, which has kitchen facilities and TV. Doubles run about NZ$70; backpackers' rooms, about $45. Information: ☎ (0516) 89-261.

The store and tea rooms down the road from the Chalet groceries and potables and serves light lunches and snacks. The Chalet has a snack bar that serves light lunches (although the proportions are generous) from 9a.m. to 5p.m.. There's a gift shop as well. The restaurant is very good, especially for dinner. Now it can be told—here is where we had our first bottle of Montana cabernet and munched on our first stewed Bambi. Lamb and venison are great, and the service is rural-Kansas friendly.

The only spot we know in Arthur's to plug in an RV is at:

Oscar's Haus Alpine Crafts down the street from the Chalet. There are also tent sites; powered sites are about NZ$10. There is also a **YHA** in the village, spots about NZ$20 a night; information: ☎ (0516) 89-230. The crafts part of Oscar's Haus has some very good handspun yarns and knit wares for sale, as good as any we saw in Christchurch or Wellington.

The Mountain House, across the street from the YHA, has bunk-style beds. Information: ☎ (0516) 89-258.

Nearby is the:

Bealey Hotel in Bealey, about 15 kilometers toward Christchurch from Arthur's. It has motel-style units with doubles going for about NZ$75; kitchen units. Information: ☎ (0516) 89-277.

Also close is the:

Otira Hotel, west of Arthur's Pass in the hamlet of Otira. Passengers aboard the Tranz-Alpine will remember Otira as the beginning of a five-mile tunnel through the Alps. In 1908, teams started from both sides of Mt. Barron and met in 1918—according to the park service, there was a bit more than an inch difference in the alignment. Because of widening work and installation of electricity and concrete, the first train went through in 1923. Because of the length and lack of ventilation of the tunnel, trains are pulled through by electric engines. The Otira Hotel, on the main highway, is a bit run down but has double and single rooms. Doubles go for about NZ$32.

THE WEST COAST

Nature walk, West Coast

The Kiwis call the narrow strip on the West Coast between the mountains and the sea Westland, and its history has mostly evolved around minerals, starting with Maori greenstone and going through the Gold Rushes to modern-day coal mines. The area is definitely laid back and rife with individualists. *It is also one of the most photogenic spots on both islands.* Along that narrow strip are grand vistas of ocean and mountain, glaciers and rain forest. The towns, such as they are, are small, many the remnants of once-booming Gold Rush settlements. The main road down the coast is Highway 6, which you pick up at the western end of the Arthur's Pass highway.

GREYMOUTH

So named because it's at the mouth of the Grey River, this city of about 12,000 is another spot that got its start as a Gold Rush settlement. *It's the largest city on the West Coast and, as the saying goes, it's close to a lot of nice places.* There's not a lot to do aside from wander the beaches and shop. *Most of the tours offered by local operators are Gold Rush-oriented,* although you can also find fishing guides and jet boating trips. Greymouth is the gateway to the largest lake on the West Coast, **Lake Brunner**. There are some nice walks around the lake, including a trail through **Moana Reserve**, a 150-acre park with many typical West Coast rainforest plants, including several species

of orchids. At **Moana Township**, there is a golf course, hotel and restaurant, as well as boat rentals, helicopter tours and fishing trips. Try
Lakeside Jet Boating Tours, ☎ (03) 738-0036 in Greymouth. The
township is a stop on the Tranz-Alpine Express. There is a very good
inn available, the **Lake Brunner Lodge**, a trout-fishing lodge with
excellent food. Rooms and three meals a day go for about NZ$220,
double. ☎ 738-0163. Most of the trout found on the West Coast
are browns; the only place with rainbows is Lake Brunner.

WHERE TO STAY

Greymouth is fairly popular with seaside tourists in the summer, so
there are a number of motels available in the city. Among them are:

Kings Hotel—Mawhera Quay on the Grey River. Restaurant with bar,
sauna, spa; some kitchenettes, some apartments. Standard doubles are
NZ$115. ☎ (03) 768- 5085.

Willowbank Motor Lodge—Two kilometers north of town, full kitchens,
laundry, courtesy car, spa, pool, breakfast and evening meals available.
Doubles are NZ$80. ☎ 768- 5339.

Ashley Motel and Motor Inn—70-74 Tasman St. Heated pool, restaurant,
bar, laundry, tea/coffee. Doubles, around NZ$100. ☎ 768-5135.

Revingtons Hotel—Tainui Street off Smith Street. Center of town, an old
hotel with private and shared facilities. Restaurant, two bars, breakfast
available. Doubles with private bath, NZ$90. ☎ 768-7055.

Greymouth Seaside Holiday Park—Chesterfield Street, south of city center on the beach. Communal kitchens, car wash, laundry, spa. *Not one
of the better Top 10 facilities but serviceable.* Tourist flats, double:
NZ$60; cabins, doubles,·NZ$40; bunkhouse, NZ$15 per person.
☎ 768-6618.

There are two hostel facilities:

The Greymouth Youth Hostel is on Cowper Street about a kilometer from
the city center. Bike hire, full kitchen, laundry. Members, NZ$16-18
per person; non-members NZ$20.

Pavlova Backpackers is at 16 Chapel St., off Tainui Street, near the train
and bus station. Laundry, kitchen, double rooms. NZ$15-18 per per-
son a night. ☎ 768-4868.

WHERE TO EAT

For our money, one of the best places in town to eat is:

Cafe Collage, which offers everything from in-season shellfish to great
lamb and venison. *The scallops are especially tasty.* It's at 115 Mackay
St., upstairs. Hours are noon-1:30 p.m. for lunch, 6 p.m.-late for dinner. BYOB, closed Sundays and Mondays. Moderate prices.
☎ 768- 5497.

The Red Wagon Wheels Restaurant and pub in Revingtons Hotel is popular and has *good quality family fare*. It's open all three meals, closed Sundays. Low to moderate prices. ☎ 768-7055.

ACTIVITIES

Like Hokitika, Greymouth is a *greenstone center*. It's the home of one of the more famous jade carvers in the country,

Ian Boustridge, whose works are on display at the National Museum in Wellington. His house/studio is at 25 Coates Street. Ask anybody in town for directions, but call first: ☎ 768-6048.

Greymouth is on the Picton-Fox Glacier train route, and is served by bus from various cities. Air service is out of Hokitika (shuttle available). There are major car rental agencies, as well as bike and moped agencies.

On the way north to Greymouth are a couple of Gold Rush attractions:

Goldsborough, on a road about 10 kilometers north, and the more improved

Shantytown, eight kilometers south of Greymouth. Shantytown offers gold panning, steam train rides, horse-drawn vehicles, a working sawmill and about 30 old buildings depicting a "typical" West Coast gold mining town in the 1890s. It costs about NZ$10 to get in; another NZ$5 to pan for gold. There's a licensed restaurant for lunch and morning /afternoon teas.

HOKITIKA

This was apparently the first place in New Zealand spotted by European explorers—the Dutchman Abel Tasman arrived here in December 1642. In Maori times, it was an important greenstone trading center, and in the 1860s, exploded during the gold rush. It was largely because of the gold madness around Hokitika that the Arthur's Pass road was developed.

It's now a peaceful town of around 3,000, just south of the intersection of Highway 73 (Arthur's Pass Road) and Highway 6. If you're interested in the history of the area, stop at the **West Coast Historical Museum** on Tancred Street, open weekdays, 9:30 a.m.-4:30 p.m., 2–4 p. m. weekends and holidays, closed weekends during the winter. It has several good **Gold Rush displays** and a 20-minute historical audio-visual program. Admission is about NZ$3. There are several **greenstone factories** in town open for tours and sales.

WHERE TO STAY

If you want to spend the night before going south to the glaciers or north to Westport and Nelson areas, there are a couple of motels:

The Hokitika Motel, 221 Fitzgerald St., has kitchenettes, laundry, a ministore, tea/coffee, spa and a courtesy van. AA discount. Doubles are about NZ$75. ☎ (0288) 58-485.

The Goldsborough has all the amenities offered by the Hokitika Motel, plus breakfast is available. It's close to the beach. Doubles are about NZ$80. ☎ (0288) 58-772 or 773.

The Hokitika Holiday Park has on-site facilities, including a laundry, communal kitchen and TV lounge. Tourist flats, equipped with cooking equipment, are NZ$50; bedding extra. Cabins are NZ$40, and a bunkhouse that sleeps 12 is NZ$10 per person. ☎ 58-172.

The Central Guest House, 20 Hamilton St. in the city center, offers budget accommodations. It has a TV lounge, coffee/tea, laundry and courtesy van. Breakfast and dinner available. Doubles are about NZ$65. ☎ 58-232.

WHERE TO GO

There are not many places to eat. Try **Fowler's Tearoom and Restaurant** on Weld Street; the **Preston Bakery and Tearoom** on Revell Street; the **Seafood Shop** on Weld Street across from the post office for fish and chips, or pub food at the **Westland Hotel** at the corner of Weld and Revell streets.

GETTING THERE

There is rail and bus service to the town, as well as regular air service from Christchurch and Nelson. From ChCh the fares are about NZ$135; from Nelson about NZ$165. There is also service from Auckland, Wellington, Dunedin and Invercargill.

ACTIVITIES

A couple of spots near Hokitika are worth a stop. About 25 kilometers southeast of town on the Kokatahi-Kowhitirangi road is the:

Hokitika River Gorge, a very pleasant spot for a walk. There's a suspension bridge over the river.

For information about the Greymouth/Hokitika area, stop at the Greymouth Information Centre in the Regent Theatre building at the corner of Herbert and Mackay streets. It's open seven days during the summer, Monday-Friday in winter. ☎ 768-5101. There are six banks in town.

About 30 kilometers south of Hokitika is the hamlet of **Ross,** another relic of the gold madness, notable for being the location where the largest nugget in New Zealand history was found. It weighed in at more than six pounds and was immediately made a celebrity. It was named "the Honourable Roddy," after a government official, then paraded all over the country. Eventually, being good little colonials, they shipped the chunk off to George V as a coronation gift. He, having no sense of style, promptly had it melted down to embellish tableware at Buckingham Palace, the twit. If you've a mind, there are several walks around the village that take you past the diggings; stay on the paths because there are mine shafts all over. There's also some gold panning to be done. There's a little museum where you can see a replica of Roddy.

About 60 kilometers on south is a spot called **The Forks**, where you can catch a dirt road that goes to the coast at a place called Okarito. Along the beach you'll see plenty of white heron, and a kilometer or so north on the coast is **Okarito Lagoon**, a tidal marsh where a white heron sanctuary is located. There's a YHA hostel and beach campground at the end of the road. Tours of the sanctuary by jet boat are available through Sanctuary Tours; rates and information are available at the Westland National Park offices in Franz Josef.

The Forks also marks the northern edge of **Westland National Park**, a 222,000-acre (348 square miles) park that has *the most elevation extremes of all the country's national parks.* It goes from sea level on the West Coast to the top of 11,500-foot Mt. Tasman. The result is a wide series of ecosystems, from rain forest to sub-alpine to glaciers. Although technically **Mt. Cook** is on the other side of the mountains (and inaccessible by road from the West Coast), New Zealand's highest mountain is still the center of attraction in the Westland National Park area. Also included in the park are the South Island's two other great tourist attractions, the **Fox** and **Franz Josef** glaciers. Mt. Cook is actually in its own national park, which abuts Westland.

What makes the Southern Alps and the glaciers so striking is that, compared to the glaciers of Alaska and Canada, they are framed by lush rain forests. Within a few miles inland from the ocean, you're at the glaciers' faces, and your first sight of them will be through the dense canopy of the coastal vegetation. They are, simply, startlingly beautiful and worth a visit to New Zealand by themselves.

Franz Josef, the farthest north of the pair, was named after the head of the Austro-Hungarian Empire in 1865 by Julius von Haast, an Austrian explorer. The glacier is about seven miles long. Fox Glacier was named after Sir William Fox, the premier of New Zealand in the early 1870s. Fox is a bit longer and wider than Franz Josef. They rise in the mountains at a height of about 8,500 feet and end at about 980 feet above sea level. The glaciers gave rise to small communities with the same names, both of which now have Westland National Park visitor centers. The centers have information not only about the glaciers, but hiking, camping, accommodations and activities in the park. *Of the two* communities, Fox Glacier is the best-equipped, as far as eateries and accommodations are concerned. Both settlements, however, offer a variety of glacier-oriented activities from helicopter trips to hikes over—and onto—the glaciers themselves. Both have medical clinics.

GETTING TO THE GLACIERS

There is no airline service to either Fox Glacier or Franz Josef, but both can be reached by train/bus or just bus connections. From Christchurch, the Tranz-Alpine train connects with a bus to both villages. There is also bus service from Queenstown, Greymouth, Nelson and Wanaka. Fares from ChCh to the glaciers are about NZ$80; from Queenstown, about NZ$80.

FRANZ JOSEF

Coming from the north, Franz Josef is the first glacier village you come to. It has a permanent population of less than 600, and like Fox Glacier, *it can be almost impossible to find a place to spend the night in the peak holiday season*. At last count, there were about a half-dozen places to stay in the village, including hostels. The village also has a grocery store, a gas station and a small church—Our Lady of the Alps. And there are at least two companies offering either airplane or helicopter rides over and onto the glaciers. The visitor center is open 8a.m.-5p.m. weekly and, in the summer, will often have evening programs on the ecology and geology of the glacier area. There are also accommodation information, souvenirs, booklets and maps available. Information: ☎ (0288) 31-796.

WHERE TO STAY

Westland Motor Inn—Just on the north of town about six kilometers from the glacier. Around 100 rooms with spa, bar and restaurant, laundry, game room and tea/coffee. Rooms range between NZ$80 and NZ$130; off-season discounts. ☎ (0288) 31-729 or 728.

Franz Josef Hotel and Lodge—A complex of lodge, motel and backpackers rooms located a few kilometers north of the village. It underwent refurbishing in 1991. There's a bar, restaurant and bottle shop. Motel rates are between NZ$80 and NZ$110; lodge and backpackers rates between NZ$15 and NZ$30. ☎ 31-719.

Glacier View Motel—Also a bit north of the village. The view is great. Rooms range from studios to family style. Coffee/tea, courtesy van, spa, breakfast available. Doubles are around NZ$80. ☎ 31-705.

Glacier Gateway Motor Lodge—Just across the one-lane Waiho River bridge south of town. Opposite the glacier access road. Units include some with kitchens and microwaves; spa, sauna, baby-sitting, courtesy van, restaurant, breakfast available. Doubles are between NZ$70 and NZ$95; off-season reductions. ☎ 31-776.

Franz Josef Holiday Park—Next to the Glacier Gateway. More than seven acres, including RV and tent sites, cabins, bunkhouses, tourist cottages and a lodge. Kitchen, laundry, game room, barbecues, pool, bus stop. Tent sites are about NZ$8; bunkhouses are NZ$10 per person; cabins are NZ$25 for two persons; lodge rates are about NZ$25 per person, and tourist flats are about NZ$40, double. ☎ 31-766.

Franz Josef Hoste—Modern and close to town, doubles and family rooms. Shop, low-cost meals available. Rates are NZ$16 per person a night, NZ$20 for non-members. ☎ 31-754.

WHERE TO EAT

Fern Room—At the Franz Josef Hotel. Family meals, licensed. Moderate. ☎ 31-719.

Glacier Store and Tearoom—Small grocery store and *place to grab sandwiches and meat pies.* Next to the gas station. ☎ 31-731.

D.A.'s Restaurant and Tearoom—Take-away as well as restaurant. *Salad bar and large proportions.* Inexpensive. ☎ 31-721.

ACTIVITIES

The highlight of your New Zealand tour, if you're not afraid of flying, is a flight to the glaciers, especially the flights where you actually land high in the mountains. Like everything else in Westland, glacier flights are weather dependent. Even on clear, sunny days, it's not uncommon to have so much cloud cover around the peak of Mt. Cook that it can't be seen.

These flights can be short or long, depending on the pocketbook, and you can either take a **ski-plane** or a **helicopter**. *We prefer the choppers because you can hover over the glaciers and take magnificent photos.* On the other hand, when's the last time you landed on snow in a ski-plane?

The two companies currently offering helicopter trips are **Glacier Helicopters** and **The Helicopter Line.** Prices are about the same for both companies. Some sample trips:

A 10-minute flight from Franz Josef up to the top of the glacier and back is about NZ$60 per person. A 20-minute trip up the glacier with a landing is about NZ$100. Both glaciers and a landing, about a half-hour, is NZ$130. The most spectacular helicopter trip, if the cloud gods cooperate, flies up the Franz Josef, over to the Fox, then a wide circle around Mt. Cook and Mt. Tasman, past the Tasman Glacier and back down Franz Josef. The trip is 40 to 45 minutes and costs around NZ$170 per person. *If you save up for no other trip on your New Zealand vacation, try to do this one. It's tremendous.* Trips can be booked at both companies' offices in the village, or from almost any tourist office or travel agency in New Zealand. It's wise to book several days in advance—and hope the weather's OK. Information: Glacier Helicopters, Box 34, Franz Josef, ☎ 31-755 or after hours, 31-745. The Helicopter Line flies only from Franz Josef; Box 45, ☎ 31-767, after hours, 774; central nationwide reservations through ☎ (09) 774-406. Ski-plane rides are about the same price and offer the same itineraries. They are offered through Mt. Cook Lines, ☎ 31-714, after hours, 746. The company flies from both villages. You can hike in the Franz Josef area by yourself or with a guided group; note, however, *you're not allowed on the glacier itself without a guide.* Some hikes:

Glacier walk—Go south just over the Waiho River bridge, and turn left onto the Glacier Road. Drive to the end where there is a parking lot and information kiosk. From the parking lot, it's about an hour to a viewing platform near the foot of the glacier. The valley walk shows you a classic glaciated valley, from the pockets of glacial debris to the gravel-bedded river to the river itself, a milky greenish-white from the deposits of ground-up rocks it carries. The fine rock particles, ground by the ice, are called glacial flour. The path is fairly level.

Alex Knob—A bit more for the serious hiker. It's listed as an eight-hour walk, but you can do it in five. It goes from about half-way down the glacier road up to an elevation of around 4,200 feet, passing through some excellent rain forest and into alpine grasslands. If the weather's clear, it's a great view of the glacier.

Lake Wombat—On the Alex Knob track, but branches off to what is called a glacier lakelet. An easy stroll through the rain forest.

Guided walks are offered by Trips & Tramps with offices next to the Helicopter Line. For about NZ$25, they'll take you on a walk onto the glacier to look at ice caves, crevasses and other attractions. Some equipment is furnished. There are normally two tours a day that take about two and a half hours each. ☎ 31-719, extension 590.

MOUNTAIN CLIMBING

Serious ice climbers and mountaineering types can book trips through several specialty companies, including Alpine Guides Westland with offices in Fox Glacier; information: P.O. Box 38 Fox Glacier, ☎ (0288) 30-825. They also have an office in Mt. Cook. Another company with icefield trips is Alpine Recreation of Canterbury Ltd., Box 74, Lake Taupo; ☎ (03) 680-6736.

FOX GLACIER

Here's where we suggest you base yourself in Glacier Country. There's more to do, the same opportunity for flights, hiking and glacier trips are available, but there's more going on here and the accommodations are better. You're only 12 miles from Franz Josef if you want to go back and do the trails and activities there.

The park visitor information center will be on your right coming into town from the north and, as noted, will have pertinent information about trails, trips and accommodations. Glacier Helicopters and Mt. Cook ski planes can be booked here, as can short or extensive glacier treks with Alpine Guides.

The prices for helicopter and plane rides from Fox Glacier are basically the same as from Franz Josef. Note that the Helicopter Line flies only from Franz Josef.

ACTIVITIES

Cone Rock Track—Of the many trails around both glaciers, we found the trip up to Cone Rock/Chalet Lookout to be unsurpassed for scenery and variety of ecosystems. Some of the overlooks down into the Fox River Valley are awesome, definitely not for folks with a fear of heights, and not recommended for small children. The Chalet Lookout portion of the trail is fairly even, but the Cone section is steep and fairly rigorous. Figure maybe 3 hours to the top of Cone Rock and back if you also do the Chalet. To get to the trails, take the Glacier Road just past the Fox River, south of town.

The Beach—There are several trails along the beach, which is reached by driving down the Cook Flat Road about 10 kilometers off the main highway. One trail goes to a seal colony, passing some old mining ruins; it's about a 3-hour round trip.

Worms—Right in the village, near the Golden Glacier Motor Inn, is a **glowworm grotto**—in case A) you care and B) you haven't had a chance yet on the trip to see the little creatures. In the summer, the information center often runs tours down to the grotto at night. The cave here is not as elaborate as some of the bigger insectual spots, but it does in fact have glowworms.

Heli–Hiking—In addition to the basic glacier flights (some with landings), Alpine Guides (with Glacier Helicopters) also has flights that combine a helicopter ride with a hike. They call it heli-hiking, and the basic drill is to fly you up around and then onto the ice. Guides then walk you back down. Here's a chance to see some real ice caves and great scenery. One trip takes you up to a mountain hut where you spend the night. The half-day heli-hike is about NZ$100 per person. The overnight stay (fly in, fly out) is about NZ$500 a couple, including equipment and food. Alpine also does twice-daily glacier walks for about NZ$30 per person for a half day or about NZ$50 for a full day, both including equipment. It's a better trek here, we think, than at Franz Josef. Alpine Guides and Glacier Helicopters are located behind the

Fox Glacier Hotel. ☎ (0288) 30-825 or 823. Mt. Cook Line is next to the Fox Glacier Hotel. ☎ : 30-812.

WHERE TO STAY

Fox Glacier Hotel—You can't miss it, a big, rambling white wooden building in the center of town. It is a bit seedy around the edges, but the rooms are good, the food is OK, and the hotel owner is tops. The hotel is now a third-generation operation and is where many tour bus groups spend the night when they come to the glaciers. The hotel has old rooms and new rooms. We prefer the older ones, which have balconies and great views; the new ones are more motel-style and are, incidentally, where the tour groups are. There is a public bar where the locals hang out, or if you prefer privacy, a guests-only bar in the hotel wing. Also available are tea/coffee, free laundry and a licensed restaurant. Rooms in the older section go for about NZ$80, double; in the newer section, about NZ$90; rates cheaper for shared bathrooms. There is a grassy area outside where on a sunny day, you can sit and sip a beer while the world goes by and the Southern Alps glisten over your shoulder. Very comfy, indeed, and for our taste the place to call home while you do the glacier bit. ☎ 30-839.

A1 Motel—Of the several motel-style units, this is probably the best. It's on the beach road, just past the Catholic Church. Laundry, spa, courtesy van, squash court, kitchens. Doubles are about NZ$80. ☎ 30-804.

Fox Glacier Motor Park—A Top 10 RV park, also on the beach road. Large range of units from motel-style to tent sites. The motel units have kitchens, the tourist flats have "rangettes." Motel units run about NZ$70 double. Four-person tourist flats are about NZ$55 double. Cabins are about NZ$35 for two. ☎ 30-821.

Hostels—Hostel-style accommodations are found at the **Fox Glacier Youth Hostel**, which shares a building with the **Golden Glacier Motor Inn**, and the **Ivory Towers**. Youth Hostel prices are NZ$17 a night, NZ$22, non-members, ☎ 30-847. Ivory Towers charges about NZ$12 per person for a double, ☎ 30-838. Motel units at the Golden Glacier are about NZ$70, double, ☎ 30-847. It has a restaurant.

WHERE TO EAT

The Fox Glacier Hotel—As we noted, ground zero. The bar opens at 11 a.m., stays open until late. Meals are moderate, cooked breakfasts available. ☎ 30-839.

Fox Glacier Restaurant and Tearoom—Does a good cooked breakfast, teas and take-away. It's across the street a block or so from the hotel. There's a pay phone nearby. Restaurant ☎ 30-868.

For sandwiches and light fare, try the **Hobnail Coffee Shop** in the Alpine Guides building back of the hotel. ☎ 30–825.

A couple enjoys the might of a waterfall near Milford

TOWARD QUEENSTOWN

The 300-odd kilometer drive from the glaciers to Wanaka is a jewel among jewels and is probably *the single-best stretch of scenic rain forest highway on the South Island*. The road basically stays inland from Fox Glacier to Lake Moeraki, and the total effect is green, green. Twists and curves, canopies of **rain forest** plants, occasional glimpses of the mountains and the sea. There are some small settlements here and there along the road with a motel or cafe, and the last stretch before the village of Haast parallels the **beaches** for a good 20 kilometers. On the way, you will pass two lakes, Paringa and Moeraki, which have rest stops with picnic tables and views of the lakes, which are home to flocks of **black swans**.

Native Bush, Minehaha

HAAST

Haast is about halfway between the glaciers and Wanaka, an easy half-day dawdle. Should you choose to call a pit stop, there are a few places to sleep and one restaurant. It also has gasoline—high priced and questionable but still gasoline.

WHERE TO STAY

Erewhon Motels—Located at Haast Beach, reached by turning right off the main highway and heading toward the ocean. Kitchens and a flock of pedigreed ponies. Doubles are about NZ$65. ☎ (0288) 32-825.

World Heritage Hotel Haast —In Haast, near the Haast River bridge. Bar, licensed restaurant, suites, tea rooms, jet boat hire available, laundry. About NZ$75, double. ☎ 32-827.

Haast Motor Camp—Take the Haast Beach road south about 15 kilometers along Jackson Bay Road to a wide spot called Okuru. Right on the beach, communal kitchen, laundry, store, some units with cooking facilities; tent and powered sites. Cabins are about NZ$45, double. Backpackers, bunkrooms are NZ$16 a night. ☎ 32-860.

HAAST PASS ROAD

Past Haast, the road turns due east and begins a 150 kilometer run through the Alps to Lake Wanaka and the Queenstown area. It is one of the more picturesque treks *on the South Island, rivaling the Arthur's Pass route.* As the road climbs slowly along the Haast River, you'll see dozens of waterfalls, including one fat and active one called **Roaring Billy.** Starting in the rain forests of the coast, the road gradually takes you up into sub-alpine and alpine vegetation. Toward the top of the pass, you'll run into stretches of unpaved but well-maintained road. Near the small settlement of Makarora at the head of Lake Wanaka, you enter the Wilkins River Valley, which has what seems like billions of sheep.

The road now goes along the eastern shore of the lake. In places the road is gravel, narrow and muddy. The road then abruptly turns east and goes through a gap to Lake Hawea. At the cut, there is a picnic area with gorgeous views of deep blue-green Lake Hawea. This is open range country, so don't be surprised to come upon flocks of sheep wandering down the highway.

WANAKA

Like Queenstown, *Wanaka is a water sports and ski area, popular in both winter and summer. Smaller, less frantic and a tad less touristy,* Wanaka is favored by many Kiwis who find the pace at Queenstown too much. It's a toss-up as to which has the best scenery—both sit on lovely South Island lakes with snow-capped mountains in the background. Wanaka is the gateway to **Mount Aspiring National Park,** which sits between Haast Pass and Fiordland National Park to the south. The centerpiece of the 710,000-acre park is **Mt. Aspiring, 9,900** feet high and a classic jagged peak in the style of the European Alps. There are a number of fairly strenuous but scenic hiking trails in the park, which is *considered to be one of the wildest parks on the*

South Island. The national park headquarters is in Wanaka; it's open weekdays 8 a.m.–5 p.m., and on weekends during the summer. It's at the corner of Main and Ballantyne roads. *One of the best views of Mt. Aspiring is from Glendhu Bay* on a paved local road west of Wanaka.

The Wanaka area is noted for **trout fishing** as well as **whitewater trips** on rivers feeding into the lake. And it's close to three major ski areas, **Cardrona, Treble Cone** and **Waioru Nordic**. Cardrona is located in three basins with lift capacity for about 6,000 skiers an hour. There are **heli-skiing** trips available through the Helicopter Line at Cardrona, as well as trips to Treble Cone and slopes in the nearby Harris Mountains. The nordic area has about 25 kilometers of **cross-country trails.** Lift passes at Cardrona and Treble Cone are about NZ$50; access charges at Waioru are about NZ$30. Heli-skiing costs, depending on the number of runs, are between NZ$450 and NZ$650; glacier trips are also available. For information, contact Harris Mountain Heli-Skiing at the Wanaka Travel Centre, across from the jetty downtown on Ardmore Street. The centre also has information about activities, food and accommodation in the Wanaka area.

Wanaka is also a base for flights to Milford Sound, Mt. Aspiring and Mt. Cook, or the Fox and Franz Josef glaciers. Flights, through Aspiring Air, run between NZ$50 and NZ$200 depending on itinerary and duration. Aspiring Air is located at the Wanaka airport on the Wanaka-Queenstown highway; ☎ (03) 443-7943.

WHERE TO STAY

The Edgewater Resort—On Sargood Drive. Hotel and motel accommodations; kitchens, spa, sauna, tea/coffee, bar and restaurant, baby-sitting, courtesy van. Doubles around NZ$185, ☎ (03) 443-8311.

Clifford's Hotel—Downtown on Ardmore Street. Restaurant, bar, family lounge, spa, coffee/tea, some suites with hot tubs. Doubles around NZ$120, depending on room type. ☎ 443-7826.

Pembroke Inn—94 Brownston St. Nice views, tea/coffee, sauna, kitchens, laundry, restaurant. About NZ$80, double. ☎ 443-7296.

Wanaka Motor Inn—Mt. Aspiring Road about 2 kilometers from town. Some hot tubs, laundry, ski-drying room, tea/coffee, bar and restaurant, courtesy van, excellent scenery. Doubles, around NZ$130. ☎ 443-8216.

Bay View Motel—Glendhu Bay Road, 3 kilometers from town. Kitchens, fireplaces, courtesy van, breakfast available. Doubles, around NZ$90. ☎ 443-7766.

Wanaka Hostel—181 Upton St., close to the lake. Ski rental and transport. NZ$16 a night, NZ$20 for non-members.

Pleasant Lodge Holiday Park—On Glendhu Bay, a Top 10 RV park. Pool, spa, laundry, barbecues, store. Tourist flats with rangettes and fridges, NZ$55, double. Cabins, NZ$32, double. Motel units, NZ$72, double. ☎ 443-7360.

Wanaka Motor Park—Brownstone Street, near downtown. Laundry, community kitchen, spa, boat park, ski room. Tourist flats, NZ$45, double. Cabins, NZ$35. Bunkrooms, NZ$13 per person. ☎ 443-7883.

WHERE TO EAT

Ripples—Pembroke Village Mall (right downtown near the lake). BYOB, Kiwi cuisine, outside dining in good weather. Lunch noon-2 p.m.; dinner from 6 p.m. Moderate to expensive. ☎ 443-7413.

Clifford's Hotel—On Ardmore Street. *Pub-style meals, good wine list,* open for lunch and dinner. Moderate. ☎ 443-7826.

Cardrona Restaurant—Near the ski fields on Highway 89, due south of town. Restored Gold Rush building, scenery, great food. Moderate to expensive. Note: the Highway 89 route between Wanaka and Queenstown is off-limits to rental RVs. ☎ 443-8153.

Edgewater Resort Hotel—Brasserie style, *lake views, colonial furnishings, seafood a specialty.* Open for dinner from 6:30-10 p.m. Moderate. ☎ 443-8311.

Rafters—At the Wanaka Motor Inn on the Mt. Aspiring Road. Open fire, casual, lamb, steaks and New Zealand blue cod. Licensed. Open for dinner 6-9 p.m. ☎ 443-8216.

Relishes Cafe—On Ardmore Street in Central Wanaka. A BYOB, cafe-style serving from 8 a.m.-11 p.m. Sometimes closed Tuesdays. *Open fire, warm atmosphere.* Excellent steaks and sinful desserts. Very reasonable prices. ☎ 443-9018.

Te Kano—Brownstone Street. Nationally-famous vegetarian place housed in a small cottage. *Great for mulled wine in the winter. Large portions, good prices.* ☎ 443- 7028.

ARROWTOWN

If you're in a car and the weather is decent, *the most scenic—and most direct route—from Wanaka to Queenstown is down Highway 89*, an unpaved road running through the Cardrona Valley. At 45 miles, the trip through the valley is shorter by about 10 miles, but probably slower due to the ruts and washboards in the road. But the scenery is great. And, as we noted, it's verboten for rental RVs.

The fast way is on Highway 6, which circles to the east and then drops into Queenstown and Lake Wakatipu from the north. Either way, you'll come within a short distance of Arrowtown, a gaggle of Gold Rush cottages and old buildings quite popular with tourists. Lots of photographs are taken along Cardigan Street—**the Avenue of Oak Trees.** The village has a very good **gold mining museum** and several good restaurants and motels. In summer, a red double-decker bus runs from Queenstown to Arrowtown for about NZ$20.

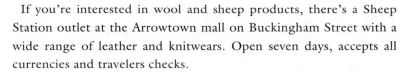

If you're interested in wool and sheep products, there's a Sheep Station outlet at the Arrowtown mall on Buckingham Street with a wide range of leather and knitwears. Open seven days, accepts all currencies and travelers checks.

WHERE TO STAY

Golden View Motel—48 Adamson Road Kitchens, laundry, car wash, store, pool. Doubles, around NZ$70. ☎ (03) 442- 1833.

Viking Lodge Motel—21 Inverness Crescent. A-frame chalets, laundry, pool, bikes for hire. Doubles, about NZ$75. ☎ 442-1765.

Mace Motel—13 Cardigan Street. Two- and three-bedroom units, kitchens, fridge, laundry, spa, store. Doubles, about NZ$80. ☎ 442-1825.

Arrowtown Caravan Park—47 Devon Street Kitchen, laundry, dining room. On-site caravans are NZ$35, double. ☎ 442-1838.

New Orleans Hotel—27 Buckingham Street Restaurant, bar, private lounge, bottle shop, tea/coffee. NZ$60, double. Bunkrooms, NZ$13 per person.

WHERE TO EAT

Courtyard Restaurant, Bar and Coffee Shop—At the mall on Buckingham Street. Licensed. Devonshire teas, homemade pies, tarts and cakes. Sandwiches, as well as full meals, such as blue cod, steaks and chicken. During the winter, it's open for dinner only on Friday and Saturday; seven days the rest of the year. Lunch from 11 a.m.-3 p.m.; dinner from 6-10 p.m. Coffee shop opens at 9:30 a.m. Moderate. ☎ 442-1828.

Bistrorant—In the New Orleans Hotel. Open seven days, **large portions**. Breakfast and lunch; dinner from 6-9 p.m. Moderate, ☎ 442-1745.

The thrill of bungee jumping can be had in Queenstown

QUEENSTOWN

Queenstown Mall

We have met some New Zealanders who refuse to go anywhere near Queenstown, it being, they say, too bloody frantic, touristy and tawdry. And by Kiwi standards, it just might be. But compared to the flashy-toothed, beautiful-people-laden ski spas around North America (Aspen comes to mind at once), Queenstown is pretty mild. *It's in a beautiful location, sitting beneath some sawtooth ridges called the Remarkables, next to one of the South Island's incredible deep lakes, Wakatipu.* As for that, we think it's a toss-up which community has the best setting, Queenstown or Wanaka.

Whatever, Queenstown is the fun capital of the South Island, close to skiing, close to fishing, close to mountain hiking, close to Milford Sound. If you care, it's also the **bungee-jumping** capital of the world and world famous for **whitewater rafting.**

Detractors will tell you that Queenstown's comportment began at its birth in the 1860s as a wild mining town. It is close to the Shotover River and claimed to be one of the richest gold-bearing streams in the world. Some of the tales that came from those days would suggest it's probably true—cooks pulling huge nuggets of gold out of the gravel with a butcher knife, two guys rescuing a dog from the river and winding up with 25 pounds of gold by nightfall—you get the idea. But gold booms are usually followed by gold busts, and by 1900, there were only 190 brave souls left in town.

The Shotover is still reputed to be full of gold, but mostly it's used for sport now.

Lake Wakatipu has always been the center of attention in the city, which sits wrapped around its edges. It's typical of the large southern lakes, carved deep by ancient glaciers—in this case, about **1,240** feet deep, going well below sea level. It's the third largest lake in New Zealand, S-shaped and stretching for more than 50 miles. It's a very popular sailing and fishing area, by North American standards very **underused**. In the Gold Rush days, there were four lake steamers bringing prospectors and supplies into the town, as well as taking supplies to the sheep and cattle stations that had been established here and there on the shores.

ACTIVITIES

BY LAND

Queenstown is a fairly compact town, easily walkable, with some very steep hills, particularly near the Parkroyal Hotel. The downtown area is compact, with lots of stores and the requisite number of sporting goods stores, boutiques, sheep shops, singles clubs, jewelry stores, hotels and more tourist information offices per square yard than almost any place we've been. It also has one of the prettiest golf courses in New Zealand. But Queenstown's main charm, really, is as a place to use as a base for some special trips around the Southern Alps and the fjords.

First, get your bearings, and the best way to do that is to walk up Brecon Street and catch the gondola that goes up to the top of

Bob's Peak in back of town. It rises 1,500 feet at a steep angle (37.1 degrees, we are told), and from the top, you can see most of the city and big chunks of lake and mountains. There's a restaurant at the top which offers a special deal in connection with a bus tour to Milford Sound. (See Restaurant section). It's also possible to walk to the top if you're feeling strong. The ride up and down by gondola will cost about NZ$10. It opens in the morning at 10. Information ☎ 442-7860.

Another great view of the area is available from atop

Mt. Coronet, which sits a few miles behind the city, facing the Remark-ables. A ski lift takes you up the 5,400-foot peak, renowned for its fine winter powder, and a great place to scope out the countryside. The lift runs all year and costs about NZ$15. Buses run to the ski area in the winter.

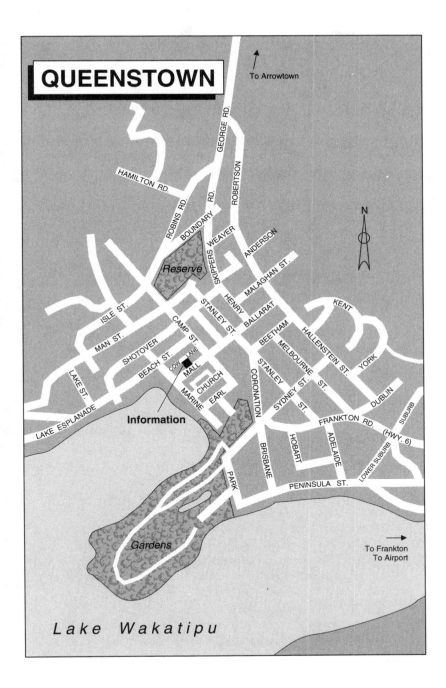

BY WATER

The other way to get your bearings is by water. The last of the lake steamers, the TSS *Earnslaw*, is an old smoker that dates from 1912. It was built in Dunedin and brought overland to the lake in pieces. The TSS, by the way, either stands for "Tourist Steam Ship" or "Twin Screw Steamer," take your pick. It was the largest of all the lake steamers, 170 feet long, 24 feet wide, and was named after the highest mountain in the region, 9,300-foot Mt. Earnslaw, at the head of the lake. Its tourist duties these days are a far cry from the days when it earned its keep hauling tick medicine and sheep dip into farms and bales of hides and fleeces out. The old tub has a very good kitchen, which is probably best enjoyed on the evening dinner cruise.

The first cruise of the day is at 12:30 p.m., and takes an hour to do a fast trip around the lake near the town; snacks available. It'll run about NZ$25 per person. The 3-hour afternoon cruise gives you a dose of station life by sailing over to the

Walter Peak homestead, where you get a shearing demo, spinning lessons and a look at some sheep dogs at work (they're worth the price of admission).

If you wish, you can go to the station for dinner, or eat aboard. Both evening meal trips leave at 5:30 p.m., dropping station folks off and picking them up at 9:30. The station dinners, at the

Colonels Homestead, are NZ$50 per person. In summer, barbecues are a specialty. To make reservations or check what's on the station menu, ☎ 442-8101. There are two evening meal cruises aboard the boat, leaving at 5:30 and 7:30 p.m. The price is NZ$50 per person. There is a well-stocked bar aboard the *Earnslaw* as well. It can be booked at any Fiordland Travel office downtown or at the wharf across from the Park Royal. Information and bookings, ☎ 442-7500. When all the sailing is done, the *Earnslaw* ties up for the night at the wharf and becomes a floating piano bar.

The female member of this team will always hold a special spot in her heart for Queenstown for it was here, on a sunny fall afternoon, that she spotted her first—and as it turned out, last—kiwi. Perhaps here we should warn you about kiwi spotting as practiced in the darkened zoolets of New Zealand. The beasts are nocturnal, and the light levels in their displays are almost non-existent. For the first 10 minutes you're blind, then rapidly disappointed because, as much as you look, you can't see the bloody bird. Here's where old hands will win out—patience, people, patience. Eventually the beast will suddenly appear from the bushes, nine parts beak, and you can go home and die in peace. But if you've seen one kiwi—it's probably not worth going more than once unless you have something about big noses.

The place in Queenstown to spot *Archie Apteryx* is the

Kiwi and Birdlife Park just down from the entrance to the gondola station. In addition to the kiwi house, there are a bunch of native and introduced birds wandering around, including Canada geese, shellback ducks and keas. About NZ$8 per person to get in. Information ☎ (03) 442-8059.

BY AIR

If you want to get your bearings by air, that's possible as well, from helicopter flights to puttering around in an old Tiger Moth bi-plane. For choppers, call the **Helicopter Line** at ☎ 442-7820. *The Moth, vintage 1938, will fly over the lake and peel around Coronet Peak for some great views for about NZ$150.* Book it by calling **Vintage Flights,** ☎ 442-3016. Local flightseeing trips on a conventional aircraft will run about NZ$50 for a quickie 15-minute buzz over town or about NZ$150 for a 1-hour flight over the whole area.

Flights from Queenstown to Milford Sound and back are quite popular, weather permitting, and will run you about NZ$150 per person, one way. But most folks either do a round trip or combine the air flight with a boat tour of the sound and return fare on a bus. The fly-boat-bus packages will run about NZ$175. A fly-boat-fly trip will cost about NZ$210.

There are also flights to Mt. Cook where you can hop a helicopter for a landing on a glacier near the mountain. That'll set you back about NZ$625. All sorts of combinations for flights around Queenstown and the southern South Island are available; basically tell them where you want to go, they'll fly you there. Contact Milford Sound Scenic Flights at ☎ 442-3065, or Mt. Cook Airline ☎ 442- 7650. Fly/bus or flightseeing trips are also available on Fiordland Travel's own planes. Flights for any air service can be booked through any travel agent or the information centre in town. About that golf course. The Kiwis rate the links at 18-hole

Kelvin Heights as one of the most beautiful in the country and "the 6th in the world for scenery." We're not sure what the first five were, and the PR folks aren't talking, but there's no denying it's a lovely stroll, especially the fifth hole from tee to green. The course is on an arm of land across from town, five minutes by water taxi from the Esplanade or 10.5 miles by car. Call the taxi at ☎ 442- 8665. The club has everything you need from rental clubs to golf carts to shoes. It opens at 7:30 a.m. For the latest green fees and reservations, ☎ 442- 9169.

THE ESSENTIAL QUEENSTOWN
HOW TO GET THERE

By bus—Buses from Christchurch run to Queenstown daily on both InterCity and Mt. Cook Landline. The trip takes about eight hours and costs between NZ$90 and NZ$95 one way. The buses from Dunedin to Queenstown run weekdays on InterCity, weekends on Mt. Cook Landline. One-way costs are between NZ$50 and NZ$60. There is a daily bus from Fox Glacier to Queenstown on InterCity for about NZ$80, and also from Franz Josef for about NZ$85. The trip from Invercargill is on InterCity weekdays and Mt. Cook Landline on weekends, and costs about NZ$40. Both bus companies have a daily route from Milford Sound, usually in the afternoon, for about NZ$70. They also make the run from Mt. Cook, also in the afternoon for about NZ$60. Daily Te Anau-Queenstown service on both lines runs about NZ$40. From Wanaka, daily on both is about NZ$30.

There is no train service to Queenstown.

By air—There is daily service to Queenstown from Christchurch on both Mt. Cook and Ansett. Most of the flights are morning and early afternoon. The price is about NZ$260 one way. Mt. Cook has three daily flights from Mt. Cook, costing about NZ$$205 one way. From Nelson, Air Nelson has daily service and Ansett has MondaySaturday service. The fare is about NZ$410.

From the North Island, Air New Zealand, Ansett and Mt. Cook have regular service from Auckland to Queenstown for about NZ$540 one way. There are also daily flights on Mt. Cook and Ansett from Rotorua for about NZ$530. Flights from Wellington are on Air New Zealand and Ansett for about NZ$410. From way up north (Kerikeri on the Bay of Islands), you can fly on a Mt. Cook puddle-jumper for NZ$720—the flight takes 7 hours.

HOW TO GET AROUND

Queenstown is so compact we can't think of why you'd want a taxi, but if you do, ☎ 442-7788. Better is to rent a bike or a moped. There are several moped places around downtown. Basically all you need is a valid driver's license. You get gas and unlimited kilometerage for about NZ$50 a day. Bikes will give you lots of exercise (it's fairly hilly), and rent for about NZ$20 a day.

INFORMATION

The **Queenstown Visitors Centre** is located at the corner of Shotover and Camp streets (P.O. Box 230); ☎ 442-7319. The area code for Queenstown is (03).

The biggest tour company in the area is Fiordland Travel; if they can't arrange it, it probably can't be done. The company has offices in Queenstown, Te Anau and Manapouri. In Queenstown, the office is at the Steamer Wharf (next to the Earnslaw) or P.O. Box 94; ☎ 442-7500

WHERE TO STAY

Queenstown Parkroyal—On Beach Street across from the Earnslaw dock. About 140 rooms, Steamers Lounge and Bentley restaurant. Pool, sauna, TV, fridge, coffee/tea makers. Good locationbut a bit sterile. Great lake views. During October-April high season, about NZ$250 a night, double. ☎ 442-7800.

Quality Inn A-Line—27 Stanley St. (up the hill a bit from the city center). About 80 rooms, bar, restaurant, spa, laundry, gym, fridges. Some units up to five persons. NZ$130 per room. ☎ 442- 7700.

The Lodges—6 The Esplanade. Kitchen units, some with microwaves; some units sleep 5-7 persons. TV, laundry. NZ$150 for two; NZ$12 per person in addition. Good for groups or skiers. ☎ 442-7552.

Holiday Inn Queenstown —Sainsbury Road, off The Esplanade and Fernhill roads. About 150 rooms. Two restaurants, bar, pool, tennis, gym, sauna, courtesy van, ski-drying area. About NZ$245 for double, $27 for each additional person. All the facilities, but still Holiday Inn-ish. ☎ 442-6600 or (0800) 655-557.

THC Queenstown (now a Southern Pacific hotel)—Corner of Earl and Marina Parade. An old favorite, done in lattices painted red, purple and yellow. Good location right next to the lake, inner courtyard and garden. About 150 rooms and 20 apartments. Bar and restaurant, TV, minibars, laundry service, tea/coffee things. High season, about NZ$190, double; NZ$135, off season. Apartments run around NZ$230.

Nugget Point—This is a sports lodge a few miles out of town on Gorge Road at Arthur's Point. 1- and 2-bedroom units with kitchen, TV, laundry, spa, pool, tennis courts, squash courts, gym and courtesy airport van. Doubles are about NZ$250; suites are about NZ$310. Excellent restaurant. ☎ 442-7630 or 7680.

Shotover Resort—Close by Nugget Point, the lodge has a pool, spa, indoor cricket, bar and restaurant. A good à la carte and barbecue restaurant. It also has some budget accommodations. About NZ$200 luxury, NZ$40 budget. ☎ 442-7850.

The Terraces—On the way to the airport at 48-64 Frankton Road. Lake view with Hilary's licensed restaurant. Doubles, about NZ$200. ☎ 442-7950.

Vacation Inn—Corner of Frankton and Adelaide streets. About 100 rooms, bar, restaurant, spa, hair salon, TV, tea/coffee, laundry, fridge, courtesy van. About NZ$135, single or double.

Mountaineer Hotel—Corner of Beach and Rees streets heart of town. One of our favorites, and a member of the Pub Hotels group. It's one of the town's oldest with foundations dating back to 1862. **Great bar**— **Horsefeathers**—restaurant, bottle shop, hustle and bustle. A double with bath is NZ$75; backpackers' bunk rooms, NZ$25 per person. ☎ 442-7400.

Lakeland Resort Hotel—14-18 Lake Esplanade. About as European-looking as you'll find in Kiwiland, popular with skiers. Next to the lake on the Esplanade. About 180 rooms, TVs, pool, bar, restaurant, ski-drying room, hair salon, sauna, tea/coffee, off-season rates. NZ$120. ☎ 442-7600.

Alpine Village Motor Inn—Toward the airport on Frankton Road. Spa, pool, chalets or lakeside suites. On the lake. Chalets are NZ$95; suites, NZ$110. ☎ 442-7795 or 7738.

Ambassador Motor Lodge—2 Man St., on the hill near the city center. Close to the gondola and kiwi park. Units sleep 2 to 6, with kitchens, balconies, laundry, spa, executive suite, courtesy rides. About NZ$95, double, NZ$16 per person extra. Suite is about NZ$110. ☎ 442-8593.

Pacific Park—On Frankton Road outside town, set on 13 acres of forest overlooking the lake. About 42 rooms, 6 with kitchens, tea/coffee, laundry, ski-drying room, tennis, bar and restaurant, courtesy bus to airport. Doubles/singles, about NZ$115. ☎ 442-6500.

Blue Peaks Lodge—Corner of Stanley and Sydney streets, close to downtown. Owned by the same outfit that runs the gondola. About 60 units, most with kitchens; children's play area, laundry, TV, breakfasts available. Single/double, NZ$8, extra persons, NZ$12. ☎ 442-9224.

Sherwood Manor Motor Lodge—Frankton Road, outside town, close to airport. About 60 units, most with kitchen; spa, sauna, pool, gym, laundry, TV, tea/coffee, ski-drying room, bar, restaurant, courtesy van. Very nice, actually. NZ$95, single/double, reductions off season. ☎ 442-8032.

Melbourne Motor Lodge—In conjunction with the Melbourne Guest House, 35 Melbourne St. Overlooking the town. 1-, 2- and 3-bedroom units, 1- and 2-bedroom kitchen units and suites, including a honeymoon suite. Laundry, spa, TV, breakfast available. About NZ$100, double, for the 1-bedroom units, $13, additional persons; NZ$125 for the larger units. ☎ 442-8431.

Hotel Esplanade—32 Peninsula St. Overlooks the lake. About 20 units, double/triple, TV, laundry, bar, pool, sauna, ski-drying area, courtesy coach, breakfast available. About NZ$25, double. ☎ 442-8611.

Melbourne Guest Lodge—35 Melbourne St. B&B, laundry, guest lounge, tea/coffee, spa, shared bath. Doubles about NZ$70. Family kitchen suite, about NZ$145. ☎ 442-8431.

Goldfields Motel and Guesthouse—41 Frankton Rd., near the Vacation Inn. Kitchen units, chalets, laundry, TV lounge, tea/coffee, breakfast available. B&B double, NZ$75; chalet with breakfast, NZ$80, double; and motel rooms, no breakfast, NZ$80. ☎ 442-7211.

Queenstown Motor Park—Man Street, steep walk to the top of the hill above town. A Top 10 RV park with other accommodations; dairy. Motel units, NZ$70, double; tourist flats, NZ$55 double; cabins NZ$33; lodges, NZ$50. ☎ 442-7252.

BACKPACKERS

Decco Backpackers—52 Man St., near the motor park. Newest place in town. Double, triple or quad rooms, NZ$15 per person. ☎ 442-7384.

Bumbles Hostel—2 Brunswick St., above the lake, near town. Good, cheap meals, very popular place. Dorm bed, NZ$14; double, $16. ☎ 442-6298.

Queenstown YHA—80 Esplanade. Next to the lake, near the wharf. About 100 beds, modern, some family and doubles. Laundry, meals at night, late-night closing (3 a.m.), courtesy van, TV, storage, popular with skiers. NZ$18 a night, non-members, NZ$22.

WHERE TO EAT

Queenstown is a tourist mecca, especially during the ski season, and like most tourist towns, the place is full of oases to feed your body and slake your thirst after a hard day's tramping or **sitzmarking**; or bungee jumping if you still have the urge to eat.

First things first. No day starts without coffee, and we found only one place open at 6:30 a.m., waiting for our bus to Milford Sound. It's the **Gourmet Express**, which serves brekkie from 6:30-noon and stays open until 9 p.m. *Reasonable prices, bottomless cup, good service.* Bay Center on Shotover St. (It's in sort of a shopping arcade.) ☎ 442-9619.

There's a **Pizza Hut** and a **McDonald's** if you're feeling homesick, but the place to rub shoulders with the locals is at **Roaring Meg's Restaurant**, situated in an old gold miner's cabin. Here's your chance to try some mutton bird, yahoo. *Basic Kiwi food;* BYOB dinners Monday-Saturday from 6 p.m. Moderate to expensive. 57 Shotover St. ☎ 442-9676.

Good Chinese food is available at the popular **Lai Sing Restaurant** upstairs in the O'Connell Pavilion. There are often all-you-can-eat specials, *the wine list is good and the drums tell us the martinis are the best in town.* (Gin is evil, thanks.) The main dishes will run you around NZ$15–18. There's also take-away. Open seven days, serves lunch 12-2:30 p.m., dinner 5:30-11 p.m. ☎ 442-7131.

The town is popular with Japanese tourists, who tend to spend more per capita than most tourists, so it's a bit surprising there's only one sushi bar. Then, checking with the local press, we found it's the only sushi bar on the South Island. Surely not. Anyway, it's called the **Minami Jujisei**, and it's *very popular and semi-expensive*. It's licensed and also serves lamb and beef Japanese-style dishes. Open only for dinner, reservations recommended. It's at 3 Rees St. in the Arcade. ☎ 442-9854.

A comfy spot in the middle of downtown is **Chico's**, with fireside dining in the winter, stone walls, **à la carte** menu, live entertainment most nights. It's licensed, moderate to expensive. Dinner weekly starting at 6:30 p.m. Located on the Mall. ☎ 442-8439.

The only Mexican restaurant in town is **Saguaro's**, which has live music at nights. Luncheon specials. Fully licensed, but you have to **BYOB** wine for dinner. Open 12-2 for lunch, 5:30-late for dinner. Sometimes closed for lunch in the off-season.

More stone walls, more fireplaces, tight spaces, cramped quarters: the ever-popular **Cow**; fittingly enough, an Italian restaurant. It's located on Cow Lane off Camp Street, hence the name. Always a line, **BYOB**. Take-away pizza. Open noon-10:30 p.m. ☎ 442-8588.

Skyline Gondola Restaurant—The place to eat above it all. It's atop Bob's Peak high above the lake, reachable by the gondola. For NZ$40 each, you get a carvery dinner featuring Kiwi meats, live entertainment, good wine list, nifty views of the harbor and the ride up and down. The dinner service starts at 6 p.m. There is also a cafeteria at the top that opens at 10 a.m. Reservations for dinner necessary. ☎ 442-7860.

A few choices, out of town:

Packer's Arms—Here's your basic 1860s trading post and hotel from the Gold Rush days, very popular with Queenstownites for dinner or garden lunches. *Venison on the menu, worthy wine list, altogether excellent.* It's on the road to Arrowtown just past Arthur's Point (Gorge Road). Open weekly from 6:30 p.m., closed Tuesdays for lunch. Reservations for dinner necessary. Expensive but worth it. ☎ 442-8999.

Arthur's Point Tavern—Another Gold Rush relic, overlooking the Shotover River. Popular for Kiwi food (rump steaks, chook and chips). *Very nice, reasonable prices.* Gorge Road toward Arrowtown. Open weekly from 6:30 p.m. for dinner. ☎ 442-8007.

And nearby is the restaurant at the **Nugget Point Lodge** which has *excellent meals at expensive prices* (some main dishes are NZ$60). Closed Mondays, dinner from 7-9:30 p.m. ☎ 442-7630.

PUBS & NIGHT SPOTS

The Mountaineer Hotel has live entertainment five days a week at least, plus an assortment of pub grub (bangers and mash, hot dogs and chips, roasts). Two bars running, no food after 10 p.m. ☎ 442-7400.

Eichardts Tavern—Vintage 1862 building, white and proud, sitting on the Mall at the waterfront. *Tends to be very rockish and loud with faint overtones of heavy metal and a touch of rap.* Anyway, it's open from noonish to latish. On the second floor is a nightclub, the Penthouse. Closed Sundays. ☎ 442-8369.

Dolphin Club—Singles and/or young couples place, *very popular*, entertainment every night. It's downtown on Shotover Street. Open 9 p.m.-3 a.m. ☎ 442-9692.

SHOPPING

The major sheep store is the **Sheep Station** on the Mall, which like its counterpart in Christchurch, has very nice, fairly expensive leather and wool goods.

A group of stores is located in O'Connell's Pavillion at the corner of Beach and Camp streets. Try **McKnight's for Mohair**, which has homespun wool and mohair, carded or already woven. **Action Downunder** carries pure wool knitwear and pure cotton goods, as well as deer-leather garments. **The Beer Essentials** has T-shirts, sweatshirts, rugby jerseys, shorts and hats with the logo of your favorite Kiwi beer. If you fancy Australian opals, try the **Opal and Jade Centre** at the corner of Beach and Rees streets. There's a workshop. Or the **Aotea Opal and Gold Bar** across from the Parkroyal Hotel carries 18- and 14-carat gold jewelry, as well as opals.

And the **Duty Free Shop** on the Mall says it has same-day mailing service to some parts of the U. S.

The Rakaia River and Mount Hutt, Canterbury

THE MILFORD EXPERIENCE

Mitre Peak, Fiordland

The Kiwis have long noted the interest in the country's fjords in general and the Milford Sound in particular, issuing such modest assessments as "hiking capital of the world" and "the eighth wonder of the world."

So it's no surprise they stand ready any time of year to cart your old carcass to the Sound by bus, boat or plane. Milford Sound is on the southwestern coast of the South Island, a territory gouged and sharpened by huge glaciers—a land that in many ways is the spitting image of the southern Norwegian coast combined with the Canadian Rockies.

The sound is an actual fjord—an arm of the sea that has filled up a deep glaciated valley—and is one of several long fjords along the coast that are the center of **Fiordland National Park**, the country's largest and probably most beautiful preserve. It ranges for 200 kilometers or so along the southwestern coast from Milford Sound to the tip of the South Island, containing something like **4,700** square miles with more than a dozen fjords. *The park has been awarded World Heritage status—meaning, supposedly, that exploitation of the area's resources will never be allowed.*

WHEN TO GO

Because of the weather around the sound, there really is no best time to go. There are some times to avoid, however: Kiwi winter and summer. In the summer, you can't move for tourists, and in the winter, you might not be able to move because of the weather.

In the winter (June-August), it snows in the Kiwi Alps, and avalanches sometimes close the road into the sound. It's not rare for busloads of passengers to be stranded at Milford because the road is closed. And sometimes there are such fierce storms blowing up the sound from the Tasman Sea that tour boats can't leave port. There are perfectly fine days in the winter, to be sure, but the South Island does freeze and it does snow. This leaves you with the shoulder seasons, September-November and March-May. The weather is sometimes chancy, as you'd expect for fall and spring, but the weather is offset by the lack of tourists. *Trying the trip in the shoulders also has advantages because of usually lower air fares and seasonal specials.*

HOW TO GO

The easiest and least expensive way to see the sound (unless you're driving yourself) is by bus, either from Queenstown or the small village of Te Anau, the jumping-off point for most Milford Track hik- ers and also a base for many Milford bus trips. By bus, it takes about 3 hours to reach Te Anau, which is about 170 kilometers southwest of Lake Wakatipu. After morning tea at a local Te Anau hotel, the bus goes on through the mountains and rain forests to the sound. Most trips include a boat tour, which takes you from the end of the highway out to the open ocean and back again. The return trip gets you back to Queenstown around 7:30 p.m. or so.

The prospect of spending a full day with a pack of strangers on a bus is normally less than dazzling—but hold on a bit; here we have one trek that even us dedicated tour-group haters can actually enjoy.

Transportation Alternatives

And the price—depending on what combination you want—is reasonable. A round-trip bus trip, combined with a cruise on the sound, will run around NZ$120 per person, including morning tea (basically a continental breakfast). Should you choose, you can return to Queenstown or Te Anau in a hurry by plane. There are several companies offering fly-coach or fly-fly trips to the sound. One common example is taking a coach to the sound, doing the boat tour and flying back. A coach-boat-fly package is about NZ$240 from Queenstown; a fly-boat-fly from Queenstown is about the same price. Some flights also go to Doubtful Sound, generally conceded to be the most beautiful of the fjords. These packages are available from travel agencies in Queenstown and Te Anau. In the shoulder season, your best bet is Queenstown; try Fiordland Travel, which has several offices in Queenstown. Or contact Mt. Cook Line in Queenstown ☎ (03) 442-7650, or in Te Anau at ☎ (03) 249-7516. Or also contact the InterCity offices in Queenstown, ☎ 442-7420. Or Scenic Flights at ☎ 442-3065.

The day-long bus trip will show you many slices of New Zealand, from the sheep-infested paddocks of flat farmland areas to the avalanche-packed mountains of the New Zealand Alps. You pass several of the country's largest lakes, and—if it's not raining—marvel at the clear, pollution-free air.

TE ANAU

You can, as we noted, start the Milford Sound tour from here. There is regular daily bus service to Milford Sound (about NZ$35 one way) plus there are offices for most of the major tour groups (especially Fiordland Travel) and transportation organizations. *The best part of the trip to the Milford Sound area, unless you're madly in love with sheep (thousands of sheep), starts in the mountains north of Te Anau.* Te Anau is on the South Island's largest lake, **Lake Te Anau**, which is 1,150 feet deep and surrounded by a vast beech forest. Te Anau is a Maori word meaning "caves of rushing water." At the north end of the lake is Glade House, where the Milford Track begins.

Te Anau is the headquarters of the Fiordland National Park, and the visitor center has lots of information about hiking, camping and other activities. Here is where you can book a Milford Track trek. It's open daily; ☎ (03) 249-7921.

Te Anau itself is not much, but sits in a nice spot next to the lake and does have the basics for hanging around a few days, including some comparatively expensive lodging and some good restaurants.

WHERE TO STAY

Te Anau Hotel—Te Anau Terrace, on the lake. Booking office for track treks, tours, boat cruises, etc. Laundry, pool, storage room, bar, two restaurants. Doubles, around NZ$250-NZ$300; villas, from NZ$300. ☎ (03) 249-7411.

The Village Inn—Mokoroa Street downtown. Family units, handicapped' units, honeymoon suite, penthouse suites, kitchens, tea/coffee, mini-bars, laundry, baby-sitting. Bar and restaurant open for dinner 6-9 p.m. Doubles, NZ$120-170. ☎ 249-7911.

Explorer Motor Lodge—6 Cleddau, off Mokoroa Street, downtown. Trip bookings, laundry, golf clubs hire, breakfast available. Off-season rate reductions. Doubles, about NZ$100. ☎ 249-7156

Campbell Motor Lodge—42 Te Anau Terrace. Kitchen, spa, laundry. Doubles, about NZ$100; off-season rates. ☎ 249-7546.

Black Diamond Motel—15 Quintin Dr., off Mokoroa Street, downtown. Kitchens, laundry, putting green. Doubles, NZ$65-80. Off-season rates. ☎ 249-7459.

Shakespeare House—10 Dusky St. Rooms with showers, some with baths. Cooked breakfasts, dinner available. Courtesy car. Doubles, around NZ$80, off-season rates. ☎ 249-7349.

Te Anau YHA Hostel—Milford Road, about 1.5 kilometers out of town. Farm setting, laundry, kitchen, store, booking facilities, storage, tent sites. NZ$18 per person, NZ$22, non-members. ☎ 249-7847.

Te Anau Backpackers—48 Te Anau Terrace. Laundry, barbecues, storage. Shared rooms, about NZ$18, double rooms, about NZ$40. ☎ 249-7713.

Te Anau Motor Park—Manapouri Road, about 1 kilometer from town. Laundry, sauna, tennis, store, sewage disposal site. Cabins, NZ$35-55; motel unit, doubles, NZ$90. ☎ 249-7457.

Te Anau Mountain View Cabin and Caravan Park—Mokonui Street. A Top 10 member. Laundry, sewage disposal site, boat park. Cabins and on-site caravans, around NZ$30. ☎ 249-7462.

WHERE TO EAT

The best food is probably in the hotel restaurants. In addition:

Bailey's Restaurant—Corner of Milford and Mokonui streets, a popular bus tour stop. *The place to buy take-away lunch for the Milford Sound boat trip.* Moderate prices.

La Toscana—Italian restaurant downtown. Pizza, pasta, good coffees, home delivery and take away. Moderate prices. ☎ 249-7756.

The Bluestone Restaurant—Lakefront Drive. Fine dining, all three meals. The dining room fireplace is made of river stone and offers a good view of Lake Te Anau. Fresh fjord crayfish, smoked eel, South Island venison and lamb. Hours are breakfast, 7-9 a.m.; lunch, noon-2 p.m., and dinner, 6-9 p.m. From May 1 to Sept. 30, closed for lunch. ☎ 249-7421.

TOWARD MILFORD

Once past Te Anau, the road parallels Lake Te Anau for about 30 kilometers then cuts inland to start its climb over the Alps to the sea. Once to the mountains—the Earl and Darren ranges—you begin to see why this stretch of highway can be so dangerous at times. There are avalanche warnings all over, and in late spring don't be surprised to drive through the remains of an avalanche that roared into the basins during the thaw.

It is against the law to stop in some danger spots. Tour bus drivers are under orders to report the license plates of offenders, so the police will be waiting to give you a pricey souvenir as you drive out of the park. The weather up in the heights is chancy with rain a very definite possibility at any time. To throw a positive shaft of light into the negative tunnel, however, some fanciers insist the only time to do the trip is when it has been raining heavily. This, of course, flushes out the hundreds of waterfalls along the route—nice if you like overcast waterfalls.

The highway eventually arrives at a dead-end basin that stopped further progress until 1935 when work began on the **Homer Tunnel,** a truly prodigious project dug through solid granite, at first by hand tools. The tunnel enters the mountain at 3,000 feet above sea level and exits at 2,000 feet. It's 354 feet wide, three-quarters of a mile long and has a 10 percent grade. Not too long after leaving the tunnel, you get a glimpse of **Mitre Peak**, a pyramid-shaped mountain that is probably the most photographed object in the Milford Sound area. Milford Sound—the community—sits at the southeastern end of the sound and is currently being redone. After years of relative disinterest, the New Zealand government finally decided that the number of tourists coming in and out of the area —not just hikers but also bus and airplane travelers—required some upgrading of services. About NZ$4 million was authorized to upgrade roads and water-sewer facilities.

Sailing on the Sound

The sound has a relatively small entrance on the ocean, but widens out enough to let cruise ships the size of the *Queen Elizabeth II* go up-fjord several miles—and turn around in one great circle. The mouth is so small, in fact, that England's Capt. James Cook managed to miss the entrance to the sound while he was doing extensive charting around New Zealand in the 1700s. The trip on the sound is normally aboard one of the so-called *Red Boats* that run daily tours and take about 2 hours to run from the dock out to the Tasman Sea and back. The fjord (usually) is flat calm, flanked by steeply rising peaks and towering waterfalls. About a third of the way down the 14-mile-long sound is a wide spot where cruise ships turn around. The big ships don't stay long because there's no place to anchor— the fjord is 1,000 feet deep at this point.

Weather permitting and waterfalls cooperating, the Red Boats usually ease their bows under a waterfall, where brave souls can get a drink of icy waterfall water. If they succeed (getting soaked in the process), they are given a shot of their favorite booze. Most people are content to just take photographs of the soakees. Food and drink are available aboard the boats, although food tends to be a bit pricey. A better suggestion is to buy a sandwich or two at Te Anau when the bus stops for morning tea. If you make arrangements ahead, you can stay at Milford a day or two before going back. Accommodations at Milford—and indeed, at all the facilities in the sound area—are owned by the Southern Pacific Hotel Corp., which purchased the Milford assets from the Tourist Hotels Corp., a government agency. The main accommodations are at the **Milford Sound Hotel,** which has 33 rooms ranging from around NZ$50 to about NZ$200 for a suite. Standard rooms are about NZ$90. The hotel has a restaurant and a pub plus a cafeteria—it's about the only thing in town. There is also a hostel. Reservations are essential, especially after the hiking track opens in early November. ☎ 249-7926. From North America, the Milford Sound Hotel can be booked by calling ☎ (800) 835-7742. Backpacker accommodations are available at the Milford Lodge near the hotel, which also has caravan sites. Room rates are about NZ$20 per person. ☎ 249-8071

THE MILFORD TRACK

The Track—meaning, of course, New Zealand's Milford Track—is rated by some connoisseurs as the best hiking trail in the world. When enthusiasts laud its greatness, they most likely are thinking of the spectacular scenery you get along the track, the relative isolation and the comradery of the trail. However, when detractors list its faults, they consider the whole thing to be a 33-mile, weeklong stretch of overpriced, bug-infested, rain-sodden trail through the New Zealand countryside—gorgeous, indeed, but not always worth the sacrifice. *There is a saying around the Milford area: It's either raining, or it's about to.* It's not unusual to get 400 inches of rain a year, and it rains an average of one out of three days—which for some hikers is about one day too much.

BUGS

Bugs? The track is infamous in summer for sand flies—nasty little varmints that are first cousins to the dreaded Canadian black fly. One guy in the know says the key is not wearing navy blue—they see blue, he says, they go crazy and start a feeding frenzy. An even better suggestion from us professional arthropod haters is to stay away from the flies in the first place. But this is mere piffle, of no moment to serious trampers. The track is, after all, the Track, and a badge most hikers would kill to wear. A small but grumbling group of democrats have always protested about government control of the track and the facilities at Milford Sound—and the fees charged to partake of its glories. The Tourist Hotel Corp., the government hotel-tourism agency, has traditionally charged a fee to walk the track, partly because hikers must stay in approved government huts along the track and partly to limit the number of hikers per day (at present only 80 a day: 40 in groups, 40 independent). The hotel at Milford was owned by THC, as were the ferries that took hikers from the end of the track (up the sound a ways) to the bus terminal at the hotel for the return trip to civilization.

Lake Quill, Milford Track

Now control of the track and the amenities at Milford is in private hands because THC has been purchased by Southern Pacific Hotels. What the end result of this will be is uncertain.

GUIDED WALKS

Many hikers choose to take one of the guided walks, which have been operated for the government by Southern Pacific Hotels for some time. The new SPH brochure offers a six-day trip that includes a visit to the Fiordland National Park headquarters in Te Anau, a trip up Lake Te Anau, use of camping huts along the track, meals, some equipment and a cruise on Milford Sound. The price per person is around NZ$700-NZ$750, not including transportation to Te Anau where the tours begin. Te Anau is served daily by air from Christchurch and Queenstown and by bus from those two cities plus Invercargill.

The age limit on the tours is 10 to 70. Guides are equipped with radios for emergencies. Tour participants are supposed to be in good enough condition to do around 10 miles a day. The tours this year begin Oct. 27 and run through the first of April. Reservations are necessary, and some periods, such as Christmas-New Year's, sell out early.

FREEDOM WALKERS

It is also possible to go on your own (as a so-called "freedom walker") by paying a NZ$40 fee and picking up your own costs for food, equipment, ferry boats and buses. The total cost will run around NZ$150 per person. Like the group hikers, you are required to stay in Southern Pacific huts along the track at night. A deposit is required. Information on both group tours and independent hiking is available in North America from **Southern Pacific Hotels**, ☎ (800) 441-3847; ask for John Saypol. The trips also can be booked through any tour agency in New Zealand, and at Fiordland Travel offices in Queenstown or Te Anau.

Mount Cook Line Treks has Milford trips from Te Anau, 6 days, 5 nights, for about NZ$700. For information in North America, ☎ (800) 468-2665. Because of the crowds, many trampers choose to ignore the Milford Track and do one of the other excellent trails in the Queenstown area.

OTHER TRACKS

Other tracks in the Milford area include the **Greenstone**, the **Route-burn** and the **Hollyford**. *Of these, serious hikers will probably like the Hollyford best—all the scenery of the Milford Track without the crowds.*

GREENSTONE

The **Greenstone** is an ancient Maori trail through alpine valleys, past lakes, rivers and gorges. Its name comes from the fact that the Maori used it to reach the rich deposits of greenstone near Lake Wakatipu. The 21-mile, all-season track usually takes about 3 days. It's the easiest of the Milford area tracks.

ROUTEBURN

The **Routeburn** is a high-level track about 25 miles long, through the Alps, with some of the best scenery in the area, that enters 2 national parks. The trek takes about 3 days, starting on the continental divide and running toward Queenstown and Lake Wakatipu.

HOLLYFORD

The **Hollyford** also starts at the divide, then goes between the **Darran Range** and **Mount Tutoko**. You'll find ferns, orchids, mosses, then along Lake McKerrow (a fjord), seals, penguins and dolphins. It's 3 to 4 days to the end of the Hollyford. Some ardent hikers then go around Big Bay, pick up the Pyke Track and return to the divide. There are several walk-in, fly-out options available.

For the truly in-shape, one of the most rewarding treks is the trail up and over Ball Pass linking the Tasman and Hooker valleys in Mount Cook National Park. The 3-day trail goes over 7,000 feet and gives magnificent views of Mt. Cook and the Tasman and Hooker glaciers. It can be rugged (crampons sometimes required), but the difficulty factor is not really high. Optional trips include guided tours over **Copland Pass**, a 5-day trek across **Tasman Glacier** itself or an overnight hike to the base of **Mount Cook**.

Town cryer reads from a scroll in Christchurch

GOING SOUTH

From the Queenstown area, you can wend your way south to Invercargill, the country's southernmost city; then east to Otago, that portion of the eastern South Island from Invercargill to Dunedin; north to Oamaru; wander back up north to Cooktown and the east side of the Alps, or head back through the farmland and pastures to Christchurch. In any direction, the land flattens out as you leave the mountains and fjords, and *the feeling becomes less scenic and a lot more pastoral.*

INVERCARGILL

Invercargill lives on sheep—the city is surrounded by meat processing plants that handle nearly 10 million animals a year, mostly lamb. Like Dunedin (as you can tell from the names), Invercargill was originally a Scottish settlement. If you've been to Scotland, you can appreciate why the Scots would feel comfortable here. *The weather can be truly lousy, and there's nothing much between you and Antarctica.* But the sheep folks admire the weather, especially the year-round rains, because there's always grass for the beasts. In New Zealand, especially around Wellington, there are always a few jokes about the south end of the South Island, a lot like the jokes Canadians have for people who live in Newfoundland and Americans have for the residents of North Dakota. But if life is slow in the South, that seems to be the way they like it. In truth, many tourists don't even blink passing through Invercargill, which they see as simply a base for trips to the much more exotic sights of Stewart Island across the Foveaux Strait.

Most of the streets in Invercargill are named after Scottish rivers, the main drag being Dee. *There's nothing either very pretentious or very exciting about the city—it's basically just a nice, quiet agricultural center.* It has a couple of things going for it, however, including a museum where you can see the extremely rare New Zealand **tuatara**. It also has several **excellent restaurants**, some of the best in New Zealand.

The tuatarium is housed in the **Southland Museum** in Queens Park, which has a pretty good **Maori gallery** as well. The museum is free, although they like donations. The chances of spotting the reptiles are usually pretty good, although babies are very hard to see. The museum also has an **observatory**, open Wednesday nights, April through October. Museum hours are 10 a.m.-4:30 p.m., weekdays, 1-5 p.m., weekends. ☎ (03) 218-9753. Weather permitting, **Queens Park** is worth a stroll. It contains about 200 acres of lawns, gardens and an 18-hole golf course. The city has two down-town-area heated swimming pools, four golf courses, tennis courts and rental facilities for bikes or horses. About 10 miles southwest of town is **Oreti Beach**, with a long stretch of good beach and sand dunes. Information about the city and the area is available at the Visitors Centre, 82 Dee Street (look for the Grand Hotel). ☎ 218-6091.

WHERE TO STAY

Gerrard's Hotel—Corner of Esk and Leven streets. For our taste, the best place in town. Small, intimate, red brick, 1890s building across from the train station. Wonderful restaurant/bar. Many rooms newly redecorated. B&B doubles with bath are about NZ$95. The restaurant is Victorian decor and is open for all 3 meals, dinner 7 nights a week. Dinner is from 6:30 p.m.; reservations necessary. ☎ 218-3406.

Ascot Park Motor Hotel—Corner of Tay Street and Racecourse Road. Four kilometers from the city on a 17-acre site. Indoor pool, spa, saunas, restaurant, bar, kitchens, baby-sitting, some motel units, some suites. Doubles are about NZ$150. ☎ (03) 217-6195.

Kelvin Hotel—16 Kelvin St., city center. Restaurant, bar, coffee/tea, handicapped facilities. Some suites. Doubles, about NZ$115. ☎ 218-2829.

Grand Hotel—76 Dee St. Old landmark building, now refurbished. Restaurant, bar, some suites. Doubles, about NZ$90. ☎ 218-8059.

Monticello Travel Lodge—240 Spey St., downtown. Restaurant, kitchens, B&B, courtesy van. B&B double, about NZ$95. ☎ 218-2503.

Colonial Motor Inn—335 Tay St., near a shopping center. Laundry. About NZ$95, double. ☎ 217-6057 or 6058.

Townsman Motor Lodge—195 Tay St., about a kilometer from the city center. Kitchens, spa, courtesy van, baby sitting, breakfast available, tea/coffee. Some deluxe units. Doubles are about NZ$90. ☎ 218-8027. ·

Invercargill Hostel—122 North Road, Waikiwi, about 3 kilometers from city center. Barbecue. NZ$16 a night per person; non-members, NZ$20. ☎ 215-9344.

Beach Road Motor Camp—At Oreti Beach. Laundry, TV lounge, store, kitchen. Tourist flats, NZ$55, double. Cabins, NZ$30, double. ☎ 213-0400.

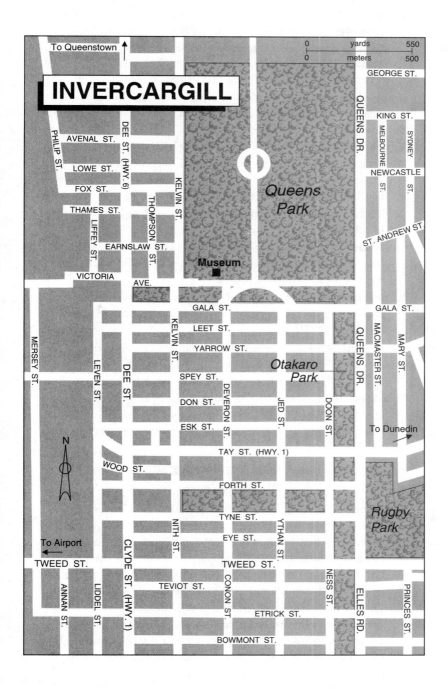

WHERE TO EAT

Donovan's—220 Bainfield Rd. Popular, honored restaurant housed in a restored farm house. *Famous for game dishes and also for the house specialty, "Whiskey Lamb Deep Creek"* (Bambi sauteed in booze). Good wine list. Tuesday-Saturday 5 p.m.-1 a.m. for dinner; lunches November and December. Reservations. ☎ 218-8156.

Strathern Inn—200 Elles Rd. Another award winner, also in a cottage. Six dining rooms show history of the area. *Specialties include Stewart Island salmon, venison, smoked eel.* Lunch noon-2 p.m. (closed Saturdays); dinner from 5 p.m. Reservations. ☎ 216-0400.

The Crystal Room—In the Ascot Park Hotel, corner of Tay Street and Racecourse Road. Weekend buffets, New Zealand a la carte menu. Lunch noon-2 p.m.; dinner 6-10 p.m. ☎ 217-6195.

Highlights Restaurant—Award winner, in the Kelvin Hotel. Stewart Island *salmon a specialty.* Reservations in high season. ☎ 218-2829.

Homestead Restaurant—Corner of Avenal and Dee streets. Family restaurant, family prices. *Many seafood dishes.* Lunch 11:45 a.m.-2:15 p.m.; dinner 4:30-10 p.m. ☎ 218-3125.

The Cosmopolitan—34 Esk St. Hamburger heaven, plus other sandwiches, venison and seafood. Open for lunch and dinner; closed Sundays and Mondays. ☎ 218-2166.

H.M.S. Kings—83 Tay St. Done up like a sailing ship; *the food makes up for the decor.* Seafood and steaks a specialty. BYOB. Closed Sundays. ☎ 218-3443.

Ainos Steakhouse—Ruru Street, off North Road. Open fire, steak and seafood. BYOB. *It's the oldest restaurant in town and the owner still does most of the cooking; many awards.* Open for dinner; closed Sundays. ☎ 215-9568.

ESSENTIALS

GETTING THERE

Invercargill has daily air service from Auckland and Christchurch and weekday service from Wellington (one Saturday flight), Dunedin, Hokitika, Nelson and Rotorua. Service is offered either on **Air New Zealand** or **Ansett**. From Christchurch, the one-way fare is about NZ$230; from Auckland, about NZ$430; from Wellington, about NZ$320, and from Rotorua, about NZ$410.

The city is also the southern terminus of **The Southerner**, a non-smoking train with a buffet car that starts in Christchurch with stops at Timaru and Dunedin. Daily service starts at 8:40 a.m., arriving in Invercargill around 6 p.m.; the return leaves at 9:20 a.m., arriving in Christchurch at 7 p.m. The one-way fare without a pass is about NZ$80. The city also has regular bus service to all parts of the South

Island. The fare from Invercargill to ChCh will run about NZ$90; to Dunedin, about NZ$40.

INFORMATION

For information about national parks and other government facilities, including Stewart Island, contact the Department of Conservation office on Don Street, ☎ 44- 589. The AA office is at 47-51 Gala St.; ☎ 218-9033.

THE OTHER ISLAND

New Zealand is actually considered to be three islands—the third being Stewart Island, south of Invercargill. Virtually unpopulated (maybe 500 people, if that), the island is lush with bird and plant life, including **brown kiwis**, herds of **feral cats, red deer, possums, rats** and flocks of **bush birds.** Sections of the island are covered with **ferns** and **podocarps**, with the odd **orchid** thrown in here and there. It gets pretty dense. Stewart Island is the permanent home of the folks who drag **lobster** and the world-famous **Bluff oysters** from the waters of the Foveaux Strait. *But the island is also a national park, one of the most popular in the whole country.* It's about 1700 square miles in area, has 450 miles of coastline and 130 miles of **hiking trails.** James Cook sighted it but thought it was part of the South Island. It was originally settled for timber, whaling and gold and other mineral mining, but now tourism and fishing are about all that's left. Judging from the look of things, fishing is still number one.

Native Tree Fern, Urewera National Park

In a nation of changeable weather, Stewart Island is even more changeable than most, with tons of rain annually but, surprisingly enough considering how far south it is, very little frost. It's not a place for folks who like their action hot and heavy, there being only one settlement of any size, but *it's a bush-walker's paradise.* The trails come in all sizes and various degrees of difficulty, and the government has placed hiking huts all over the island.

The main settlement is called **Oban**, which sits in a little inlet called Halfmoon Bay. *It usually reminds people of the sort of seafaring village you see along the coasts of New Brunswick or Nova Scotia, weathered and wooden and 50 years behind the times.* But it's too green and not rocky enough to be anywhere in the Maritimes. It looks—well—very New Zealandish. Information about the island is available either at the information centre in Invercargill or at the Stewart Island Visitor Centre on the island (right downtown, you can't miss it). ☎ (03) 219-1130. The island has a total of about 25 miles of paved roads, but give a Kiwi a road and he'll put a bus tour on it, in this case less than an hour but good for island backgrounding. Or you can rent mopeds or mountain bikes.

It does get busy in the summer, and reservations are a must. There are only a couple of restaurants, and accommodations are limited. There is a food store, but the prices are about what you'd expect on an island.

WHERE TO STAY

Stewart Island Lodge—At Halfmoon Bay. These are the best—and most expensive—digs on the island. The lodge has 4 units and rates include all meals. It's licensed. Summer rates (November-April) are about NZ$180 per person a night, double; winter rates (May-October) are about NZ$130 per person, double. Courtesy pickup at the dock or airport; fishing/diving boat available. ☎ (03) 219-1085.

South Sea Hotel—Downtown on the waterfront. Restaurant, TV lounge, public and private bar, restaurant. Room rates do not include meals. Doubles are about NZ$85 plus tax. Budget doubles are NZ$50 plus tax. Meals are moderate.· ☎ 219-1059.

Rakiura Motel—About a mile from town. Kitchens, laundry. Doubles about NZ$70. ☎ 219-1096.

Shearwater Inn—Downtown. A new complex and an associate YHA member. Restaurant, bar, laundry, kitchen, lounge. Doubles, about NZ$70. Backpackers, about NZ$16. ☎ 219-1114.

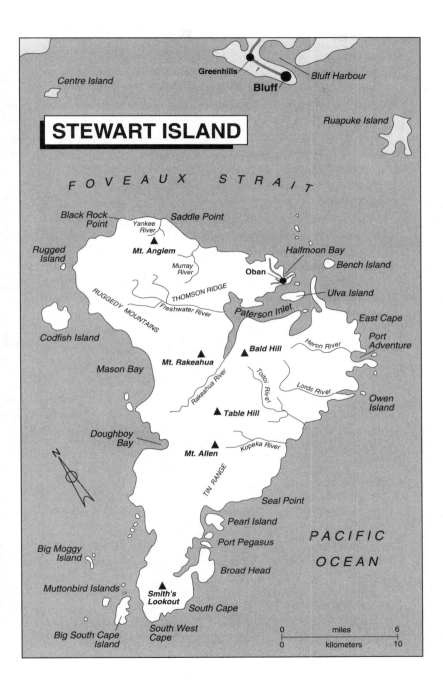

Stewart Island Holiday Homes—An interesting alternative. The homes sleep up to 10 persons, but you have to supply your own linens and food. The homes are a few blocks from the wharf with a view of Halfmoon Bay. Rates for 2 persons are about NZ$65 a night; extra folks, NZ$16 each. ☎ 219-1057, or in Invercargill, 217-6585.

Jo and Andy's B&B—One double, one triple, corner of Main Road and Morris Street. Cooking facilities and laundry available. NZ$18 per person with linen supplied. ☎ 219- 1230.

Horseshoe Haven—On Horseshoe Bay about two miles from the wharf. Tent sites, A-frame cabin, bunkhouse. Cabins with everything provided except food are about NZ$45, double. ☎ 219-1565.

In addition, a number of private homes have rooms to rent. These can be arranged through the island information centre or by contacting Stewart Island Travel, P.O. Box 26, Stewart Island, ☎ 219-1269 or 1293.

WHERE TO EAT

The best restaurant in town is probably **Annie Hansen's Dining Room** in the South Sea Hotel. Seafoods are tasty, or you can try venison or a muttonbird, the island specialty. Reservations necessary. Lunch from noon to 1 p.m.; dinner from 6-7 p.m. ☎ 219-1059.

For lighter fare, try the **Travel Inn** tearooms down the street (run by the same folks who own Stewart Island Travel).

ACTIVITIES

In addition to hiking or just lolling about, you can book helicopter trips in advance, look in on a **fish processing factory**, shoot deer (including some American whitetail) or better, **take a cruise** around the area to look at the seals and other local residents. There are several boats for charter at Oban with rates around NZ$50 per person for a full day. Overnight trips, meals included, are around NZ$500 per day for a party of 4. These can be booked in Invercargill or on the island itself.

GETTING THERE

By boat or by plane. Like its big brother up north between Picton and Wellington, the Foveaux Strait is open to the westerlies and can get very rough. The small ferry that makes the trip runs at odd times during the off season but daily during the height of the tourist season. Check times with the Stewart Island Charter Services offices in Bluff or with the Invercargill information centre. The one-way fare is about NZ$35, less for YHA members. If you just want to go over and come back, you'll have about 3 hours on the island before the return trip.

The fastest (and usually the smoothest) way over is the 20-minute flight aboard one of Southern Air Ltd.'s small planes. During the winter, there are 3 flights a day going and coming; more in summer. The round trip fare is about NZ$230, double; singles are NZ$140, kids, about NZ$70. The airline office can also book accommodations, charter a boat, set up bus tours or reserve whatever you want on the island. The office is at the Invercargill airport, ☎ 218-9129, toll free (0800) 658-876.

The Almost-Antarctic Experience—From Bluff, the seacoast city south of Invercargill, Southern Heritage Tours runs cruises to some of the isolated near-Antarctic islands south of Stewart Island. The company, a New Zealand natural history travel company, has 11- to 15-day cruises which hit about 6 island groups. The cruises are aboard the 140-foot *Pacific Ruby*, which has a crew of 15, including a professional chef and a medical officer. The cruises run between December and February and cost about NZ$2,400 per person, including meals—air fares extra. Information is available through the New Zealand Tourism Board in Santa Monica.

Helicopter tour of dramatic scenery near Milford Sound

HEADING NORTH

Penguins at Sandfly Bay

From Invercargill toward Dunedin, you have a choice of fast and farmy or slow and scenic.

Two highways branch from Invercargill to the settlement of **Balclutha**. The coast road, Highway 92, is worth the drive. At **Fortrose**, the land is grass-covered dunes as far as you can see, and at low tide, the whole country is out digging for shellfish. The locals are slowly claiming the ocean verge as new farmland, what they call down here "winning the land," but much of it remains rugged and pristine. The drive takes you along cliffs and rain forest, and if you have time, it might be worth stopping along the way at any of the several reserves and nature walks available. One good one is the trail up to **Purakaunui Falls**, about 15 kilometers east of **Owaka**. This is also the area of the **Catlins Forest Park**, just about midway between Dunedin and Invercargill. *The park, about 144,000 acres, is mostly virgin coastal forest, with hiking trails to secluded bays where you can see Hector's dolphins, seals and penguins.* Information and maps for the park are available at the Department of Conservation office in Owaka; ☎ (03) 415- 8341. There's a very nice beach along the coast highway between the **Tautuku Peninsula** and **Papatowai**, which also has a good beach and a nice RV park.

At **Balclutha,** the roads converge to become Highway 1, which runs north through Dunedin to the tip of the South Island. Balclutha is of note because it sits on the Clutha River, the largest river in New Zealand in terms of discharge. *Clutha* is the Celtic form of the Clyde, a river back in Scotland.

DUNEDIN

Dunedin proclaims itself the "Wildlife Capital of New Zealand," a bit of a boast, but allowable.

Northern Royal Albatross

The two most famous members of the wildlife set live out at the end of the **Otago Peninsula**, which juts north of the city—**the royal albatross** and the endangered **yellow-eyed penguin.** The city, population about 120,000, also calls itself the "Edinburgh of New Zealand," and indeed, *Dunedin* is the Celtic form of Edinburgh. It started life aptly enough as a Presbyterian colony (no doubt as far away as possible from the leftist Anglicans up in Christchurch).

The harbor, formed by the peninsula and the east shore, was a favorite of early whalers because it's about the only decent anchorage on this stretch of the South Island. It had a fairly unsavory reputation as a place where whalers got eaten by Maoris and Maoris got slaughtered by whalers, but all was basically placid by the middle 1840s. The hills rise steeply from the harbor, giving Dunedin a sort of San Francisco look. And like San Francisco, Dunedin got its start as a base for gold-mad miners, in this case part of the mobs who rushed to Queenstown and Arrowtown in the 1860s. A lot of gold

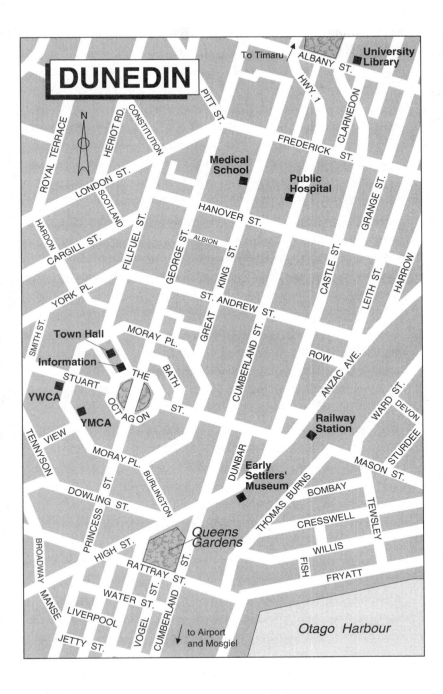

fortunes were spent building gaudy Victorians all over town, and the city also became a banking center.

The heart of the city is the **Octagon**, a garden area flanked by several city landmarks, including an almost compulsory statue of **Bobbie Burns**. Also nearby is **St. Paul's Cathedral**, the signature church in the city which, amusingly, is Anglican. Near it is **First Church**, the Presbyterian seat. Both are worth a look; First Church (1875) is currently being refurbished. St. Paul's, built in 1915, is probably the more dramatic of the two with fine roseate windows and a huge organ. Evensong performances, open to the public, are held Tuesday, Wednesday, Thursday and Sunday. Information is available at the cathedral office, open 9:30-12:30, Monday-Friday.

Another Dunedin landmark is the **railway station** on Cumberland Street, an old Edwardian hulk now a bit chipped around the edges. It was built in 1904 and of some note is the mosaic tile floor with railroad motifs, plus gilt-edged mirrors and genuine Thomas Crappers in the loos. The guy who designed it was knighted. *De gustibus et coloribus non est disputandum.*

Some other relics are the **Municipal Chambers,** opened in 1880; the **Law Courts**, 1902; the **Otago Boys High School**, 1884; **St. Joseph's Catholic Cathedral**, 1886; a **Dominican priory**, 1877; **Knox Church**, 1876; **Southern Cross Hotel**, 1883, and the **Otago Star building**, built in the 1870s and still housing the newspaper it was named after.

Three of the major tourist targets in town are the many rhododendron gardens, the Olveston mansion and the Cadbury Chocolate Factory. The gardens are scattered all over town, so much so that the third week in October is celebrated as Rhododendron Week. One of the better gardens is the **Rhododendron Dell** at the Botanic Gardens, started in 1914. The gardens are off Great King Street (northbound Highway 1). Look for the statue of Peter Pan and Wendy. Information is available at ☎ 474-3309. The Dunedin Rhododendron Group maintains a private garden, which you can tour for NZ$2.

Olveston is a time capsule of how the posh got along around the turn of the century. It's a Jacobean mansion, filled to the gunwales with antiques, period paintings and collectibles. It was built between 1904 and 1906 and was left to the city by the family in 1966. The billiard room looks like an aircraft carrier, and the Great Hall, all oak and darkness, oozes money. Hour-long guided tours are available

Monday-Saturday and Sunday afternoon. Reservations are suggested; the tours, about NZ$10 for adults, can be booked at the visitor's centre. Information also available by calling the mansion at ☎ 477-3320.

The Cadbury factory *might be the most popular attraction on the South Island.* It's almost impossible to get a tour because they are booked months in advance, especially during the school holidays. Of course, they give you free samples. One-hour tours run Monday-Thursday, and can be booked, maybe, at the visitor's centre.Or try a visit to **Speights Brewery**. More free samples on one-hour tours. Information: ☎ 477-9480. The city also has an excellent museum, with a really fine display of Maori art and architecture. The **Otago Museum** is on Great King Street, adjacent to the university. One of its major attractions is a Maori meeting house, carved in 1872. It's a classic—remember to take your shoes off before going in. There are also displays of canoes, greenstone carvings, and relics from other Pacific cultures. The museum, built in 1877, is also noted for a remarkable collection of classic works from Greece and Rome. Admission is free. Hours are 10-5, Monday-Friday; 1-5 p.m., weekends. Information ☎ 477-2372.

The Otago Peninsula draws many visitors every year to see the wildlife and enjoy the raw coastal scenery. The drive from the city to the tip at Taiaroa Head runs through country that reminds us of the Yorkshire dells with fewer stone walls. It's about 25 or 30 kilometers from the city to the head with some fine views and some fairly curvy roads.

It can be a bit confusing getting to the peninsula road. From the Octagon, get on Princes Street south, go about 1 kilometer, then turn left on Anderson's Bay Road. The road takes a sharp left, becoming Musselburgh Rise, then goes left again to become Ravelston Street. Soon after, at Silverton Street, turn right, and soon you should see a sign for Larnach Castle. Proceed. The tourist spots on the peninsula are signposted.

The first major attraction you come to is **Glenfalloch Gardens**, about 10k out of town. There are 30 acres of woodlands and gardens, with a licensed restaurant, the Chalet Cafe. Open for teas, lunches, dinners and some buffet dinners. Monday-Tuesday, 9:30-5:30; Wednesday through Sunday, 9:30 a.m.-10 p.m. Moderate. ☎ 476-1006.

Larnach Castle

Soon after is **Larnach Castle***, supposedly the country's only castle. But it ain't really a castle, but more like a big, rambling Victorian mansion.* The place does not live up to its descriptions. It's impressive enough, but for the NZ$9 charged per person to get in, not really worth it. It has 40,000 square feet of rooms, plus about 1,000 acres of land. There is a verandah for light repast, and if you stay at the lodge, evening meals and breakfast are available in the castle. The castle's ballroom is often used for public occasions. The castle folks do have a couple of nice places to spend the night if you want to stay on the peninsula. **The Stable**, a century-old building, has budget accommodation, as well as RV spaces. The four-person rooms go for NZ$30, double. The **Larnach Castle Lodge**, a re-created farm building, has better doubles starting at about NZ$75; shared kitchens, tea/coffee. Castle tours,half price for guests. Information is available at the city visitors centre or at the castle; ☎ (03) 476-1302.

For a look at the sealife that inhabits the Otago Peninsula area, stop in at the **Portobello Marine Museum** run by the Otago University Marine Research Station. Displays of marine life, touching pools, a tuatara. It's on a peninsula to the left past Larnach Castle. Open weekends and holidays, noon-4:30 p.m. Fee NZ$5.

At the tip of the peninsula is the **Royal Albatross Colony**, where the huge seabirds have one of their few rookeries near civilization. Adults can fly 75 miles an hour, migrate more than 120,000 miles a year and have wingspans of nearly 11 feet. Entry permits, available at the colony's visitor centre, are about NZ$15; reduced rates in the winter. The viewing season opens Nov. 24, closes Sept. 16 the next year. Information at the Trust Bank Royal Albatross Centre, ☎ 478-0498 or 0499.

Next to the colony is an old fort, which draws the curious to look at the **Armstrong Disappearing Gun**, an 1886 wonder that was aimed underground, raised to fire, then disappeared below again for a reload. It could fire a 100-pound shell 5 miles. Tours of the fort and the colony are often combined. Bookings through the Dunedin visitors centre. Entry fee is NZ$10, or for both colony and fort, about NZ$20.

Also at the head is **Penguin Place**, where you can see southern fur seals and the endangered yellow-eyed penguins. The last 4 hours of daylight are the best viewing hours for the birds. Bookings through the Dunedin Visitors Centre. Fee NZ$5.

ESSENTIALS

GETTING THERE

Dunedin has regular air service from cities in the south, as well as the North Island. Daily service is offered by Air New Zealand from Auckland for about NZ$400 one way. Other prices: Wellington, NZ$270; Rotorua, NZ$370; Christchurch, NZ$190; Hokitika, NZ$230, and Invercargill, NZ$135. Train service is available on the Southerner Express from either Christchurch or Invercargill. The fare from Christchurch one way is about NZ$50; from Invercargill, about NZ$40. There is bus service to Queenstown, Timaru and Te Anau. The one-way fare to Queenstown is about NZ$50. The train/bus office is at 200 Cumberland St.; Mt. Cook Landline bus offices are at 67 Great King St.

GETTING AROUND

Dunedin Taxis will take you around town, get you to the airport or, for about NZ$40 an hour, tour you around. They claim they will compete with airport shuttles. ☎ 777-777.

TOURS

Otago Harbour Cruises has a couple of packages designed to show the full glories of the bay and the peninsula. You can cruise out to Taiaroa Head on the *M.V. Monarch* and bus back, or bus out and cruise back. The first plan is probably the best because you see the albatrosses and the penguins; the second stops at Larnach Castle. The cruise out/bus back is about NZ$60. It takes 6 hours. The bus out/cruise back is about NZ$40 and takes 4 hours. Other packages are available. Information: Otago Harbour Cruises Office, corner Wharf and Fryatt streets, ☎ 477- 4276 or 4215.

Newtons Coachways offers peninsula bus tours with stops at most of the popular spots. The tour to the albatrosses and penguins is about NZ$35. Information, Newtons, 105 Melbourne St.; ☎ 477-5577.

A very nice train trip runs from the historic railroad station to the Taieri Gorge north of the city. Lots of canyons and scenery, often compared to the narrow gauge trip in Durango, Colorado (which, incidentally, was built by one of the author's great-grandfathers). The trip out and back runs about 4 hours. There's wheelchair access and a bar/snack car. If you're camping, they'll drop you off and pick you up later. Tickets are available at the train station, the city visitor centre or any InterCity booking office. The adult ticket is about NZ$40. Information: Otago Excursion Train Trust, ☎ 477-4449.

INFORMATION

The **Dunedin Visitor Centre** is located in the Octagon. Hours are 8:30 a.m.-5 p.m. weekdays, 9-5, weekends. ☎ 474-3300.

WHERE TO STAY

The city has for its size a remarkable number of good hostelries and eateries for a wide range of purses. We like the Southern Cross because of its style and location, but some lodgings toward the peninsula and beaches are quite comfy as well. A number of good units are in the university area, which is shady and peaceful.

Southern Cross—Corner of High and Princes streets, close to the Octagon. Satellite TV, tea/coffee, dry cleaning/laundry service. Three restaurants: The Lobby, a la carte gourmet; the Deli-Cafe, open 7 days, 24 hours, and the classy old Brasserie and Exchange Bar with pub-style food. Doubles are about NZ$150. ☎ 477-0752.

Abbey Lodge Motor Inn—680 Castle St, nice location near Otago University and the Botanical Gardens. Luxury and honeymoon suites, spas, indoor pool, sauna, laundry facilities, bar, restaurant, fridge, tea/coffee, baby-sitting, some kitchens. Hotel rates are about NZ$160, double; motel rates about NZ$100, double. ☎ 477-5380.

Pacific Park Dunedin—21-24 Wallace St. Hillside location overlooking the harbor, about a kilometer from city center. Honeymoon and deluxe suites, 2.5 acres of native bush, restaurant/bar, tennis courts, miniature golf, barbecue/picnic area, tea/coffee, minibars, baby-sitting. Doubles, about NZ$110. ☎ 477-3374.

Quality Inn Dunedin—Upper Moray Place, right on the Octagon. Minibars, tea/coffee, valet service, spa, sauna, restaurant/bar, baby-sitting. Doubles, about NZ$140. ☎ 477-6784.

Cargill Motor Inn—678 George St., close to the university and Otago Museum. Some luxury suites, spas, minibars, tea/coffee, laundry, bar/restaurant. Doubles, about NZ$125. ☎ 477-7983.

Leisure Lodge Motor Inn—30 Duke St., university area. Original site of a brewery—stones from the old building were used in the bar, and the dining room is named after the oast house. Large landscaped garden, fine ambiance. One deluxe suite, family units, tea/coffee, laundry. Doubles,. about NZ$100. ☎ 477-5360.

High Street Court Motel—193 High St., near the Octagon. Kitchens, laundry, gardens, breakfast available. Doubles, about NZ$90. ☎ 477-9315.

Alglen Motor Hotel—137 St. Andrew St., city center. Tea/coffee, baby-sitting, some suites with spas, family-style cafe and house bar. Doubles, about NZ$110. ☎ 477-0572.

Commodore Luxury Hotel—924 Cumberland St., near the university and botanical gardens. Kitchens, courtesy van, baby-sitting, breakfast available, licensed restaurant. Doubles, from NZ$75 to NZ$110. ☎ 477-7766.

Regal Court Motel—755 George St., near the Otago Museum and university. Kitchens, laundry, breakfasts available. Doubles, around NZ$90. ☎ 477-7729.

Alcala Motor Court—George and David streets near city center. Rooftop units, executive and honeymoon suites, spa, laundry, breakfast available. Doubles, about NZ$85. ☎ 477-9073.

Aberdeen Motel—46 Bank St., first motel off the northern motorway about 3 kilometers from town. Kitchens, laundry, tea/coffee, morning paper, breakfast available. Doubles, NZ$80-100. ☎ 473-0133.

Law Courts—Corner Stuart and Cumberland streets. A favorite moderate-priced hotel. Funky Art Deco building with a Cobb & Company restaurant. Great staff, great urban neighborhood, comfortable bar, one of the Pub Hotel group. Private baths, coffee/tea. Doubles, about NZ$60, singles, NZ$30. ☎ 477-8036.

Ocean View Motor Lodge—14 The Esplanade, St. Clair Beach, south of the city center. Ocean views, kitchens, garages, breakfast available. Doubles, about NZ$80. ☎ 455- 7941.

Sahara Guesthouse and Motel—619 George St., about a kilometer from city center. B&B, laundry, motel and lodge units, some kitchens. Guesthouse doubles, about NZ$53; motel doubles, about NZ$75. ☎ 477-6662.

Wains Hotel—310-314 Princes St., close to bus terminal and city center. Dining room, house lounge and public bar, bottle shop, B&B. Doubles, about NZ$80; suites, NZ$100. ☎ 477-9283.

Leviathan Hotel—65 Lower High St. Private baths, house lounge/bar, laundry, minibars, restaurant, some rooms with rangettes. Doubles, around NZ$70. ☎ 477- 3160.

Alvand House—3 Union St. Very tiny, city center. B&B, laundry, coffee/tea. Doubles NZ$65. ☎ 477-7379.

Stafford Gables Hostel—71 Stafford St., five minute walk to the Octagon. YHA facility close to a supermarket. Doubles, twins, triples and family rooms. Cafe open in summer. NZ$18 per person a night; non- members, NZ$22. ☎ 474-1919.

Aaron Lodge Motel and Holiday Park—162 Kaikorai Valley Rd., about 2.5 kilometers from town. Top 10 member. Kitchen, laundry units, barbecue, linen hire. Motel units about NZ$70, double. Tourist NZ$60, double; cabins, NZ$35; ☎ 476-4725

WHERE TO EAT

Good hotel restaurants worth a try, in addition to the Southern Cross and the Oast Room at the Leisure Lodge, include the **Settlers Inn** at the Quality Inn, BYOB, specializing in lamb, fish and steaks; the **Carv-**

ery in the Wains Hotel, which has a reasonable Sunday smorgasbord; the **Abbey Motor Lodge restaurant**, which has a seafood and meat smorgasbord, weekends, and **Aggie's Restaurant** in the Pacific Park, which specializes in sinfully rich crayfish.

OTHERS

95 Filleul Restaurant—95 Filleul St. *One of the classiest places in Dunedin.* Housed in an old Victorian mansion, open fires, real china. Menu changes with the seasons, but lamb, venison, fresh fish and seafood are the norm. Lots of fresh veggies. Very popular, reservations essential. Dinner from 6:30 p.m. ☎ 477- 7233.

Blades—450 George St. *Another award winner, French in flair.* BYOB, emphasis on fresh foods. Monday-Saturday, from 6 p.m. ☎ 477-6548.

Orient Chinese Restaurant—320 Princes St. *Gourmet Chinese food, very tasty.* Lunch Tuesday-Friday noon-2 p.m.; dinner Monday-Saturday from 6:30 p.m. Moderate. ☎ 477- 5897.

Palm Cafe—84 High St. Colonial furnishings, overlooking the Queen's Gardens. *Pasta specialities,* as well as vegetarian dishes and fish and lamb. Closed Sunday and Monday. ☎ 477-6534.

Unique Cuisine—395 Princes St. Tough name to live up to, but *the lamb and venison dishes are very good.* BYOB, 5-course meals. Dinner from 6 p.m., 7 days. ☎ 477-0640.

Los Gatos—199 Stuart St. Especially suited for Californians in need of a burrito fix. *Very popular,* reservations essential. Lunch Thursday-Monday 11:30-2; dinner, Friday-Sunday 6-10 p.m. ☎ 477-3930.

Glorious Food—367 George St. Take-aways and pastas and egg-and-bacon breakfasts 7 days a week. Very reasonable. ☎ 477-6959.

Foxy's—370 George St. Great pub food, Victorian decor with live entertainment some nights. Lunch and dinner, closed Sundays. Budget prices. ☎ 477-8100.

Potpourri—97 Lower Stuart St. *Vegetarian, special dish every day. Good salad bar.* Open Monday-Friday 9 a.m.-8 p.m.; Saturdays 10-2; closed Sundays. ☎ 477-9983.

Captain Cook—Albany and Great Kings streets. Garden bar, pub food. *Where the university crowd hangs out. Very crowded.* Open for lunch noon-2 p.m. Student prices.

NORTH TO TIMARU

Roughly 60 miles north of Dunedin along the coast highway, No. 1, is **Oamaru**, which is primarily known for the production of a creamy white limestone, which has been used in the construction of several notable New Zealand buildings, including the Town Hall in

Auckland, Wellington's old Customs house and the cathedral in Christchurch. *The town itself has a wealth of limestone buildings, so many in fact, that efforts are underway to create a working Victorian town* around what was the original trade center of the city. Worth a look is the so-called **Victorian Street** (Harbour and Tyne streets) where white stone buildings stand, a bit forlorn, testimony to the once-thriving Gold Rush economy that flourished in the 1860s. The harbor here is artificial, constructed of the gravels that line the ocean bed, close to shore. It was from Oamaru in the 1880s that the first shipments of refrigerated mutton and other sheep products were sent to England, creating a boom in the Kiwi farm business that lasted until England joined the European Common Market.

Oamaru is also the intersection of Highway 83, en route to Mt. Cook and the Southern Alps. *It is the commercial center of the fertile Waitaki River Valley where many fruits are grown.* The area also produces some excellent cheeses; try the Whitestone cheddar. The river marks the boundary between the Otago and Canterbury districts. South of town about halfway to Dunedin are the famous **Moeraki Boulders**, a clutch of huge rock spheroids of special significance to the Maoris. The rocks, the legends say, are food baskets that washed ashore after one of the founding canoes of the first Maoris crashed onto an offshore reef.

About 80 kilometers further north is the city of **Timaru**, the agricultural center of South Canterbury. It has one famous son, Robert Fitzsimmons, the boxer who beat Jack Dempsey in 1891 and Gentleman Jim Corbett in 1899. It is also the home of one of the most famous horses in history (at least in Australia and New Zealand), **Phar Lap**. The horse won almost every race he entered, so much so that the Aussies tried to get him banned from the Melbourne Cup. He was poisoned and died while on a trip to the United States. A very entertaining movie about the horse was made not long ago.

Caroline Bay

The heart of the city is **Caroline Bay**, where there is a very popular annual carnival held during the Christmas-New Year's holidays. The beach is described as "fine and sandy," but we found it to be pretty muddy and not very attractive. It is a safe swimming spot, however, and very crowded in the summer. *Like the other settlements along the east shore of the South Island, Timaru has a collection of old stone Victorians,* including **St. Mary's Anglican Church**, made of local basaltic rock and limestone from Oamaru. The city's harbor is the central bulk handling area for the South Island, including facilities that reportedly can load 5,000 sheep an hour onto transport—many, it is reported, headed for the dining rooms of Saudi Arabia. There is a huge DB brewery here and what is billed as one of the largest tanneries in the world.

Timaru lies about halfway between Christchurch and Mt. Cook, which is reached by taking Highway 8 east past Lake Tekapo and into the Alps. *It's probably the best place to stop between ChCh and Dunedin.* While nothing fancy, there are some motels and good restaurants for those who want to haul in for the night. Information about the city, the region and some attractions (including some Maori rock paintings) is available from the South Canterbury Information Centre, 14 George St.; ☎ (03) 688-6163.

WHERE TO STAY

Hibernian Hotel—4 Latter St. A Tudor-style hotel near center of town. The place we suggest you stay. It's a member of the Pub Hotel group. Cobb & Co. restaurant. Doubles about NZ$65 with bath. ☎ 688-8125.

DB Grosvenor Hotel—Cains Terrace, near city center. Restaurant, bar, tea/coffee, B&B. Doubles about NZ$90. ☎ 688-3129.

Aaron Court Motel—27 Evans St. Close to Caroline Bay. Laundry, spa, garages. Doubles about NZ$85. ☎ 688- 0079.

Aorangi Motel—400 Stafford St. Close to Caroline Bay. Kitchens, laundry, breakfast available. Doubles about NZ$70. ☎ 688-0097.

Cedar Motor Lodge—36 King St. Kitchens, laundry. Doubles about NZ$80. ☎ 684-4084.

Elizabeth House (YHA)—14 Elizabeth St. Doubles and family rooms. Fishing, tennis and cycle rentals. NZ$15 per person a night. ☎ 688-4685.

Hydro Grand Hotel—360 Stafford St. Public bar, house lounge, laundry, restaurant. About NZ$60 double with bath. ☎ 684-7059.

Jan's Place—4 A Rose St. B&B. Rooms about NZ$35 per person. ☎ 688-4589.

Selwyn Holiday Park—Selywn Street, north end of town. A Top 10 RV park. Kitchens, laundry, canteen. Tourist flats with rangettes and showers, NZ$60; cottages, NZ$35 double; cabins, NZ$22 double. ☎ 684-7690.

WHERE TO EAT

The Boat House—335 Stafford St. *Good view, great seafood.* Specialties are king prawn, mussels and scallops. Dinner 6-9 p.m., closed Sundays. ☎ 688-3981.

Casa Italia Restorante—Strathallan St. *Grand old building, home-made pastas, good Italian wine cellar.* Dinner from 6 p.m. Closed Mondays. ☎ 684-5528.

Bunch O' Grapes Cafe—10 Variety Lane. Morning and afternoon teas, smorgasbords, lamb kebabs. Open 9 a.m.-4 p.m., Monday-Friday; from 6 p.m., Saturdays, closed Sundays. ☎ 688-0329.

Royal Garden—134-136 Stafford St. Cantonese fare, smorgasbord lunches, family smorgasbord Sunday nights. Lunch noon-2 p.m. Monday-Friday; dinner seven days from 5 p.m. ☎ 684-8844.

Dusty Miller Restaurant—18 A Hobbs St., in the Northtown Tavern. Family dining, bottle shop, pub food and dinner menus. ☎ 688-0065.

Charlie's Coffee Shop—Stafford Mall. *Maybe the place to stop for lunch on the road.* Full menus or take- aways. Bargain daily specials. Open 8:30-5 Monday- Thursday; 9:30-2 p.m. Saturdays, closed Sundays. ☎ 688- 3955.

MT. COOK

If you're on the eastern side of the Southern Alps, it seems almost criminal not to go to Mt. Cook, which has probably the most famous hotel in New Zealand (the Hermitage), and arguably one of the best views of the mountains on the whole South Island. As the crow flies, it's less than 10 miles from Mt. Cook to Franz Josef, but the crow has to fly over 10,000-foot mountains and the glaciers. *Mt. Cook Village is the base of* **Mt. Cook National Park**, *probably the most spectacular national park in the country, and one that rivals most scenery you'll see in the European Alps.* The park, 270 square miles, contains more than 20 peaks over 10,000 feet, including, of course, Mt. Cook, the tallest mountain in Australasia. The Maoris called it *Aorangi*—the Cloud Piercer. It also contains the world's longest temperate-zone glacier, the *Tasman*. The view from the village is such that Mt. Cook is just one of a bunch of tall, snow-clad peaks, meaning the whole vista is spectacular.

Lake Pukaki, Mount Cook

Information about the park is available at the Mt. Cook National Park Visitor Centre right next to the Hermitage. ☎ 562-1818 or 1819.

ESSENTIALS

GETTING THERE

There is daily air service to the Mt. Cook airport, about 5 kilometers from the village, on Mt. Cook Airlines. From Wellington, about a 2-hour flight, the one-way fare is about NZ$390; from Rotorua, about NZ$500; from Auckland, about NZ$530. South Island fares are Queenstown, about NZ$200; Christchurch, about NZ$220, and from Nelson, about NZ$345. There is no direct air service between Fox Glacier, Franz Josef and Mt. Cook, but charter flights can be booked. Bus service is available from the airport to the village.

Daily bus service is provided by both InterCity and Mt. Cook Landlines from Christchurch. The trip, about 5 hours on InterCity, costs about NZ$60 one way. There is daily Mt. Cook Landline service to Queenstown for about NZ$55 and from Timaru for about NZ$45.

WHERE TO STAY

The Hermitage is the third of its name. The original was washed away in a flood in 1913; the second burned down in 1957. The new one, all picture windows and stone, is the premier place to stay, but reservations long in advance are usually necessary. It was formerly owned by the New Zealand government, but is now a member of the Southern Pacific Hotels group. All rooms have baths and phones. There is also a cinema, restaurant, cafe, sauna, coffee/tea. Doubles go for around NZ$280. ☎ (03) 435- 1809. There is a coffee shop, usually open all week from 9- 5. The expensive Panorama Room (great views, OK food) is open all week, with dinner served until 10 p.m. Things like venison stews, mussel chowders, cod patties are on the menu.

Glencoe Lodge—About a kilometer from the Hermitage. Operated by the same company that owns the Hermitage. B&B, tea/coffee, reservations also essential, usually open only in the summer. Doubles around NZ$210. ☎ 435-1804.

Mt. Cook Chalets—Also a Hermitage property. Hot plates, frypans, showers, singles. Doubles are about NZ$75. Book through the Hermitage. Note: Guests staying at the chalets and the Glencoe are allowed to use Hermitage facilties.

YHA Mt. Cook Youth Hostel—Pool table, food shop, central heating, barbecue, handicapped facilities. Advance bookings needed in the summer. NZ$18 per person. ☎ 562-1820.

Glentanner Park—Outside the park, about 23 kilometers south of Mt. Cook on the shores of Lake Pukaki. Kitchen, laundry, camp store, helipad, barbecue area. RV spots, tent sites. On-site unequipped rental caravans, NZ$14 per person. Cabins, some with showers and kitchens, NZ$55 double. ☎ 435-1855.

WHAT TO DO

If you're a couch potato, just sit and stare at the mountains (provided, of course, the ever-changeable weather permits). For the more active:

HIKING

Get maps and info at the park headquarters. There are several easy hikes, a few more strenuous. The best easy trek is probably

Governor's Bush, which goes through a small beech forest. Another good one is the

Hooker Valley trail, a bit more strenuous but good because it takes you up the Hooker River to the face of the Hooker Glacier, all the way to the beginning of the very tough

Copland Pass track. Look for bunches of sassy keas in the area, and watch out for the famous Mt. Cook lilies, in reality mountain buttercups. The petals are pure white.

For serious hikers, Alpine Recreation Canterbury Ltd. based in Lake Tekapo, about 60 miles from Mt. Cook Village, offers a three-day excursion across

Ball Pass, which connects the Hooker and Tasman valleys in the heart of the park. The company owns its own hut, and the route, while strenuous, is not technically difficult—the company says fit folks in their 60s and 70s have made it. The trip starts either at the Lake Tekapo bus stop or the visitors centre at Mt. Cook village. The trip, including the hut, all food, guides and equipment (including boots if you wish), is about NZ$600 per person for the full 3 days. Information: Alpine

Recreation Canterbury Ltd., P.O. Box 75, Lake Tekapo; ☎ (03) 680- 6736.

In the village, Alpine Guides has a rental office, as well as guide services. The company offers everything from simple hikes to full-scale climbing expeditions to the top of Mt. Cook itself. Some of these obviously require advanced mountaineering skills. The company also operates

Climbing Schools. They ain't cheap, however. A guide for the day runs about NZ$250; the climbing schools up to NZ$2,000 per person and serious expeditions begin at about NZ$2,000. Mt. Cook, by the way, was first climbed on Christmas Day 1894. Information: Alpine Guides Mt. Cook, P.O. Box 20, Mt. Cook; ☎ 435-1834.

SKIING

One of the more popular skiing trips in the South Island, for intermediates or experts, is to hop a ski-plane and fly from Mt. Cook to the

Tasman Glacier and ski down. Alpine Guides has a trip down the 27-kilometer-long glacier that involves 2 ski runs, 3 snow landings and a gourmet lunch. Including guide fees, the cost per person is about NZ$450. The company also takes ski parties into the

Ben Ohau Range, with 3 runs, 4 helicopter flights and a total vertical drop of 9,800 feet. Price, about NZ$450.

FLIGHTSEEING

As we said when we were on the other side of the mountains, coming to the South Island and not doing a flight around, through and into the Alps is unforgivable. It doesn't matter much which side you do it from, because there are air services aplenty basically taking in the same territory.

The Helicopter Line, operating from Glentanner Park, will circumnavigate Mt. Cook, look at the western and eastern glacier fields, do a snow landing and get you back in 45 minutes for about NZ$210 per person. A quick flight up to a landing on Richardson Glacier and down (30 minutes) is about NZ$150. There's a courtesy coach to take you from the village to Glentanner.

If a fixed-wing is more to your taste,

Air Safaris, booked through the Helicopter Line, flies in and around the Alps from Glentanner or Lake Tekapo for about NZ$110 an hour per person; a combination trip with a helicopter landing is about NZ$210. Information: Helicopter Line, Box 19, Mt. Cook; ☎ 435-1801. Or try Mount Cook Line, ☎ 435-1848.

TOP OF THE SOUTH

Many visitors coming south miss much of the northern area of the South Island, opting usually to head for Christchurch or taking the Westport Highway toward the west coast and the glaciers. However, *area residents think Nelson, west of the Picton ferry dock, might be one of New Zealand's better-kept secrets.* The sunsets around the area are justifiably famous, and Nelson has, on the average, more sunny days than any other part of the country. Nearby are the lovely fjords of the **Marlborough Sounds** country, which Capt. James Cook used as his primary base during his explorations of New Zealand and Antarctica. Much of the area is now a **national maritime park**. The fjords are not technically fjords, but ocean-drowned river valleys. The Marlborough area between Picton and Christchurch is *the nation's third largest wine-producing area,* home to the always good Montana line of wines and other vineyards scattered around Blenheim. In addition to huge catches of seafood and fish, the northern end of the island is also known for the production of fruits of various sorts.

MARLBOROUGH SOUNDS

The Sounds are a boater's and fisher's paradise with thousands of hidden and protected coves, miles of hiking trails, campgrounds and even some roads. But many of the special places are available only by boat, float plane or long hikes. Passengers on the **Interislander** ferries see only a piece of the whole picture, although **Queen Charlotte Sound** is one of the most beautiful of all the routes through the Sounds. There are a number of adventure and recreational companies located in Picton or Havelock, the tiny settlement 10 miles west of Picton, that do various trips around the Sounds.

Included are Charter Link in Picton, with boats sailing all over the Sounds for about NZ$180 per day per vessel; ☎ (03) 573-6591. Or Marlborough Sounds Charters in Picton with a variety of craft starting about NZ$100 a day; ☎ 573-7726. Or Portage Bay Charters in Picton, with prices starting around NZ$90; ☎ 573-4445. In addition, there are water taxis and a mail boat that you can hop.

There are some fairly fancy lodges stuck in remote areas, but the most famous place is probably **The Portage**, on Kenepuru Sound across Queen Charlotte Sound and a peninsula from Picton. It can be reached by twisty road, float plane or boat. It has a variety of water sports equipment available; a good bet for backpackers. It has a restaurant, bar, pool, spa, baby-sitting and bunkrooms. Doubles are around NZ$100; 4-person bunkrooms, about NZ$25 per person. ☎ 573-4309.

Another good choice is the **Punga Cove Tourist Resort** on Endeavor Inlet, north of Queen Charlotte, also accessible by road (long drive) or boat. It's a good spot located not far from Ship Cove, where Cook anchored and where there is a memorial to the famous captain. The units are self-contained chalets set in a bush environment with licensed restaurant, pool, barbecue area, beach, fishing access and glow worms. Doubles are around NZ$100. ☎ 573-4561.

The mail boat and also water tours of the Picton area are available through Beachcomber Cruises, 8 London Quay in Picton; a variety of cruises are available in the NZ$25-40 range for 2-hour jaunts. ☎ 573-6175 or 573-6844.

Information about other services, including dive shops, scooter rentals, air transport and tours, is available at the Marlborough Promotions Information Center toward town from the Ferry Dock; ☎ 573-7513.

WHERE TO STAY

For those wanting to haul in at Picton, especially if you're coming over on a late ferry, there are a number of reasonably priced motels. Most have courtesy coaches, and most can be booked from Wellington or actually aboard one of the Interislander ferries.

The Americano Motel—Our favorite, probably because of the name. 32 High St., middle of the shopping area, near London Quay. Kitchens, laundry, spa, bike and canoe hire, courtesy van. The motel **restaurant** serves all meals 7 days a week; family style or candle light. Nice view of the harbor. Seafood, venison and a free dessert. Rooms are about NZ$85 double. ☎ 573-6398.

Anchorage Lodge—Waikawa Road. Kitchens, laundry, pool, spa, barbecue area, coffee/tea, breakfast available, courtesy van. Doubles about NZ$90. ☎ 573-6192.

Best Western Koromiko Park Motel—Six kilometers south of town. Next to Picton Golf Course, kitchens, pool, spa, laundry, breakfast available, courtesy van. Doubles about NZ$80. ☎ 573-7350.

Picton Whaler's Inn—Waikawa Road. Pool, spa, restaurant and bar, baby-sitting, courtesy van, backpackers' rooms. Doubles about NZ$95; backpackers NZ$20 per person. ☎ 573-7002 or 7202.

Admiral Lodge—22 Waikawa Rd. B&B, close to bus and train station. Shared baths, tea/coffee. Doubles about NZ$77. ☎ 573-6590.

Tourist Court Motel—45 High St. Kitchens, laundry, tea/coffee, courtesy van. Double rooms between NZ$55 and NZ$70. ☎ 573-6331.

Terminus Hotel—Corner London Quay and High Street. Restaurant and three bars, tea/coffee. Doubles about NZ$60. ☎ 573-6452.

Wedgewood House—10 Dublin St., city center. YHA associate. Older-style guest house. Kitchens, laundry, some units with private baths. NZ$15, non-members, NZ$20. ☎ 573-7797.

Picton Pavlova Backpackers—34 Auckland St. No curfew, laundry, kitchens. Doubles about NZ$16. ☎ 573-6598.

Blue Anchor Holiday Park—Waikawa Road. Top 10 RV park. Laundry, pool, community kitchens. Motel unit double about NZ$75; tourist flats, NZ$55 double; cabins, NZ$30-42 double. ☎ 573-7212.

WHERE TO EAT

Ship Cove—33 High St. Specializes in seafood and Marlborough wines. Open 7 days for lunch and dinner. ☎ 573-7304.

Fifth Bank—Wellington Street. Seafood, shellfish, steaks. Open for dinner only. ☎ 573-6102.

Bakery and Lunch Bar—46 Auckland St. Filled rolls, sandwiches, pies. Open 7 days.

NELSON

Nelson, the city of sunsets, is the gateway to two fine preserves, **Northwest Nelson Forest Park** and **Mount Richmond Forest Park**, as well as the very popular **Abel Tasman National Park**. Not far to the south is **Nelson Lakes National Park**, an alpine area with hiking and many glacial lakes. It's a popular mountaineering area. The city dates its history back to the early 1840s and was a center for German immigration to New Zealand. A local boy who made good was Nobel laureate Ernest Rutherford, the noted atomic scientist. It's a popular summer vacation spot and has many gardens, art galleries and carnivals. The beaches are crowded, and there are many outdoor activities available including water sports, caving, hiking and fishing. The centerpiece of the city is **Christ Church Cathedral**, started in 1925 and finished in 1967. Around town are a few stately old homes, including **Isel House** (1850), **Broadgreen House** (1855) and **Fellworth** (1880).

In addition to tourism, the area is dependent on fruits, fishing and forestry—and, with **Blenheim,** is becoming an important wine growing area. It is also known as an **artists' colony**. Information is available from Nelson Regional Promotions, corner Trafalgar and Halifax streets; ☎ 548- 2303. Information on the parks, including Marlborough Sounds, is available from the Department of Conservation office, 186 Bridge St.; ☎ 546-9335.

Nelson has regular air service to most of the major cities on both islands, using either Ansett or Air Nelson. One-way fares from Auckland are about NZ$250; from Wellington, NZ$130; from Christchurch, NZ$170; from Queenstown, NZ$405.

Regular train/bus service is also available from Christchurch (one-way fare about NZ$65), and there is also bus service to Dunedin and Invercargill to the south and Greymouth to the west.

WHERE TO STAY

Quality Inn Nelson—Trafalgar Street. Rooms and suites, pool, spa, sauna, gym, restaurant and bar, tea/coffee. Double/single rooms about NZ$145. ☎ 548- 2299.

California House—29 Collingwood St. No-smoking facility, B&B, tea/coffee, courtesy van. Doubles from NZ$105- 140. ☎ 548-4173.

Beachcomber Motor Inn—23 Beach Rd., Tahunanui, 4 kilometers from the city center, near the beach. Some kitchens, laundry, pool, tea/coffee, spa, restaurant and bar, baby-sitting, courtesy coach. Doubles between NZ$100 and NZ$130. ☎ 548-5985.

Courtesy Court Hotel—26-30 Golf Rd., Tahunanui, near the beach. Best Western, kitchens, laundry, pool, spa, breakfast available. Doubles around NZ$100. ☎ 548-5114.

AA Nelson Motor Lodge—8 Ajax St., on the banks of the Maitai River. Kitchens, honeymoon suite, laundry, breakfast available. Doubles about NZ$100. ☎ 548-8214.

Anchor Lodge Motel—7 Roto St., Tahunanui, near the beach. Pool, coffee/tea, laundry, baby-sitting, courtesy van. Doubles about NZ$65. ☎ 548-6007.

Pavlova Backpackers—Corner of Trafalgar and Bridge streets. No curfew, laundry. NZ$15 per person. ☎ 548- 9001.

Pavlova Backpackers Farm Hostel—Still inside city limits; kitchen, laundry, courtesy van. NZ$15 per person. ☎ 548-9906.

Nelson YHA Hostel—42 Weke St., about a kilometer from city center. Bike hire, kitchen, laundry. NZ$15 per person, NZ$20 non-members. ☎ 548-8817.

Tahuna Beach Holiday Park—70 Beach Rd., Tahunanui. Said to be the largest RV park in Australasia, capable of handling almost 5,000 tourists a day. In addition to tent sites and RV pads, it has 6 kitchens, laundry, store and a car wash. Motel units are about NZ$80 double;

tourist flats, NZ$50 double; cabins, NZ$45 double; lodge, NZ$32 double. ☎ 548- 5159.

WHERE TO EAT

Junipers—144 Collingwood St. Fine dining in a century-old house. Specialties include smoked snapper chowder, quail and venison. Dinner from 6:30 p.m.; closed Sundays. ☎ 548-8832.

The Brown House—52 Rutherford St. Another historic house (1880), but this one has a ghost. Dinners only, BYOB, closed Wednesdays. *Specializes in domestic and wild game.* ☎ 548-9039.

City Lights—142 Hardy St. Liveliest place in Nelson. International cuisine, live music from jazz to Cajun. *Watch for Nelson scallops; also great lamb dishes. It's very casual and tends to get a tad noisy.* Dinner from 5:30 p.m.; closed Sunday. ☎ 548-8999.

Cobb & Co. Family Restaurant—In the Wakatu Hotel, corner of Bridge and Collingwood streets. Usual family menus, senior discounts, specials. Open 7:30 a.m.-10 p.m., 7 days. ☎ 548-4299.

Chez Eelco—296 Trafalgar St. Always popular, almost always open. Sandwiches, coffee, some hot-plate specials. Open 6 a.m.-11 p.m.

BLENHEIM

The largest community in the Marlborough area, Blenheim is becoming the capital of the South Island's growing wine industry. The industry began in the area in 1973 when Montana planted its first vines and is starting to rival the more famous wine areas on the North Island. (See the section on *Wine Producing Regions* for specifics). And as the wines become better known and more popular, the quality of inns and restaurants in the area is bound to get better. Besides, how can you go wrong—they grow a lot of garlic around here and harvest a lot of mussels—and that's most of the major food groups right in one spot.

You can reach Blenheim on the Coastal Pacific about a half-hour ride from Picton, or by bus. Information about the city and wine tours is available from Marlborough Promotions, Arthur Street; ☎ 578-4480. Or from the Vistors Information Centre at 1C Main St., ☎ 578-9904.

WHERE TO STAY

Blenheim Country Lodge—Seymour Square, corner of Alfred and Henry streets. Pool, minibars, restaurant and bar, tea/coffee, courtesy van. Rooms about NZ$115 double or single. ☎ 578-5079.

Chateau Marlborough—High Street, city center. Studios, suites, kitchens, handicapped facilities, pool, laundry, tea/coffee, breakfast available, courtesy van. Doubles about NZ$95-130. ☎ 578-0064.

Bing's Motel—Corner Maxwell Road and Seymour Street. Three acres of grounds, tennis courts, spas, pool, indoor bowling, kitchens, laundry, Chinese restaurant, handicapped facilities; breakfast available. Doubles about NZ$80.

Aorangi Lodge Motel—193 High Street. 578-2022. Kitchens, laundry, pool, BBQ, hanidicapped units, baby-sitting, courtesy van; breakfast available. Doubles about NZ$90.

Blenheim Al Holiday Park—78 Grove Rd., north end of town. ☎ 578-3667. Community kitchens; pool, laundry. RV park. Tourist flats. NZ$50 per double; cabins NZ$30-40 per double.

RESTAURANTS

Rocco's—5 Dodson St. ☎ 578-6940. Scampi, fresh fish, lamb. Lunch noon-2 p.m.; dinner starting at 5 p.m. Closed Sun. Expensive.

Hunter's Wine Village and Restaurant—Rapaura Rd. north of town off Highway 1. ☎ 572-8803. Popular spot to check out the wine business and try one of the restaurant's game meals. Blackboard menus, a la carte, the local grape. Lunch Sat./Sun. noon–2:30 p.m.; dinner Thurs.–Sun. from 6 p.m. Moderate to expensive.

Grove Mill Cafe—1 Dodson St. ☎ 578-9199. Wine bar, tasting bar; seafood cooked in wine a specialty. Lunch daily noon-2:30 p.m.; dinner Thurs.–Sat. from 6 p.m. Moderate to expensive.

Cobb and Co.—in the Grosvenor Hotel, 91 High St. ☎ 578-1109. Two bars, a wine tasting area, pub meals, the usual Cobb and Co. family fare. Budget to moderate.

THE NORTH ISLAND

Prince of Wales Geyser, Whaka

A place of volcanic fire and history. Home to the nation's two largest cities including the capital. Land of roaring geysers and bubbling thermal pools with *some of the best soaking in this or any other world.* Land of easy sailing, great fishing—and the economic and population center of New Zealand. Not as pretty, we insist, as its southern sibling, but still managing to please the eye and placate the palate.

The North Islanders, being comparatively urbanized, sometimes look down on their bumpkin cousins down south as slow and perhaps a bit cloddish. The southerners, for their part, are quick to eschew the pressures and noise of living in the swirl of urban madness in Wellington and Auckland. But remember, this is New Zealand, so any fears about big city tensions must be put into perspective. By North

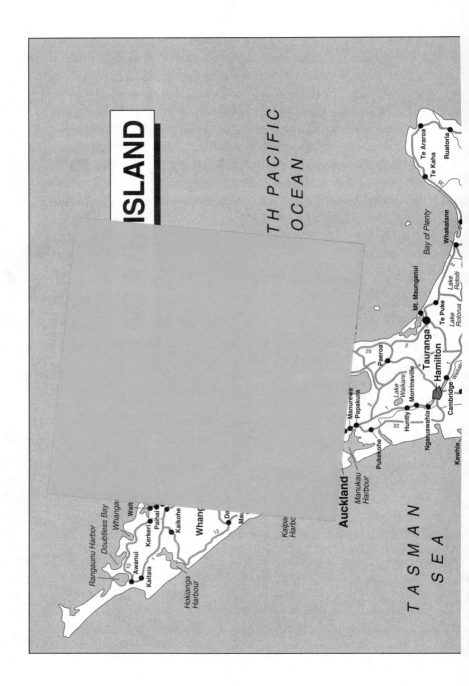

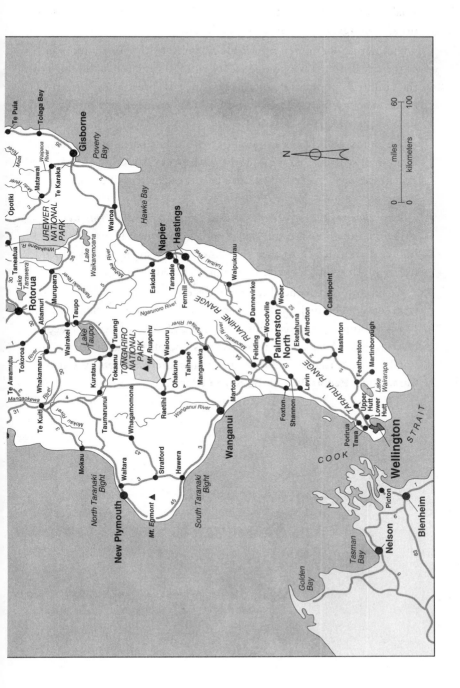

American standards, the two biggest cities here are relatively small—Auckland's population is about 700,000 not counting suburbs; Wellington's is only about 325,000.

The metropolitan area of *Auckland*, lying to the north and south of the city center, has a population of close to a million, a full third of the country's population and, like Sydney, is spread out all over the place. The tourism folks say the city and environs are more than 2,155 square miles in area.

The influx of Polynesian peoples from other parts of the Pacific, combined with the native Maoris, have made Auckland the largest Polynesian city on earth. But once past these metropolitan spots, *the open country of the North Island is every bit as rustic as the south.*

Being closer to the equator, the North Island tends to be warmer than the south. But there are still skiing and other winter sports here, and it's not unusual to have a winter snowstorm block major north-south roads between Wellington and Auckland.

Wellington is the official capital of the country, but Auckland is the true center. The major international airport is here, so the first spot of Kiwi country most visitors see is Auckland. A nice enough place in its own right, Auckland is also close to some of the major attractions on the North Island, including the major thermal areas, the lovely **Coromandel Peninsula** and the **Bay of Islands.**

AUCKLAND

Pohutukawas, Devonport

In the early days before English colonial settlement started in earnest, the base of European operations was the **Bay of Islands** area near **Russell,** a whaling center and, in the early days, a raunchy settlement with an international bad-boy reputation. After the Treaty of Waitangi was signed in the early 1840s, the colonial administration decided to move the capital to a more central location, and picked a spot further south on a narrow isthmus between two lovely bays. *The English, a la Manhattan Island, bought the city site from the Maoris for about US$35.* The new city was named in honor of Lord Auckland, a viceroy of India and mentor of the new colony's first governor, William Hobson. It did not start to develop into the largest urban center in New Zealand until well into this century. Other attractions, such as the **1860s gold rushes,** kept most of the interest and most of the population on the South Island. Eventually, better weather and better trade moved the population center to the Auckland area. In the early days, however, Auckland was far from the center of things and Wellington, closer to the South Island and endowed with an excellent—if windy—port was chosen to be the new capital in 1864.

The Auckland metropolitan area sits on and among more than 50 or so dormant or extinct volcanoes. **Rangitoto Island,** just to the northeast of the city center in the Hauraki Gulf, is believed to have last erupted about 800 years ago. In Maori times, the area was covered with **pas**, and one of the reasons the site was chosen by the English was the relative ease of interdicting Maori land movements. Only about 5 miles separate the Tasman Sea to the west and the Pacific Ocean to the east. For most of its history, Auckland grew south of Waitemata Harbour. Getting to the other side of the harbor—the North Shore—meant hopping a ferry or making a long detour around. It wasn't until 1959 that the new **Harbour Bridge** was built. As is true in many cases, the bridge was already too small when it was completed. Population on the North Shore grew in great leaps, and so did bridge traffic. (Something like 100,000 vehicles cross each day). Congestion got so bad that in the end, the four-lane bridge was expanded by adding two lanes on each side. A Japanese firm did the work and of course the new lanes became known as the "Nippon Clip-Ons." The bridge looks a little like the Coathanger—the Sydney Harbour Bridge—meaning a lot of people think it's pretty ugly. *Auckland is definitely a water-orientated place,* as befits its location. The official city boosters say it's New Zealand's most beautiful harbor city, which is, of course, a view not necessarily shared by some other Kiwi ports. Anyway, *Auckland's official nickname is "The City of Sails."*

The heart of the city is bustling **Queen Street**, which runs uphill from the harbor to the area around Karangahape Road. Several large parks are scattered about, including the Auckland Domain and Albert Park at the city center. Many of the major hotels and restaurants are in the Queen Street area near the harbor, and Queen Street is lined with cafes, shops, shopping centers and office buildings. The central downtown area is compact enough to get around by foot.

Our best cure for jet lag is to ignore it. Chances are you'll land early in the morning in Auckland from Honolulu or Los Angeles. So check into the hotel (or get your RV) and then head downtown and do the **Coast-to-Coast**, a 13-kilometer stroll that takes you across the isthmus from sea to shining sea. The route takes you past several of the best viewing areas in the city, including some interesting parks, which actually enclose volcanic cones. The sides of the cones still carry scars caused when early Maoris constructed extensive terraced

fortifications. *The highest spot in town (about 640 feet above sea level) is* **Mt. Eden**, *with a deep crater and a view that takes in the whole isthmus, both oceans and the lands to the north and south of the city—it's probably the best view in town.* Another good spot is **One Tree Hill**,

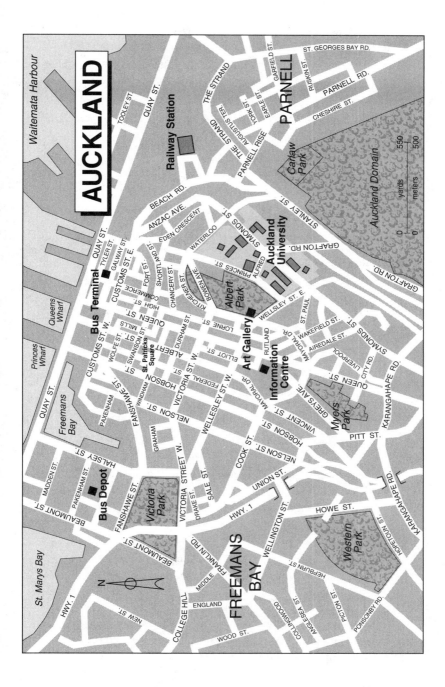

which was *the largest Maori settlement in the area* (estimates say around 4,000 population or so). The hill was named after a huge native totara tree that once stood on its summit; it's been replaced by a big fir. Next to it is a tall obelisk honoring the Maori people. The One Tree park is also the site of the **Auckland Observatory**, which has public programs Tuesday and Thursday nights, 8-10. Information: ☎ 365-6945. Both One Tree and Mt. Eden are on the coast-to-coast hiking trail, or can be reached by bus or car. Trail maps and information are available from any of the many visitor centers scattered around town. The trail starts at the Ferry Terminal building on Queen Street and ends up at Manukau Harbour. It's signposted all the way.

THE ESSENTIAL AUCKLAND

WHAT TO SEE

Auckland Domain—In the Domain is a small spring which, we are told, was used to raise the first rainbow trout in New Zealand. These trout—the Adams and Eves of the Kiwi rainbow world—were raised from eggs taken from the Russian River north of San Francisco. A popular attraction is enclosed areas with displays of plants from around the world. The Domain is also home to the **Auckland War Memorial Museum,** which has probably the country's best collection of Maori art and artifacts. Included among the ground floor displays are a meeting house, storage house and a magnificent 82-foot-long war canoe. On the first floor are displays of New Zealand arts and crafts, native animals and geology, and on the second floor is the war museum, which includes two Halls of Memory where are inscribed the names of all those who died in the World Wars and later. *(Note: the Kiwis use the European system. What would be the first floor in the U.S. is called the ground floor, and our second floor is called the first floor, etc.)* Admission is free; donations welcome. Hours are 10-5 daily. There is a gift shop and cafe. ☎ 377-3932.

The Aotea Centre—*One of New Zealand's most famous citizens is Dame Kiri Te Kanawa, a Maori with international opera credits.* She sang at Chuck and Di's wedding, and might be familiar to PBS viewers who saw her sing Paul McCartney's "Liverpool Oratorio" in 1991. She once announced that she would never sing opera in New Zealand until a decent opera house was built. Along came the Aotea Centre, opened in 1990. The 2,500-seat theatre has banquet facilities, meeting rooms and conference areas, and is located on Queen Street in the center of the city. Kiri Te Kanawa proceeded to come back to New Zealand to sing opera, and how did they treat her? After a performance of "La Boheme," the reviewer for a Wellington newspaper allowed as how "Te Kanawa was dramatically insipid but vocally rewarding." Anyway, now the country has a world-class performing arts center. Information: ☎ 307-5050.

Albert Park—This is the closest park to downtown, just a few blocks off Queen Street. It was the site of barracks for imperial troops until the 1860s. Coming up Queen Street from the harbor, hang a left on Victoria Street.

Auckland City Art Gallery—*This is one of the most important archives of New Zealand art in the country.* Originally opened in 1888, the gallery is a center for research and exhibits of Kiwi artworks. Except for special exhibitions, admission is free. The gallery, located at the corner of Kitchener and Wellesley streets, is open daily from 10-4:30. Information: ☎ 379-2020.

The Zoo—*The 35-acre Auckland Zoological Park* in Western Springs, a few kilometers from downtown, is your first best bet to see some native New Zealand animals including kiwis and tuataras. There's also the usual collection of beasts from around the world. There are cafe and picnic areas. Admission fee is about NZ$10. Hours are 9:30-5:30 daily; last admission at 4:15 p.m. Information: ☎ 781-620.

Parnell—*One of the more popular shopping areas in the city.* Parnell Road, a short walk east from Queen Street, has been restored as a Victorian village, and is very busy on weekends. One place worth a stop is the Elephant House, where the works of about 300 local artists are displayed.

Relics—*You can't have a settlement in New Zealand without a stash of old buildings, and Auckland has its share.* Among them are Alberton (1862), a mansion built from the proceeds of a gold fortune, located in the suburb of Mt. Albert; Highwic (1862), whose owner sired 21 children, located in Epsom; Ewelme Cottage (1863) in Parnell, made from kauri wood, and the Kinder House (1856), also in Parnell, which is a gallery and museum devoted to the works of clergyman/artist John Kinder.

North Head—Across the harbor from downtown is North Head, *a military site first used for gun emplacements in the 1880s.* It's now a park and offers excellent views of the city and the harbor area.

Beaches—One of the reasons Aucklanders love to live where they do is the easy access to a number of good beaches on both coasts. *The best ones are on the North Shore north of Devonport,* easily reached by ferry or bus from the city center. Among the the more popular northern beaches are Takapuna, Milford, Mairangi Bay and Browns Bay. A popular beach for surfers (and thus not really good for swimming when the surf's up) is at Muriwai Beach on the western shore about 30 miles northwest of the city off Highway16.

CLIMATE

Auckland, the country's northernmost major urban area, is generally fairly pleasant, with winter highs in the 60s, lows in the 50s. In the summer, highs will normally be in the upper 70s, with a fair amount of humidity. Annual rainfall hovers around 50 inches. Nights, even in summer, tend to be cool. In a winter rainstorm, it can get downright chilly.

INFORMATION

The central tourism office is the

Auckland Visitor Centre on Aotea Square near the intersection of Queen and Wellesley streets. Hours are 8:30- 5:30, Monday-Friday and 9-4 on weekends and holidays. ☎ 366-6888. *There is also a visitors center at the international airport terminal*, open 24 hours a day. ☎ 275-6467.

For information about the South Island, contact

South Island Information and Travel, Endean Building, 2 Queen Street; it's open 8:30-5:30 Monday-Friday, ☎ 303- 0473. *Handicapped information is available from the Disability Resource Centre*, 14 Erson Ave, Royal Oak; ☎ 658-069.

For details on regional parks, contact the

Parks Information Service, Ground Floor, Regional House, corner of Pitt and **Hopetoun** streets. Hours are 8:15-4:30 weekdays, ☎ 366-2166 or 379-4420. On weekends and holidays, ☎ 817-7134. Another useful source for area facilities, as well as national parks around the country, is the *Department of Conservation Centre*, corner of Karangahape Road and Liverpool Street. Open weekdays, 1-4:30 p.m. ☎ 307- 9279.

The Auckland City Council also has a computerized data base listing 10,000 organizations and clubs in the city, both tourist and other businesses. You can contact the library by calling ☎ 377-0209.

If you're planning to hit the beaches or just do some touring on the North Shore, contact the **North Shore Information Centre**, Hurstmere Road, Takapuna; ☎ 486- 0060.

The central *post office* is on Queen Elizabeth II Square near Quay Street. Hours are 8-5, Monday-Friday; ☎ 302- 1059.

The *Automobile Association* office is located at 99 Albert Street. Hours are 8:30-5 p.m., ☎ 377-4660. For emergency road service, call the AA at ☎ 379-6107.

The telephone area code for Auckland is (09).

GETTING THERE

If Auckland is not your entry point in New Zealand, you can reach the city by air or ground transportation from anywhere in the country. *Air New Zealand* and *Ansett* have daily service from Wellington for about NZ$240 one way. From Christchurch, daily service is about NZ$320. From elsewhere in the South Island (Invercargill, Dunedin, Queenstown), expect to pay between NZ$400 and NZ$500. It'll cost about NZ$200 to fly to the northern parts of the North Island from Auckland. In addition to North American carriers, Auckland is served by most of the major South Pacific airlines, as well as JAL, UTA, Thai International, Garuda, Singapore and British Airways.

By train, there are two choices from Wellington. **The Silver Fern,** which has rail car service, runs Monday- Saturday and takes about 12 hours. The one-way passenger fare is about NZ$110. The fare includes complimentary lunch. There is bar service; it's a non-smoking train. It leaves Wellington around 8:30 a.m., arriving in Auckland at 6:30 p.m. Overnight service Sunday-Friday is available on the **Northerner Express**, which has no sleepers. Refreshment and snacks are available, but no alcohol. Smoking seats are available and a video is shown each night. The train leaves Wellington at 8 p.m., arriving in Auckland at 6:50 a.m. One-way fare is about NZ$75. Daily bus service from Wellington is offered by InterCity and Newman's. The one-way fare is about NZ$90 and takes about 11 hours.

Intercity buses arrive at the **Downtown Airline Terminal** on Quay Street. Trains arrive at the Auckland Central Railway Station on Beach Street. The central station for inner-city buses is behind the central post office.

GETTING AROUND

The airport is a ways out of town (about 13 miles). A taxi ride will run about NZ$35 (no tipping). The *Airporter Bus Service* runs daily every half hour from 6:30 a.m.-8 p.m. from the airport, and from 6:45 a.m.-8:45 p.m. from the city to the airport. It stops at most—but not all—major hotels and at major bus stops. The one-way fare is about NZ$10 per person. Information: ☎ 275-7685 or 275-9396. There are also several shuttle bus companies offering door-to-door service for around NZ$15. These can be booked at information counters at the airport.

Taxis normally don't cruise, so look for a taxi rank or go to a major hotel. For information, contact Auckland Co-Op Taxis at ☎ 379-2792.

For information about

buses around town or suburban, contact Buz-a-Bus, the city's bus information service. Hours are 7:30 a.m.-5 p.m., Monday-Saturday; ☎ 379-7119. The city also has a bus information counter at the corner of Victoria Street West and Hobson Street. One bus—the Street Car—starts from the Ferry Building on Quay Street and runs up Queen Street through the heart of downtown to Karangahape Road and back. The one-way fare is about 50 cents and the service runs every 10 minutes from 7 a.m.-6 p.m. Many shuttles and buses leave from the Downtown Airline Terminal Building on Quay Street near Albert Street.

Ferries to the North Shore run every hour on the hour from the Ferry Terminal and cost about NZ$7 per person one-way. Information from Fuller's, ☎ 377-1771 or ☎ 377-4074.

BANKS

Auckland banks are open Monday-Friday 9-4:30. Most have currency exchanges, and there is a currency exchange office at the airport.

TOURS

Using Auckland as a base, you can easily arrange a tour to nearby attractions. A number of options are available. These include:

United Airlines Explorer Bus runs a *circuit of the city* from the Downtown Airline Terminal to major stops, including the Victoria Park Market, Mission Bay Beach, the Auckland Museum and Parnell Village. An all-day pass (get on and off as much as you like) runs about NZ$10, and can be purchased at the terminal or from the driver. Scenic Tours has a *3-hour tour of the city* that hits all the high spots for about NZ$30 per person, which includes pickup at your hotel. Included is a guided tour of the Maori exhibits at the War Memorial Museum. For details and hours, contact the office at the Downtown Airline Terminal ☎ 640-189.

Gray Line New Zealand has an Auckland tour that includes free admission to Kelly Tarlton's Underwater World, a popular attraction where you walk through and under an aquarium full of marine life including sharks (wheelchair accessible). The tour leaves the Downtown Airline Terminal at 9:15 a.m. and costs about NZ$35 per person. Information: ☎ 309-5395.

A free harbor cruise is part of a full-day bus tour of the city offered by ABC Tours. Or the company also has *half-day trips*. The full day is about NZ$60; the half-day trips go around the city in the morning, coast to coast in the afternoon. Information: ☎ 302-1100.

Further afield, Gray Line also has a *day trip to Rotorua*, which takes in the thermal attractions, plus a stop at the *New Zealand Agrodome* for a 60-minute show on sheep. An optional luncheon cruise is also offered. The trips cost about NZ$120 per person and leave the Downtown Airline Terminal at 8:15 a.m. and return at 8:40 p.m.

Scenic Tours has a similar package for about the same price. In addition, you can book longer trips, such as a two-day affair that goes to the *Waitomo Glow Worm Caves*, lets you feast at a Maori hangi, takes you trout fishing, puts you up in a hotel in Rotorua and tours the thermal areas for about NZ$350 per person, all meals included. *A one-day trip to the glowworm caves* is about NZ$110 per person. Similar trips are offered by Vanway Tours Ltd., 15A Scotstoun Place, Glen Eden; ☎ 817-8046. Or try Thrifty Tours, ☎ 478-3550, which has essentially the same itineraries.

If water is your taste, there are several companies offering *tours and cruises around Waitemata Harbour*. Fuller's, which operates the ferries to the North Shore, has an hour tour at noon that hits the East Coast bays and goes around *Rangitoto Island*, the volcano which erupted 800 years ago. The cost, including lunch, is about NZ$35 per person, and can be booked through Gray Line or through Fuller's at ☎ 377-4074 or ☎ 377-1771. The company also has longer trips to such destinations as *Great Barrier Island and Waiheke Island*.

Very popular trips are offered by the sailing vessels of the Pride of Auckland company, which operates *luncheon and dinner cruises around the harbor*. The 3-hour dinner cruise is about NZ$70 per person, and can be booked at the Downtown Airline Terminal or at ☎ 373-4557. Several of the land tour companies offer *Pride of Auckland excursions* in some of their itineraries.

SHOPPING

O'Connell Street, a couple of blocks east of Queen Street, and the streets leading off, is a maze of small arcades filled with boutiques, eateries, pubs and speciality shops.

Vulcan Lane, *with a cobbled street, is our favorite*, but explore and pick your own spot. Great for shopping or people watching.

Once upon a time, there was a tract of land that had a garbage disposal plant, power station, stables and a blacksmith shop—all gone now except a *38-meter-high chimney*. The area now houses

Victoria Park Markets, open seven days and full of stores, an international food hall, licensed restaurants, Rick's Cafe Americain and a McDonald's. The market, located on Victoria Street West, about 2 miles from downtown, operates a free shuttle bus—the Bus-A-Bout—from the Downtown Airline Terminal. It runs every hour from 10:45 a.m.-4:45 p.m. daily; on weekends and holidays, every 15 minutes. Information: ☎ 309-6911.

The China Oriental Markets on the waterfront are housed in an old railway warehouse and offer 140 stalls, Asian foods and Kiwi products. The warehouse is at the corner of Britomart Place and Quay Street, not far from the bus terminal. The markets are open daily from 10-6. Karangahape Road—known around town simply as *K Road*—is at the opposite end of Queen Street from the harbor and is the Polynesian center of the city. It's within walking distance of the Sheraton Hotel, and offers a wide variety of South Pacific goods. Check out the Polynesian Bookstore at 3 K Road, where you can get books, posters, music and Maori dictionaries.

A good spot on the North Shore is the

Compendium Gallery at the corner of Clarence and Victoria streets in Devonport. It has a nice supply of greenstone and other artworks.

There are scads of places selling *sheepskin products*. Many of the larger places will ship the fleeces home and you don't have to pay the general sales tax. Try Breen's at 8 Quay Street on the waterfront. Or if you can forgive the name, *Woolywood* at 94 Quay Street next to the Travelodge. There are several places in the Ferry Building, which also has a number of other stores and eateries.

The *antique center* of the city is out near the airport on Manukau Road in Epsom. There are about 20 stores within walking distance of each other. Start at the corner of Manukau and Arcadia; check out Yvonne Sanders and Chatham Antiques.

If you're either not driving or unsure of the bus schedules, there's a solution: Julie Steele's Shopping Tours. These half-day excursions take you to warehouse shops, factory outlets, designer shops and bargain basements, everything from sheepskin to lingerie. A tea stop is included. One-day advance reservations are necessary. The cost is about NZ$20 per person. Information: ☎ 309-7442 or ☎ 397-442.

WHERE TO STAY

Regent of Auckland—Corner of Albert and Swanson streets. The city's premier hotel, an 11-story building with harbor views. It has several restaurants and bars, roof-top swimming pool, health club, luxury suites, spa, courtesy coach, baby-sitting, tea/coffee. More than 300 rooms, with doubles starting around NZ$375. ☎ 398-882.

Hyatt Kingsgate Auckland—Corner of Princes Street and Waterloo Quadrant near Auckland University. Located on a steep hill with harbor view; easy walk down, a hike back up. Luxury suites available. Two restaurants and a very nice bar, the Champs. Doubles start around NZ$275. ☎ 366-1234.

Auckland Park Royal—Corner of Queen and Customs streets. Nice central downtown location, close to shopping. Some rooms overlook the harbor. Two restaurants, three bars. Doubles start around NZ$265. ☎ 377-8920.

Sheraton Auckland Hotel and Towers—83 Symonds Street, near Karangahape Road. Excellent view of the city looking toward the harbor, supposedly the largest hotel in New Zealand. Two restaurants, three bars, pool, spa, laundry, health club, minibars, handicapped facilities, luxury suites, breakfast included. Doubles about NZ$230, suites start at NZ$350. ☎ 379-5139.

Auckland City Travelodge—96-100 Quay Street on the waterfront. Two restaurants, a bar, underground parking, spa, baby-sitting. Doubles about NZ$220. ☎ 377-0349.

Auckland Airport Travelodge—Corner of Ascot and Kirkbride roads about 5 kilometers from the airport. Restaurant/bar, pool, spa, sauna, handicapped facilities, baby-sitting, coffee/tea. Doubles about NZ$200. ☎ 275- 1059.

Auckland Quality Inn Anzac—150 Anzac Ave., close to the railroad station. Some harbor views, some suites. Restaurant/bar, live entertainment, sauna, tea/coffee, baby-sitting. Doubles about NZ$200. ☎ 379-8509.

Quality Inn Rose Park—100 Gladstone Rd., Parnell, across from the Parnell Rose Garden. On bus route to city. Some villas (self-contained units with kitchens). Restaurant/bar, pool, spa, tea/coffee. Doubles from NZ$180. ☎ 377-3619.

White Heron Hotel—138 Stephens Ave., Parnell. On a hill with great harbor views. Standard rooms and villas. Restaurant, poolside grill and bar. Pool, tea/coffee, courtesy van, baby-sitting. Doubles about NZ$140; villas NZ$300. ☎ 379-6860.

Barrycourt Motor Inn—10-20 Gladstone Rd., Parnell. Three restaurants, two bars, tennis, four private spas, some harbor views. Laundry. Suites have kitchens. Standard doubles start at NZ$118. ☎ 303-3789.

Park Towers Hotel—3 Scotia Place, off Queen Street in central downtown. Restaurant/bar, laundry, tea/coffee, courtesy van, baby-sitting. Some rooms with shared baths. Doubles about NZ$85. ☎ 392-800.

Abby's Hotel—Corner of Wellesley and Albert Streets. Renovated B&B, licensed restaurant, tea/coffee. Doubles about NZ$90. ☎ 303-4799.

Aachen House—39 Market Road, Remuera. Near One Tree Hill close to the train station, a restored Victorian B&B. Large rooms, scenic views, expansive grounds, no smoking. Coffee/tea, courtesy van, dinners available. Doubles about NZ$78. ☎ 520-2329.

Albion Hotel—Corner Wellesley and Hobson streets downtown. A restored 1870 hotel, all rooms with private bath. Licensed restaurant and bars, minibars, tea/coffee, breakfast available. Special rate on airport shuttle. Doubles about NZ$80. ☎ 379-4900.

Bavaria Guest House—83 Valley Road, Mt. Eden. A B&B about three kilometers from city center and close to a bus stop. Parking, tea/coffee, all rooms with private baths. They speak German. Doubles about NZ$75. ☎ 368-9641.

Railton Travel Hotel—411 Queen St., upper city center. A B&B with kitchens, laundry, rental cars, restaurant. Some rooms with shared bath, one penthouse suite. Doubles start at NZ$70. ☎ 379-6487.

Auckland City YHA Hostel—Corner of City Road and Liverpool St., close to Queen Street. Mostly double and triple rooms. TV/video lounge, sun deck, travel service, kitchen, in-house cafe. About NZ$22 per person. ☎ 392- 802.

Auckland City Centre Kiwi Hilton—A hostel at 430 Queen St., center of town. No curfew, kitchen, laundry, linen hire. NZ$17 per person. ☎ 358-0188.

Auckland Pavlova Backpackers—3 Princes St., center of city. New facility. Kitchen, laundry, shop, linen hire. NZ$18 per person. ☎ 379-3965.

North Shore Caravan Park—52 Northcote Road, Takapuna. The closest RV park to the city. Laundry, kitchens, close to shops and restaurants. Tent sites, motel units, dormitories. Motel doubles about NZ$75; dorms around NZ$20 per person. ☎ 418-1024 or 419-1320.

WHERE TO EAT

First, some hotel restaurants:

Meridian—On the top of the Auckland Parkroyal, 8 Customs St. Lunch noon-2 p.m. Dinner 6-10:30 p.m. Closed Sundays. ☎ 377-8920.

Longchamp—In the Regent on Lower Albert Street. Dinner 6:30-10:30 p.m. Tuesday-Saturday. ☎ 398-882. Also in the Regent is the Ariake with sushi bar and Japanese cuisine. Lunch noon-2:30. Dinner 6-10 p.m. Closed Sunday. ☎ 379-2377.

St. Moritz—In the Pan Pacific on Mayoral Drive. Swiss and continental. Lunch noon-3 p.m. Monday-Friday. Dinner 6:30- 11 p.m. Monday-Saturday. ☎ 366-5623.

Sakura—In the White Heron Hotel, Parnell. Japanese. Call for hours. ☎ 379-6860.

Delmonico's—In the Hotel De Brett, corner of Shortland and High streets. *Nice Art Deco decor, plus a very good wine bar.* Sunday brunches. Call for hours. ☎ 303-2389.

Palace Carvery—In the Railton Hotel, 411 Queen St. Smorgasbord seven nights a week, 5-8 p.m. Not licensed. ☎ 379-6487.

The Brasserie—In the Albion Hotel, corner of Wellesley and Hobson streets. *A meat and potatoes sort of place, some ethnic foods, large quantities.* Open seven days; breakfast 7-9 a.m., lunch noon- 2:30, dinner 5:30-9:30 p.m. ☎ 379-4900.

Some good bets around town include:

Cin Cin on Quay—99 Quay Street. One of the *in spots* for the luncheon crowd, but also popular for dinner. Located in the historic Ferry Building. Happy hour (very popular) from 5-7 p.m. *Good lunches, specializing in seafood and grilled fish, but also offering ethnic foods.* Licensed. Probably a good idea to call ahead for dinner because seating is limited. Open 8 a.m.-1 a.m.; summer, 8 a.m.-3 a.m. ☎ 307-6966 or 6967.

Fisherman's Wharf Restaurant—2 Queen Street, Northcote Point across the Harbour Bridge. *Best view in town,* overlooking Waitemata Harbour. Licensed. Shellfish, fresh fish, steaks, poultry. Lunch noon-4 p.m. Monday-Friday; dinner seven days from 6-10:30 p.m. ☎ 418-3955.

Harbourside Seafood Bar & Grill—Second floor of the Ferry Building. In the summer, balcony seating with a harbour view. In season, a crayfish tank where you can pick your own; otherwise, seafood specialties. Licensed. Lunch from 11 a.m. Monday-Thursday; 11:30-11:30 Friday and Saturday; 11:30-10 Sundays. ☎ 307-0556 or 307-0486.

Jurgen's Restaurant—12 Wyndham St. Classy old building, specializing in seafood, especially crayfish and whitebait. Also European fare with flambe at your table. Licensed. Lunch from noon Monday-Friday; dinner 6- 11 p.m. Monday-Saturday. ☎ 309-6651.

Papillon—170 Jervois Road near the zoo. Award-winning lamb dishes and a large cellar of Kiwi wines. Continental style, licensed. Dinner only from 6:30 p.m., Monday-Saturday. Reservations required. BYOB for wine. ☎ 376-5367.

Sails Restaurant—The Anchorage on Westhaven Road. Yachting ambiance, near the Westhaven Marina and Yacht Club. *Nice setting, specializing in seafood and lamb.* Licensed. Lunch noon-2 p.m. Monday-Friday; dinner Monday-Saturday 6:30a.m.-10:30p.m. ☎ 378-9890.

Union Fish Company—16 Quay Street. Housed in an old warehouse, with the bar in a boat tied to the dock. Crayfish tank to pick your own. Licensed, reservations. Lunch noon-2:30 Monday-Friday. Dinner 6-10:30 p.m. seven days. ☎ 379-6745.

Alhambra Restaurant—3 Lamps Plaza, 283 Ponsonby Rd. *One of our favorites, situated in an old movie theater where you can catch live jazz and blues, plus a great view of the harbor.* Good seafood (especially the mussels), good cellar, excellent lamb. Lunch from 11:30 a.m. Dinner from 6 p.m. Closed Mondays. ☎ 376-2430.

Armadillo Bar and Grill—178 Symonds St. Yahoo and yippee, etc. Cowpoke motif, grilled grub, barbecues. Licensed and popular. Lunch noon on Wednesday-Thursday- Friday.

Cajn'ts—96 Albert St. in Finance Plaza. Cajun and creole, using ingredients imported from New Orleans. Also a deli and grocery shop. Open for lunch and dinner from noon-1 a.m.; closed Sundays. ☎ 377-3524.

Corfu—44 Ponsonby Rd. The smells alone will stop you in your tracks. *Great Greek goodies, great place for lunch. BYOB.* Lunch from 11:30 a.m. Monday-Friday; dinner from 5:30 p.m. seven days. ☎ 378-8676.

Java Jive—Pompelier Terrace off Ponsonby Road. We first heard about this place because of the juke box and the photo gallery of old jazz and blues players. *Lots of variety on the menu, from ethnic stuff to vegetarian. Great coffee.* **BYOB.** Dinner from 6 p.m. seven nights. Sunday brunch 11:30-2:30. ☎ 376-5870.

La Trattoria—259 Parnell Road. Decent Italian cuisine, Italian and New Zealand wines, big salads. Licensed. Lunch noon-2:30 Monday-Friday; dinner from 6 p.m. Monday-Saturday, closed Sundays. Moderate. ☎ 379-5358.

Mekong—295 Queen Street, next to Aotea Square, fourth floor. *Very popular and excellent Vietnamese fare.* Good lunch buffet (finger foods, soup, etc) for about NZ$10. Many seafood specialties. Lunch noon-2 p.m. Monday-Friday; dinner from 6 p.m. seven nights. Licensed but you can **BYOB** wine. ☎ 379-7591.

New Orient—Strand Arcade on Queen Street. Luncheon buffet, music and dancing most nights. Popular Sunday brunch, reservations required. Lunch noon-2:30 p.m. Monday-Friday; dinner from 6 p.m. seven days. ☎ 379-7793 or 7794.

Ramses Bar & Grill—435 Kyber Pass Road. *Relaxed, casual atmosphere,* highlighted by huge floor-to-ceiling windows. Usually four fish specials daily, happy hour 5-7 p.m. Licensed. Lunch noon-3 p.m.; dinner 6-11 p.m. ☎ 522-0619.

Tony's—A chain of good steakhouses. The original is at 27 Wellesley Street West; others on Manukau Road on the way to the airport and at Mission Bay on Tamaki Drive. Huge steaks for moderate prices. Lunch from noon; dinner 5:30-10 p.m. ☎ 374-196.

Caravanserai Tea House—430 Queen St., corner of Mayoral Drive. Good Near Eastern fare, kebabs and vegetarian platters. **BYOB**. Open noon-9 p.m. Monday-Wednesday; noon-10:30 p.m. Thursday-Friday; 6-10:30 p.m. Saturday; 6-9 p.m. Sunday. ☎ 302-0244.

Mexican Cafe—67 Victoria Street West. Mexican food, taped Mexican music. *Margueritas a specialty at happy hour,* 5-7 p.m. Lunch noon-2:30 p.m. Monday-Friday; dinner from 5 p.m., closed Sundays. ☎ 373-2311.

Rick's Cafe Americain—Victoria Park Market. *The place for American-style brekkie.* Licensed, blackboard lunch menu. Hours 9 a.m.-7 p.m. Monday- Saturday; 10 a.m.-7 p.m. Sunday. Budget breakfast, moderate otherwise. ☎ 309-9074.

Shakespeare Tavern—Corner of Albert and Wyndham streets. The city's oldest private brewery with *wide selection of brews and some very good counter meals,* including steamed mussels. If you drink enough of their product (and can still walk) they give you a certificate. Live music Monday and Friday. If the owner, Peter Barraclough, is around, tell him we said howdy. Call for hours. ☎ 373-5396.

NIGHT SPOTS

The Old Customhouse—Customs Street near the harbor. Live music and disco Tuesday through Saturday; live jazz Friday noon. ☎ 358-2185.

Club Singalong Karaoke—35-51 Nelson Street. They play taped music, you get up and sing along. Hours 7 p.m.-3 a.m. seven nights. ☎ 303-1630.

Abby's—Corner of Wellesley and Albert streets. Live music Thursday, Friday, Saturday, 8-11 p.m. ☎ 303-4799.

Burgundy's—289 Parnell Road. Cabaret and restaurant, dancing. Reservations required. Open Thursday through Saturday. Call for hours. ☎ 309-5112.

Cactus Jack—96 Albert Street (Finance Plaza). Texican saloon and eatery; live music Tuesday through Saturday. Hours 11 a.m.-1 a.m. ☎ 302-0942.

The Cotton Club—222 Ponsonby Road. Live jazz from 8 p.m. Friday and Saturday. ☎ 378-7888.

Kestral Ferryboat—The Kestral, an old ferry, runs from the ferry building to Devonport and back offering live music by the Riverboat Ramblers. It normally sails at 7 p.m. Friday and Saturday nights. Snacks and light meals available. Information: ☎ 377-4074.

Herding sheep at Hawkes Bay

THE COROMANDEL PENINSULA

About 120 kilometers by road from Auckland (and directly east as the crow flies) is one of the North Island's better-kept secrets—at least for many foreign visitors. Most folks around Auckland, as well as other parts of New Zealand, know the secret. It's called the *Coromandel Peninsula.*

Swimming hole

The peninsula juts northeast into the sea, separating the Bay of Plenty to the south from the Hauraki Gulf on the north, and creating the Firth of Thames directly to the west. In Maori legend, the peninsula is a giant canoe with the prow at Cape Colville and its stern at Te Aroha. *It is one of the North Island's most popular vacation spots, containing several excellent beaches, some great bushwalks, lots of scenery and an assortment of places to stay.* It's roughly 100 kilometers long, and is crisscrossed by roads, some good, some pretty rough. It's an easy drive from Auckland to Thames, the so-called gateway to the peninsula.

Capt. James Cook came calling in the area in the 1770s at a place now called *Mercury Bay* on the peninsula's east coast. There is evidence to suggest that the area was one of the first settled by the Maoris who immigrated from the South Pacific more than 1,000 years ago, and there are several pa sites that date back to around 750 A.D. European history in the peninsula began in earnest during a gold rush in the 1860s. At the peak, it is estimated that more than 70 mines were operating and according to official estimates more than 2 million ounces of gold were pulled from the ground during the mining era. At one point, Thames was the largest city in New Zealand, with 18,000 population, 100 hotels and three theaters. The peninsula was also at one time covered with kauri trees, which were all but wiped out by eager lumberjacks.

These days, Thames has about 6,500 population and large chunks of the peninsula are part of forest preserves and parks. The rugged scenery and excellent beaches make both sides of the peninsula a great place to spend a few days.

Getting to Thames and beyond is easy if you're driving. The motorway south of Auckland (Highway 1) is four-lane all the way to the peninsula turnoff (Highways 2 and 25). Figure a maximum 3-hour drive. To really do the Coromandel area, you need a vehicle, but there are a number of companies offering trips from Auckland.

Bush and Beach Ltd., for example, has a one-day tour from the city that hits the major spots on both sides of the peninsula, including a picnic lunch, for about NZ$150 per person. The more extensive two-day tour costs about NZ$350, which includes accommodations, meals and entertainment. Information: Bush and Beach, ☎ (09) 413- 9261.

WEEKEND TOUR

Or PC Tours will take you on a weekend tour of the peninsula for about NZ$250 per person, including wine tastings, hikes, all meals and accommodations. Information: Paul Campbell, 7 Lowery Ave., Mt. Roskill, Auckland; ☎ 615-693.

However, if you want to try it on your own, there is bus service from Auckland, Monday through Saturday. Buses leave from the Auckland Railway Station at 1:45 p.m., arriving at Whitianga on Mercury Bay at 5:30 p.m. Once on the peninsula, there is a loop bus service that can take you around to the major spots. For about NZ$90, you can get a ticket good for three months that takes you from Auckland, does the loop, then goes back to Auckland. The ticket lets you get on and off as much as you like and can be purchased through any InterCity agent. For more information on peninsula bus services, contact Sunkist Lodge, 506 Brown St., Thames; ☎ (0843) 88808. Once on the peninsula, contact Murphy Buses in

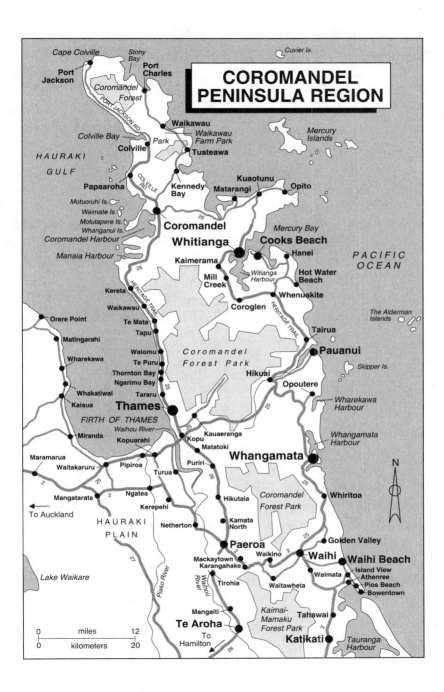

COROMANDEL PENINSULA REGION

Kerepehi, ☎ (0843) 76829 or Travel Options in Whitianga, ☎ (0843) 64356.

You can also fly from Auckland to almost any place on the peninsula on Air Coromandel for about NZ$150 per person round trip. Information: ☎ (0843) 64016. Helicopter service is available through Peninsula Helicopters in Pauanui; ☎ (0843) 47020. There is also limited rail service as far as Thames.

Most transportation and accommodations information is available at the Auckland information centers. To help you find your way around, there are several visitor centers scattered around the peninsula. They include Coromandel, on Kapanga Road ☎ (0843) 58598; Whitianga, on Albert Street ☎ (0843) 866-6555; Whangamata, on Port Road ☎ (07) 86-58340; Pauanui, at the shopping center, ☎ (0843) 48-395; Paeroa, on Belmont Road, ☎ (07) 862-8636; Te Aroha, on Whittaker Street, ☎ (07) 884-8052, and Thames, 405 Queen St. ☎ 868-7284.

AROUND THE PENINSULA

Thames got its names from James Cook, who looked at the Waihou River nearby and thought it looked like the one back in London. If you go to the part where there's a lot of mud flats, you might see his point. Modern Thames is your basic small New Zealand town with a few extra places to stay and eat because of the tourist boom. Nothing very special.

VISIT A GOLD MINE

If you're interested in the *mining history* of the town, go to the gold mine and stamping battery complex at the north end of town across from the Cable Price Foundry. The complex, part of the original Thames goldfields, offers *underground tours* of some mines plus a look at the stamping machinery used to crush the ore. The tours, operated by the Hauraki Prospectors Association, take about 45 minutes and cost about NZ$5 per person. They can be booked through the Thames Information Centre, Queen Street, ☎ (0843) 868-7284; open daily 10-4.

The best part of a Coromandel Peninsula tour will be the drive from Thames up along the east coast to the village of Coromandel. The road (Highway 25) hugs steep cliffs as it goes along the beach-ridden coastline, past small settlements, RV parks, hiking areas and often dense bush. The road lies at the base of the *Coromandel Range*, a line of peaks running down the spine of the peninsula, now mostly part of the *Coromandel Forest Park*. The park, about 185,000 acres, contains groves of protected kauri trees, as well as other indigenous trees and plants. Near Waiomu, on Highway 25 about 10 miles north of Thames, is the *Waiomu Kauri Grove,* the largest stand of trees on the peninsula. East of Tapu, a few miles further on, is the famous *Square Kauri Tree,* one of the oldest in the area, estimated to be 1,200 years old. You reach the tree by taking the Tapu-Coroglen road about 30 kilometers east.

For campers, hikers or just folks who want to get out into the open country, the best first stop on the peninsula is the Department of Conservation office at Kauaeranga, reached by taking the Kauaeranga Valley Road southeast from Thames. The DOC has maps and information about hiking, camping, off-road vehicles, camping huts and horse-riding areas. At the headquarters is a theater where you can see a film about the history of kauri logging in the area. It's open daily 8-4; ☎ (0843) 86381 or 89732.

ROAD CONDITIONS

Depending on your rental car or RV agreement, you might be forced to stay on the main road that circles the peninsula, since *many of the secondary roads are dirt,* but in most cases, the roads will be acceptable under the contract. (Part of the main road itself is unpaved). Be sure to ask, because *some of the better beaches are reached by unpaved road.*

Coromandel is a small village with a few old Victorians left over that is pretty active during the tourist season. From Coromandel, you can either go northwest to Long Bay and the excellent beach at *Oamaru Bay,* or northeast to *Kennedy Bay,* a popular crayfishing and yachti harbor. The paved portion of the main highway (25) ends near Coromandel, starting again at Whitianga. The road between is wash-boarded in places, but basically good. You will pass lots of pine forests, as well as ranch land plus some nice beaches at Whangapoua Harbour and Kuaotunu Bay.

The Whitianga area around Mercury Bay is probably the best beach area on the peninsula, as is the small headland opposite which contains *Cook's Beach, Cathedral Cove* and *Hahei.* The locals say it's the best scenery in New Zealand, and they're not far wrong. *The rugged*

seacoast is worth a stop, but it is hard to get to. There are roads that go
to Hahei, generally considered to be the best beach on the peninsula, from a point about halfway between Coroglen and Whenuakite
on Highway 25 southeast of Whitianga. Also at this point is the road
to the famous *Hot Water Beach,* where there are thermal streams just
below the beach sand—dig a hole, sit down, instant hot tub. *Whitianga* has a permanent population of around 3,000, which rises to
as much as 25,000 during the school holiday period. You can also
reach the Cook's Bay/Cathedral Cove area by ferry from Whitianga.
The ferry runs from 7:30 a.m. to noon and from 1-6:30 p.m. During school holidays, it runs from 7:30 a.m.-7:30 p.m. The fare is
about NZ$2 round trip.

The various settlements on both sides of the peninsula earn a share
of their living from the sea, and fresh seafood is readily available. At
Tairua, south of Whitianga, we bought what were *absolutely the best
fresh scallops we've had anywhere at a local fish market.* Not cheap
(about US$12 a pound), but fabulous. There is an excellent beach
there as well, long and uncrowded.

WHERE TO STAY

THAMES

Brian Boru Hotel—200 Richmond St., downtown. Built in 1868, the
hotel is now home to popular *mystery weekend packages* (30 guests,
8 actors spend the weekend solving a crime). Licensed restaurant, bar,
courtesy van. Normal doubles are NZ$80. The mystery package,
which includes two nights' accommodations, a tour of the peninsula,
a fancy dress dinner and the mystery, is about NZ$350 per person.
Information about the hotel or the mystery package, ☎ (0843)
86-523.

Avalon Hotel—Jellicoe Crescent, south of Thames. Kitchens, sauna, BBQ,
laundry, breakfast available. Doubles about NZ$80.   ☎ (043)
87-755.

Crescent Motel—100 Fenton St, corner of Jellicoe south of Thames. Best
Western, kitchens, BBQ, courtesy van, breakfast available. Doubles
NZ$75. ☎ (07) 868- 6506.

Rolleston Motel—105 Rolleston St., 1 kilometer from city center. Pool,
spa, tour desk, courtesy van, BBQ, breakfast available. Doubles
NZ$85. ☎ (0843) 88-091.

Coastal Motor Lodge—Highway 25, 2 kilometers north of Thames. Chalets with sea view, spa, laundry, rangettes, close to restaurant. Doubles
about NZ$100. ☎ (0843) 86-843.

Sunset Motel—Highway 25, 4 kilometers north of town. Kitchens, laundry, spa, tea/coffee, courtesy van, breakfast available. Doubles NZ$75. ☎ 88-573.

Dickson Holiday Park—Off Highway 25, 3.5 kilometers north of Thames. Pool, linen rental, kitchen, courtesy van, laundry. On-site RVs, NZ$35 double; tourist flats, NZ$56 double; cabins, NZ$40-50 double; dorm beds, NZ$12 per person. ☎ 87-308.

Waiomu Bay Holiday Park—Off Highway 25, 13 kilometers north of Thames. A "Top 10" park. Kitchen, recreation hall, laundry, beach, pool. Cabins about NZ$70 double. ☎ 78-777.

Sunkist Lodge—506 Brown St., north Thames. Maybe the only hostel in New Zealand with a ghost. The lodge was built in 1868. Doubles and dorm rooms. Laundry, bike hire, courtesy van. Between NZ$15-20 per person. ☎ 88-808.

ON THE PENINSULA

Firlawn House—Kapanga Road, central Coromandel. Gracious old manse with a BYOB restaurant. Check out the antique Chinese wedding bed. Shared baths, doubles about NZ$100. ☎ 58-947.

Angler's Lodge Motel and Camp Park—Amodeo Bay, about 18 kilometers north of Coromandel. Pool, spa, laundry, camp store, tennis, dinghy rental. Motel doubles NZ$90; cabins, NZ$70. ☎ 58-584.

Coromandel Colonial Cottages—Rings Road, 2 kilometers from town center. Kitchens, spa. NZ$80 double. ☎ 58-857.

Coromandel Hotel—Kapanga Road, city center. À la carte restaurant/bar, tea/coffee, breakfast available. NZ$70 double.

Tui Lodge—On Highway 25 just east of Coromandel. A hostel set in an orchard, with rooms in a chalet and a dorm. Bus service, bike hire, laundry, courtesy van, friendly folks. NZ$34 double; dorm beds, NZ$14 per person; chalets, NZ$25 per person. ☎ 58-237.

Mercury Bay Beachfront Resort—111-113 Buffalo Beach Rd., Whitianga. Safe beach, kitchens, courtesy van. Doubles about NZ$100. ☎ 65-637.

Buffalo Beach Tourist Resort (also the Marlin Motor Lodge)—13 Buffalo Beach Rd., corner of Eyre St., Whitianga. Top 10 facility, *probably the best on the peninsula*. Seven acres of park, within walking distance of seven beaches. Waterfront motel units, Champagne Hot Springs thermal pool, cold pool, backpackers lodge, kitchen, laundry. Close to restaurants and wharf. Motel units, NZ$80 double; on-site caravans, NZ$40 double; backpacker's bunks, NZ$16 per person. ☎ 65-854.

Homestead Park Resort—At the ferry landing near Cook's Beach across from Whitianga. Secluded beach, tanning rooms, windsurfers and dinghies for rent, courtesy van. Doubles about NZ$115-200. ☎ 65-595.

Hahei Holiday Tourist Park—Hahei Beach, near Cook's Beach across from Whitianga. On the beach, laundry, BBQ, close to restaurants. Tent and RV sites. Cabins, NZ$40 double; flats, NZ$45 double. Backpackers welcome. ☎ 63-889.

Aotearoa Lodge—Highway 1, 17 kilometers south of Whitianga near Coroglen. An upscale lodge offering a variety of packages, including fishing, rafting, bush treks, diving and hunting. Tea/coffee, courtesy van. Rates are about NZ$75 per person a night, including breakfast and dinner. A three-day adventure package with various options is about NZ$230 per person, including meals and accommodation. ☎ 63808.

Puka Park Lodge—Pauanui Beach, Highway 41 across from Tairua. One of New Zealand's premier lodges, very posh, with licensed restaurant and bar, pool, helicopter service. Golf, tennis, fishing and boating nearby. Access to Slipper Island, private facility about 10 kilometers offshore. Deluxe "treetop" units with private balconies, tea/coffee, minibars; meals and drinks not included. Standard doubles are about NZ$310. ☎ 48-088.

Cedarwood Motor Hotel—Port Road, Whangamata. Licensed restaurant, tennis, pool, spa, sauna, kitchens, tea/coffee. Doubles about NZ$95. ☎ (07) 865-9211.

Whangamata Motel—Barbara Ave. Pool, spa, kitchens, doubles from NZ$75. ☎ 865-8250.

Whangamata Backpackers—227 Beverley Terrace. Close to town and beach. Kitchen, laundry, tour bookings. NZ$16 per bed. ☎ (07) 865-8323.

Whangamata Motor Camp—Barbara Avenue, close to beach. Kitchen, laundry, BBQ, dairy store. Cabins NZ$45 double. Backpackers welcome. ☎ (07) 865-9128.

WHERE TO EAT

IN THAMES

Old Thames Licensed Restaurant—704 Pollen St. Natural wood panelling with photos of the good old days, lots of farm machinery hanging around. Menu outside the door (very civilized), specializing in seafood and lamb. Lunch noon-2 p.m., dinner 5-midnight seven days. ☎ 87-207.

Brian Boru Hotel Restaurant—Corner of Richmond and Pollen streets. À la carte, buffets and set menus. Licensed. Lunch noon-2 p.m., dinner 6-10 p.m. ☎ 86-523.

Cotswold Cottage—Maramarahi Road. Set menus on Sunday; popular, so call ahead. Seafood, lamb and chicken specialities. Lunch Wednesday through Friday, noon-2 p.m.; dinner from 6 p.m. Tuesday through Sunday. ☎ 86-306.

Regency Room—Hotel Imperial, 476 Pollen St. Licensed, good Sunday carvery. Dinner 5:30-9:30 p.m. Moderate. ☎ 86-200.

The Bakery—326 Pollen St. The place for breakfast; fresh baked goods. Also meat pies and other take-aways. Hours 7:30 a.m.-4 p.m. seven days. ☎ 86-719.

ON THE PENINSULA

La Casa Restaurant—Te Puru, Highway 25, 14 kilometers north of Thames. Lovely white Spanish adobe style building on a hill, *(specializing in Tex-Mex,* but also seafood). BYOB. Limited seating, call ahead. Lunch noon-2 p.m.; dinner 6-9 p.m. ☎ 78-326.

Firlawn House—Kapanga Road, Coromandel. Devonshire teas, outside dining in summer, seafood and lamb. Lovely building, nice setting. Open seven days a week, dinner from 6 p.m. ☎ 58-947.

Coromandel Hotel —Kapanga Road, city center. *Good selection of fresh seafood, especially mussels and exquisite scallops.* Reservations necessary. Breakfast 8-9 a.m. Monday-Saturday; dinner 6-8 p.m. Monday-Saturday. ☎ 58-760.

The Falls Restaurant and Tearooms—On Highway 309 between Coromandel and Whitianga near Waiau Falls Scenic Reserve. *One of our favorites mostly because of the location.* Close to a waterfall swimming hole and several bush tracks. Outdoor dining in the summer; reservations required. Hours 11 a.m.-8 p.m. ☎ 58-683.

Kingfisher Restaurant—37 Albert St., Whitianga. Licensed, à la carte, specializing in Mercury Bay seafood. Call for hours. ☎ 64010.

Snapper Jacks—Corner Albert and Monk streets, Whitianga. Another seafood place, but also has take-away fish and chips and such. The speciality is the Seafood Bazaar, using whatever's fresh that day. Lunch 11:30a.m.-2p.m.; dinner from 6 p.m., open seven days. ☎ 65-482.

Coroglen Tavern—Highway 25. Pub food but also BBQ meals in the outdoor beer garden in the summer. Hours vary. ☎ 63-809.

Keith's Licensed Restaurant—Pauanui Boulevard, Pauanui. Award-winning à la carte restaurant, featuring seafood. Dinner from 6-10 p.m., closed Monday and Tuesday (unless it's a holiday). ☎ 48-825.

Port City Restaurant—606 Port Rd. in DJ's Mall, Whangamata. Cantonese BYOB and take-aways. Very popular. Lunch noon-2 p.m. Monday-Saturday; dinner (reservations required) from 6 p.m. seven nights. ☎ 865-9121.

Whangamata Hotel — Highway 25, 3 kilometers north of town. Family dining; in the garden in the summer. Pub food but also lots of seafood. Bottle shop and live entertainment some nights. ☎ 865-8521.

A colorful Poi display in Rotorua

ROTORUA

We don't like Rotorua much, because it is over-touristed, commercial and fairly unattractive, but there's no denying its popularity as a major draw for visitors coming to New Zealand, as the rows of tour buses will attest. In fairness, it is worth a short stop to see the geysers and hot mud pools, but we think, for enjoyment of the North Island's geothermal wonders, there are better places.

Green & white terraces, Waiotapu

Rotorua is about 220 miles southeast of Auckland, and sits in the middle of what is called the **Taupo Volcanic Zone**, which goes from northeast to southwest across the North Island. The area has long been a *popular spa area*, and the locals make use of the hot steam that rises to the surface for heating their homes, cooking and building their own private hot pools. Over the years, the amount of thermal activity has slowed. Some of the blame is put on all the homes and hotels and pools that have tapped into the hot underground water and steam sources, but a large part of the reduction is often blamed on the big geothermal power plant at Wairakei near Taupo, *one of the largest geothermal power plants in the world.* At least one other plant on the volcanic zone is planned, adding to fears that the golden goose might be in danger.

The usual focus for all 600,000 or so tourists who visit the city each year is the **Whakarewarewa Thermal Reserve**, which has the country's biggest geyser, **the Pohutu**, which goes off with no set schedule and sprays anywhere from a half hour to several hours. It shoots water 100 feet or so into the air and is fairly spectacular. Also within the reserve are mud pools, hot springs and mineral pools. The reserve is also a **Maori cultural center**, where you can see dancing or watch Maori artists carving and creating other artifacts. The front door of the reserve is an elaborately carved Maori gateway, and there is a replica of a Maori pa on view where you can see food cooked in thermal springs and other activities. *There is also a nocturnal house where you can spot a kiwi or two.* Daily concerts at the pa are given at 12:15 p.m. November-April and during school holidays. Guided tours of the **New Zealand Maori Arts and Crafts Institute** on the grounds are run hourly from 9 a.m.-4 p.m. daily. The tour takes about two hours, and you get to see works in progress, as well as finished pieces. There is a gift store. The reserve is about 3 kilometers south of the city on Highway 5 (Fenton Street). Hours are 8:30-4:30 p.m. daily; admission is about NZ$8 per person, which includes the crafts center tour. The concert is extra. For information, ☎ 348-9047. By the way, don't bend your teeth trying to pronounce the name—the locals just call it "Whaka."

THERMAL POOLS

Being a spa city, Rotorua has a number of places where you can plunk your body into thermal waters. The biggest and probably most popular are the *Polynesian Pools*, situated near the Hyatt Kingsgate Hotel and the Government Gardens. There are three famous springs here—**Priest, Rachel** and **Radium**—all having different mineral content and alleged to aid in your health. There are also about 30 private and family pools available, as well as massage and hydrotherapy services. The large public pools cost about NZ$5 per person; the private pools about NZ$7 per person. Towels and suits can be rented. The pools are on Hinemoa Street on the lakeshore. Hours are 9 a.m.-10 p.m. daily. Information: ☎ 348-1328.

A bit further afield, another popular Rotorua-area spa is at **Waikite**, about 35 kilometers south on Highway 5. Boiling hot water is cooled by three cascading pools into the main pool, which is set in a park-like area. There is a private pool and a kids' pool. Light refreshments are available. Hours are 10-10 daily; admission is about NZ$8.

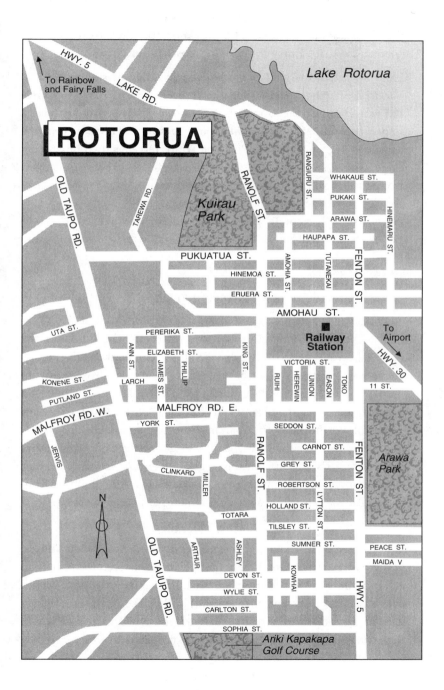

If you didn't get your fill of thermal activity at Whaka, another popular spot is the **Waimangu Volcanic Valley** southeast of the city about 30 kilometers. Take Highway 5 south, then turn left onto Waimangu Road. Entry to the valley costs about NZ$8.

Among the attractions is the **Waimangu Caldron**, supposedly the *world's largest boiling lake*, and the Inferno Crater, a lake that rises and falls about 30 feet a month. For another NZ$5, you can take a launch trip on **Lakes Rotomahana** and **Tarawera**. The launch passes the site of the once famous **Pink and White Terraces**, two huge silica ledges on the shores of Lake Rotomahana, which drew visitors from around the world. But on June 10, 1886, nearby Mt. Tarawera, supposedly an extinct volcano, erupted, burying the terraces and also the nearby village of **Te Wairoa**. The village, reached by a second launch, has a small museum with photos taken before and after the eruption. The valley is open 9-5 seven days. Information: ☎ 348-9137.

A PEEK INSIDE A CRATER

It's possible to take a trip to the top of the mountain to look into the crater. The trip, combining a boat trip with four-wheel drive up the mountain, can be booked with several companies through the city information center. If you have your own vehicle, drive south on Highway 5 to Highway 38 toward Lake Rerewhakaaitu, turn left on Rerewhakaaitu Road, left on Bretts Road to Ash Pit Road, then turn right, follow the signs to a parking lot. The summit is about two hours up. Wear a jacket because it can get really cold on top, and carry water. It's not difficult, just a good hike. *The view is incredible.* The mountain is Maori trust land, so you need permission first from the Te Arawa Trust Board on Pukuatua Street. ☎ 348-9498.

EXCAVATED VILLAGE

With your own vehicle, you can also drive to the **Buried Village**, going past Blue and Green Lakes. The village, covered by more than 6 feet of mud and debris from the blast, has been partially excavated. There is a cafe and souvenir shop, and bush walks around the village take in waterfalls and streams. Take Highway 30 east from town, then turn onto Tarawera Road about 3 kilometers from the city. You can catch the launch here for the trip over to the Pink and White Terraces, as well. There is also a trail up to Mt. Tarawera on the narrow neck of land you walk over to get from launch to launch.

Another popular geyser is the **Lady Knox***, which, like Old Faithful, erupts regularly—in this case, at 10:15 a.m.* The geyser is part of the Waiotapu thermal area about 30 kilometers south of town off Highway 5. Other attractions are the *Champagne Pool* (hot springs) and *Bridal Veil Falls.* Entry to the area costs about NZ$7. It's open from 8:30 a.m. to dusk all year. Information: ☎ 348-5637.

Finally, for some lively thermal activity (sorry, no geysers) try **Hell's Gate**, a small but very interesting thermal area about 15 kilometers east of town on Highway 30. Smaller and more intimate than Whaka, it's also not as crowded but just as fascinating. Hours are 9-5 daily; admission is about NZ$9. Information: ☎ 345-3151.

LAKE EXCURSIONS

Rotorua is set amid a number of lakes, so there are plenty of water-oriented activities for visitors. One popular excursion is to the "Romeo and Juliet" island of *Mokoia* in the middle of Lake Rotorua. The lovers, in this case Maoris named Hinemoa and Tutanekai, were involved in the same basic plot except, in their case, they lived happily ever after on the island. The Ngaroto takes you from the lakefront jetty to the island and back on a 2-hour tour for about NZ$25 per person. There are several trips a day; check for hours. Information: ☎ 348-0233.

Another way to do the lake is aboard the **Lakeland Queen**, a paddlewheeler that has a number of day and evening cruises with snacks or dinner; prices NZ$15-40. There are about four trips a day. Information: ☎ 348-6634.

TROUT FISHING

The Rotorua area, combined with Lake Taupo to the south, is one of the finest trout fishing regions in the world. If you don't bring your own equipment, there are many guides in the area who can supply gear, boats and licenses. As a rule, the guides will run you about US$30 an hour for stream fishing (minimum of 3 hours) or about US$35 an hour for boat trolling (also 3-hour minimum). Licenses, if not issued by the guides, are available at the Department of Conservation office at the corner of Tutanekai and Pukaki streets or at sporting goods stores. The cost is about US$4 a day. A couple of guides to check with are Bryan Colman, 32 Kikwi Street in Rotorua, ☎ 348-7766, and Roger Forrester, ☎ 347-9299. Other guide services are available through the city information center.

If you want your fishing with a little upscale relaxation, there are several excellent lodges in the Rotorua area that can set up fishing trips or other activities. Nonfishers can just enjoy the high quality service and cuisine. Our favorite is the **Moose Lodge**, on Lake Rotoiti about 15 kilometers east of town on Highway 30. The lodge was built as a getaway home for a very rich contractor, Noel Cole, and has been visited by all manner of swells, including Queen Elizabeth and Charles and Diana. The 18-acre site includes tennis facilities, and the lodge has its own bubbling thermal pool. *It's a very special place* and has a fishing boat of its own. Rates are around NZ$620 for a double, meals included. Information: ☎ 27-823.

A couple of other lodges, for fine service or for use as a fishing base, are the *Solitaire Lodge*, a secluded place on the shores of Lake Tarawera. The tariff of about NZ$675 per couple includes all meals and liquor. It's smoke-free. Information 28-208. And the *Muriaroha Lodge*, located in Rotorua, featuring private garden suites. The price of about NZ$600 per couple includes most meals and liquor. These lodges can be booked in North America by contacting Shoreline International, 1004 Willow St., San Jose, Calif. 95125; ☎ (800) 932- 5055.

The main museum area in town is at the so-called **Tudor Towers**, an old hulk that used to house the Government Bath House but now is home to the **Rotorua District Museum** and **the Rotorua Art Gallery**. The museum has a good display about the Pink and White Terraces, plus a re-creation of the old mud baths that used to draw the crowds. The gallery houses an extensive collection of national art, including some fine studies of Maori life. The two facilities are open 10-4 weekdays, 1-4:30 p.m. weekends. Admission is NZ$2. Tudor Towers is situated in the Government Gardens, a 100-acre preserve. On most sunny afternoons, the grounds are crawling with lawn bowlers.

MORE SHEEP

One Rotorua attraction that should be hokey but manages to pull it off anyway is the Agrodome, where you can get a really good look at how the New Zealand sheep business operates. There are three shows a day (9:15, 11 and 2:30), and you'll get to see sheep dogs do their thing, plus watch a champion shearer in action. The facility is about five miles north of town on Highway 5. Tickets are about NZ$8. You can also ride horses and milk a cow, if you're really bored. There's a store selling sheepskin and other souvenirs. Information: ☎ 74-350.

For those who like to look at fish but not necessarily catch them, there are several *trout springs* around town, full of some truly humongous fish. The best is probably **Rainbow and Fairy Springs**, a couple of miles north on Highway 5. There is also an aviary, as well as a nocturnal kiwi house. For the kids, there's a bunch of farm pets and some deer. Hours are 8-5:30; admission is about NZ$9. Across the road is the *Rainbow Farm*, another sheep show, which costs about NZ$5 but isn't as good as the Agrodome. Information on both facilities, ☎ 347-9301.

Next door to the Rainbow facilities is the **Skyline Skyrides**, a gondola that goes up Aorangi Peak with views of the city and the lakes. There's a licensed restaurant on top. If you're absolutely mad, you can try the so-called luge track, a kilometer-long sidewalk you ride down on little blue cars with handlebars, a dandy way to scrape your nose and bang your butt. It's very popular, however. The round trip on the gondola is about NZ$8; the luge rides are NZ$5 a pop. Information: ☎ 347-0027.

There are four golf courses in the city, two of which—the Rotorua Golf Club and the Springfield—are 18-holers. *A very popular reason for coming to Rotorua is the large number of hangi feasts and Maori concerts held at local hotels. Hangi* means cooking pot in Maori, but the basic idea is the same as a *luau*. One of the things they'll force on you is the traditional hongi, the Maori nose-to-nose greeting, plus maybe a try at a haka or two—the war dance of greeting. *The food will be traditional Maori: sweet potatoes, mussels, pork, lamb, venison, and it'll fill you up.* Everybody in town seems to have a favorite place to do the hangi, but your best bet is the party at the **THC Rotorua International** at the corner of Tryon and Froude streets off Highway 5 near the Whaka thermal area. The tab for the hangi and the entertainment is about NZ$40 per person and might be the best you'll see in New Zealand. There are also hangi/concerts at the Sheraton, the Geyserland Resort Hotel, the Hyatt Kingsgate, the Quality Inn and the Travelodge. In addition, there is a hangi at the Tudor Towers. Check with the hotels for time and prices.

You can also just take in Maori concerts without the food. In addition to the noontime show at Whakarewarewa, there are evening concerts at the Maori Cultural Theatre in the Civic Theatre Building on Haupapa Street at 8 p.m. daily, or at the Tamatekapua Meeting House. These concerts will run you about NZ$10 and can be booked at the visitors centre.

THE ESSENTIAL ROTORUA

INFORMATION

The New Zealand Tourist and Publicity Office (NZTP) is located at 67 Fenton St. (corner of Fenton and Haupapa). The office is open 8:30-5 daily; ☎ 348-5179.

The Automobile Association office is at the corner of Hinemoa and Hinemaru streets. Hours are 8:30-5 Monday-Friday; 24 hour service. ☎ 348-3069.

The Department of Conservation office in the Whakarewarewa State Forest Park is a little tough getting to, but it's on the same road you take to get to the Buried Village. Go on Highway 5 to the Sheraton, turn east onto Sala Street, go to Te Ngae Road, turn right to Tarawera Road, then right again to Long Mile Road and another right. It's open 8-5 Monday-Friday and 9-5 weekends; ☎ 346-1155. Disabled information: ☎ 348-5121. For emergencies, dial ☎ 111.

BANKS

Most of the major banks are located along Hinemoa Street (two blocks south of the tourist information office). Banking hours are from 9-4:30, Monday-Friday.

POST OFFICE

The Rotorua GPO is also on Hinemoa Street, corner of Tutanekai Street. Hours are 8:30-5, Monday-Friday. The area code for the Rotorua area is ☎ (07).

HOW TO GET THERE

Mt. Cook Airlines flies several flights from Auckland to Rotorua for about NZ$180 one way. The airline also flies from Christchurch (NZ$290); Wellington (NZ$200); Queenstown (NZ$525), plus other cities.

Regular Bus service is available on both Newman's and InterCity buses with connections to most North Island cities. The fare from Auckland is about NZ$40 one way; from Wellington, about NZ$70. The Auckland-Rotorua trip is about 4 hours, and it's about 8 hours from Wellington. The InterCity terminal is on Amohau Street (Highway 5) near the Air New Zealand office in the center of town; ☎ 348-1039, after hours, ☎ 379-9020. Newman's is in the information center at the corner of Fenton and Haupapa streets near Government Gardens; ☎ 348-0999.

GETTING AROUND

There is regular bus service that hits most of the major tourist spots, from Whaka to the Rainbow Farm. There is a one-day, unlimited pass for about NZ$10 you can buy from the driver. Information: ☎ 347-0098.

Taxis can be obtained by calling ☎ 485-079. Mount Cook Landline operates a half-day tour of the city, including stops at Whaka, the Agrodome and Rainbow and Fairy Springs. The fare is about NZ$40 per person. The Mount Cook office is on Amohau Street next to the Air New Zealand office. ☎ 347-7451.

WHERE TO STAY

Sheraton—Corner of Fenton and Sala streets near the Whaka thermal area. Rooms include eight suites with private spas and balconies. Three restaurants, bar, pool, thermal facilities, handicapped facilities, minibars, coffee/tea, baby-sitting. Standard doubles, NZ$225; suites NZ$300 and up. ☎ 348-7139.

Hyatt Kingsgate—Eruera Street near the lakeshore and the Polynesian Pools. Rooms include suites and spa rooms. Two restaurants, two bars, coffee/tea, minibars, handicapped facilities, indoor/outdoor pool, thermal pools, baby-sitting, courtesy van. About NZ$180 for a double; suites and spa rooms, NZ$250 and up. ☎ 347-1234.

Rotorua Travelodge—Eruera Street, near the Hyatt. Some rooms have balconies overlooking the lake. Restaurant/bar, pool, spa, tea/coffee, baby-sitting. Doubles about NZ$160. ☎ 348-1174.

Quality Inn Rotorua—Corner of Fenton and Maida Vale streets near the Sheraton. Pool, spa, sauna, restaurant/bar, tea/coffee. Doubles about NZ$140. ☎ 80-199.

Geyserland Resort Hotel—Fenton Street next to the Whaka thermal area. Pool, spa, sauna, gym, restaurant/bar, children's activities, baby-sitting, dancing weekends. Doubles about NZ$140. ☎ 348-2039.

THC Rotorua International—Corner Tryon and Froude streets next to the Whaka thermal area. Standard rooms plus villa apartments. Pool, spa, tea/coffee, two restaurants, bar, kitchens in villas, baby-sitting. Standard doubles and villas NZ$150. ☎ 348-1189.

Wylie Court Motor Lodge—345 Fenton St. Two-acre site. Each unit has a private hot pool. Restaurant/bar, laundry, tea/coffee, courtesy van, breakfast available. Doubles NZ$120. ☎ 347-7879.

Ambassador Thermal Hotel—Corner Whakaue and Hinemaru streets downtown. Best Western. Pool, spa, thermal pools, kitchens, some two-bedroom units. Standard double NZ$82. ☎ 347-9581.

Heritage Rotorua Motor Inn—349 Fenton St. Some rooms with private spas. Restaurant/bar, pools, kitchens, tea/coffee, BBQ area, tennis courts, courtesy van. Standard double NZ$100. ☎ 348-9184.

Four Canoes Hotel—273 Fenton. One luxury suite. Restaurant/bar, laundry, pool, spas. Doubles NZ$90. ☎ 348-9184.

Grand Establishment Hotel—Hinemoa Street, city center. Cobb & Co. restaurant, two bars, sauna, tea/coffee. Doubles NZ$75. ☎ 348-2089.

Eaton Hall Guesthouse—39 Hinemaru St. Eighty-year-old, thermally heated B&B. Thermal pool, tea/coffee, laundry, dinner available. Doubles NZ$65. ☎ 347-0366.

Tresco International Guest House—3 Toko St., near the InterCity station downtown. Thermal pool, laundry, tea/coffee, courtesy van. Doubles NZ$66. ☎ 348-9611.

Colonial Inn Hostel—Corner Eruera and Hinemaru streets downtown. YHA facility. Thermal pool, some family rooms, kitchen, bike hire. NZ$18 per person. ☎ 347-6810.

Rotorua Thermal Holiday Park and Lodge—Old Taupo Road near the Whaka thermal area. Kiwi Kamp facility. Several active mud pools on site. About 45 acres, with pool, kitchens, laundry, store, linen hire, BBQ. Next to golf course. Tourist flats NZ$55 double; log cabins and regular cabins from NZ$35; bunkrooms NZ$13 per person; lodge bunks including breakfast NZ$18 per person. ☎ 346-3140.

Holden's Bay Holiday Park—Off Highway 30 near the airport. Top 10 facility, close to Lake Rotorua. Pool, private hot pools, laundry, linen hire, store. Tourist flats NZ$50 double; cabins NZ$35. ☎ 345-9925.

WHERE TO EAT

Landmark—Fenton and Meade streets, next to the Geyserland Hotel. *French cuisine in an old robber baron's Edwardian mansion.* Four separate dining rooms. Licensed but you can BYOB wine. Reservations. Dinner 6-10 p.m. ☎ 348-9386.

Aorangi Peak Restaurant—Atop Aorangi Peak. *Tough to find but great view.* Go north on Highway 5 to the traffic lights at Clayton Road. Go left on Clayton to Mountain Road, turn right and climb to the top. Specialties include lamb and venison and Bay of Plenty scallops in season. Large wine selection plus imported beers. Open seven days; cocktail lounge opens at 5:30 p.m. Lunch noon-2 p.m.; dinner from 6 p.m. ☎ 347-0046.

Poppy's Villa Restaurant—4 Marguerita St. a few blocks north of the Quality Inn. Award-winning seafood restaurant housed in an old Edwardian villa amid a landscaped garden. Dinner 6-10 p.m., seven nights. ☎ 347-1700.

Skyline Restaurant—On Aorangi Peak, not to be confused with the Aorangi Peak Restaurant. Cafe and dinner service. *Evening meals include the gondola ticket* (price about NZ$20 per person). Lunch noon-2 p.m.; dinner from 6:30 p.m., seven days. ☎ 347-0027.

Lakeside Bar and Grill—Memorial Drive on the lakefront next to the jetty. Outdoor dining overlooking the lake. *Grilled meats a speciality, including rabbit, venison and wild boar.* Licensed and BYOB. Lunch noon-2:30 p.m.; dinner 6:30-10:30 p.m. Closed Monday. ☎ 348-3700.

Lewishams—115 Tutanekai downtown, one block west of Fenton Street. One of the oldest buildings in town, with courtyard dining in the summer. Seafood and spicy meat stews using lamb, veal and venison. *Small and popular.* Open for lunch 11:45-2 p.m. Monday, Wednesday, Thursday and Friday; dinner Wednesday-Monday. ☎ 349-1786.

Cobb & Co.—Grand Establishment Hotel on Hinemoa Street. Senior discounts, family dining, two bars, no-smoking section. Open seven days 7:30 a.m.-10 p.m. ☎ 348-2089.

Passage to India—44 Hinemoa St. As the name suggests, *curries and other Indian dishes as hot or mild as you want.* Music on Friday and Saturday night; take-aways. Call for hours. ☎ 348-5258.

Gazebo—45 Pukuatua St. BYOB. Burgers, curries, pies. *Popular with the locals.* Open from noon until late. Big servings. ☎ 348-1911.

Pavillon—In the Sheraton on Fenton Street. Brasserie, with a dining area overlooking a native plant garden. *Ethnic specials every week, plus basic meat and spuds dishes.* Open lunch and dinner 10 a.m.-10 p.m., seven days. ☎ 348-7139.

Tour coach north of Punakaiki

THE BAY OF PLENTY

Captain Cook named this bay when he sailed in, and to his delight, found friendly natives and lots of food to replenish his stores. And the Bay area is still supplying stores today, especially kiwi fruit, but also citrus fruit, apples, strawberries and macadamia nuts. The region is also becoming a popular tourist area, with several excellent beaches.

The town of **Te Puke**, southeast of Tauranga, proclaims itself to the be *the kiwi fruit capital of the world*, and if you're interested, you can call in at *Kiwifruit Country*, an orchard/factory/showroom about 6 kilometers east of Te Puke on Highway 2. Look for the giant sliced kiwi fruit sign. They'll haul you around the orchards on little kiwi fruit cars, let you have some kiwi fruit wine and generally tell you more about kiwi fruit than you'll ever remember. Information: ☎ (07) 573-6340. Tickets are about NZ$7.

The major center of activity on the Bay of Plenty is at **Tauranga**, about an hour's drive northwest of Rotorua on Highways 33 and 2. The city is built on a peninsula with bays on either side, and is a game-fishing and recreation center, as well as bustling port. *The best beach in the area, one of the best on the North Island, is along another peninsula to the east, Mt. Maunganui.* There's a trail to the top of the small 700-foot peak, which gives views of the harbor area and the beaches. **Mt. Maunganui Beach** runs east for about 3 miles, running into another good beach area at Papamoa. Also in the area is the Mt. Maunganui Golf Club, home of the New Zealand PGA tournament.

Highway 2 skirts the sea all the way to the bay's second major tourist center, Whakatane. *The main draw here is the excellent beach at nearby* **Ohope**. Offshore a few miles is **White Island**, an active volcano known for its dense plumes of smoke. Boat tours to the island are available.

Information on the area is available from the Tauranga Public Relations and Information Centre, The Strand, ☎ (07) 578-8103; hours 9-5 weekly; holidays 10-2. In Whakatane, contact the Information and Promotions Association, Boon Street, ☎ 308-6058.

TAUPO

Perhaps the most beautiful part of the North Island is the area around Lake Taupo and the Tongariro National Park to the southwest. Here is the showcase of the North Island's fiery volcanic history.

Lake Taupo itself is the remains of two giant craters, and the whole countryside is dotted with old cones, as well as active geothermal areas. A few miles north along the **Waikato River**, feeding into the lake, is the **Wairakei Natural Thermal Valley** and, alongside, a large geothermal power station. Part of Taupo's popularity is the lake's trout fishing, widely acknowledged to be some of the finest in the world. *It's not unusual to hook into a 10-pound rainbow*, and the lake's pure water seems to be a perfect environment for the fish. At 230 square miles, it's also the country's largest lake. There are times it's tough getting to the shore because fishermen are lined up elbow to elbow.

BASE OF EXPLORATION

The Taupo area is so attractive, in fact, that we suggest you use this as the base for your explorations of the central North Island. You're about an hour from Rotorua, a couple of hours for the winery areas of Hawke's Bay and, as noted, next door to one of the finest national parks in New Zealand. The view across the lake at the volcanoes in the park is worth the price of admission.

Compared to Rotorua, Taupo is pretty low-key, and there's nothing around town to compare with either Whakarewarewa or Hell's Gate for geothermal wonders. There are a few places worth a look and, not far away, a great place to take the waters.

You can take a look at the *geothermal power plant* at Wairakei, about 10 kilometers north of town on Highway 5. There's an information center with displays and an audio-visual program, and a nearby lookout area where you can see the plant operating. Guided tours can be arranged. The center, on the west side of the road just before you get to the plant, is open daily 9-noon and 1-4:30 p.m. The plant generates about 200,000 kilowatts, roughly five percent of the country's electric power.

Just north past the information center (over the bridge) is a road going west to the **Wairakei Natural Thermal Valley**, a region of sulphurous fumes and mud pools, a geyser or two and lots of steam. There's a small RV park and tent camp. Entry is about NZ$5. Critics point to this area when they talk about the effects of the power plant. Once, the valley supposedly had dozens of geysers; now only a couple of fairly tame spurters remain, the rest the victim of steam being drawn off for the power plant. Near the geothermal information center is the 18-hole **Wairakei International** Golf Course, *one of the best in the country and one with an international reputation.* There's also a 9-hole facility nearby. Clubs and carts are available for hire; non-members welcome. For fees and information: ☎ 374-8152.

North of Wairakei is what used to be one of the best-kept thermal secrets in the country, a marvelous little place called **Orakei Korako**. There are silica terraces that look like the White and Pink Terraces at Rotorua before the volcano buried them. There are caves. There's a sacred Maori swimming hole. There are geysers and mud pools. The area sits next to the Upper Waikato River near a lake created by a **hydroelectric** dam. There is a **tearoom**, souvenir shop, boat hire, gas station and picnic area. *It might be the prettiest thermal area in the country.* Admission is about NZ$10. There are cabins for rent (about NZ$20) and a camping area. To get there, take Highway 1 north from Taupo to Tutukau Road about 15 kilometers north, then go east. The valley is open 8:30-4:30 (4 p.m. in the winter). Information: ☎ 378-3131 in Taupo.

BLUE-GREEN RIVER

Another popular spot near Taupo is **Huka Falls**, where the Waikato River plunges over an 80-foot cliff. *Here you can see the blue-green color of the river at its best.* There's a footbridge across the river near the falls. Downriver a piece is Huka Village, a re-creation of a colonial English village, complete with cottages, restaurants and working crafts centers. There's also a deer park and aviary. Hunting, fishing and river rafting services are available. The village is open from 9-5 daily. Admission is NZ$5; children free. Information: ☎ 378-5326.

Just a bit south of the falls is what many travelers think is *one of the best hostelries in New Zealand*, the **Huka Lodge**. Set among 17 acres of trees, lawns and garden next to the river, the lodge has suites set in private chalets. In the old days before it was extensively remodeled, the lodge was home to such visitors as Charles Lindbergh and James Michener. *The dining is elegant, the service up to international standards, the furnishings of the rooms and main buildings superb.* There are tennis courts, a spa pool, library and a helipad. The tariff of about NZ$430 per person double a day includes breakfast and a five-course dinner, cocktails, airport transfers from Taupo, use of the fishing boat and kayaks. The fly fishing right in front of the lodge is often excellent. ☎ 378-5791. It can be booked through Shoreline

International, 1004 Willow St., San Jose, Calif. 95125; ☎ (800) 932-5055.

If you want to try a **lake cruise**, there is the slow and ancient (but interesting) **Ernest Kemp**, an old steam ferry that does two-hour scenic cruises around the lake and also can be hired for picnics and meals. The fare is about NZ$20. In the summer, there are trips at 10 a.m. and 2 p.m.; in the winter at 2 p.m. only. Tickets and information are available at the city information office or by calling ☎ 378-3444 or ☎ 378-3218. Faster and more elegant is the 82-foot catamaran *Taupo Cat*, an air-conditioned vessel that goes into the remote areas of the lake reached by boat only. Tours depart at 9:30 a.m. and 2 p.m. Tickets are about NZ$45. The Cat also has a nightly smorgasbord cruise departing at sunset. The fare is about NZ$55. Bookings can be made at the city information center or by calling ☎ 378-6052.

If you're keen to try for a trout or two, there are a number of guide services operating from Taupo and also from Turangi at the south end of the lake. A good bet is to contact the Taupo Commercial Launchmen's Association Inc. in Taupo, which represents more than a dozen skippers. Guide fees run about US$25 an hour for rivers and streams, minimum of 3 hours; trolling around $30 an hour, minimum of 3 hours. Most guides supply tackle and can sell licenses. The association can be reached at ☎ 378-3444 (24 hours).

FISHING PACKAGES

Lake Taupo fishing packages can be booked ahead from North America. For example, a 5-day fishing trip, using Taupo as a base, will run about US$600 and includes two days with a professional guide, breakfast and dinner, transfers from the airport, and accommodation in a motel. (No international or internal air fare is included.) Upscale, staying at the Huka Lodge (and all the amenities), a 5-day trip will run about US$1800. These can be booked through Shoreline International, mentioned above.

As for soaking the tired bod in the waters, there are **essentially** *two places*: the **A.C. Thermal Pools** in town and **DeBrett's**, about 3 kilometers from town.

The A.C. is so named because the Armed Constabulary used to come for a dip in colonial times. It has one large pool—the Lido —which is not actually a mineral pool but Lake Taupo water treated and heated to about 95 degrees F. There are some private mineral pools where the water is kept at 40 degrees C—104 degrees F. There's a waterslide for the kids plus picnic and barbecue areas. Admission is about NZ$5. ☎ 378-7321.

DeBrett's is our favorite soaking spot in the whole country, not only for the pools but also for the hotel/restaurant and RV park complex available. There are two large pools, one about 104 degrees F, the other about 97F degrees. The pools are in a wooded area downhill from the hotel complex, and at night, with steam rising to blot out the stars, the spot is about as relaxed as it gets. There are also a number of private pools, which come in varying degrees of heat. Admission is about NZ$5. Information: ☎ 378-8559.

For a spectacular look at the Taupo area, try a flight with Taupo Air Services that goes down the lake, around Tongariro National Park and back for about NZ$100. Information: ☎ 378-5325. Or DeBrett's Aviation, ☎ 378-8559. Ten to 90-minute flights, NZ$25 to NZ$150.

If you want a tour around, contact Paradise Tours, which operates minivan trips around the immediate area and also runs to Rotorua. The Taupo-area trip is about NZ$30. Tours can be booked through the city information center.

There is no direct air service to Taupo, the nearest service being to Rotorua, where you can catch a bus to Taupo for about NZ$25. At present there are three daily buses, leaving at 9, 11 and 1:30, arriving in Taupo about an hour later. The fare from Wellington is about NZ$60; from Auckland, about NZ$45.

The Taupo Information Centre is located on Tongariro Street near the waterfront, and is open from 8:30a.m.-5p.m. ☎ 378-9000. The Turangi Information Centre is on Ngwaka Place. ☎ 376-8999.

The area code for the Taupo area is ☎ (07).

WHERE TO STAY

Huka Village Estate—Huka Falls Road next to the Historic Huka Village. Restaurant/bar, pool, spa, kitchens, tea/coffee, courtesy van. Doubles about NZ$200. ☎ 378-5326.

Manuel's Resort Hotel—Highway 1 on the lakefront to the south edge of town. Pool, sauna, licensed restaurants, tea/coffee. Doubles about NZ$155. ☎ 378-5110.

Cascades Motor Inn—Highway 1, a bit past Manuel's. Pool, kitchens, tea/coffee, courtesy van. Studios for NZ$100; suites from NZ$140. ☎ 378-3774.

THC Wairakei Hotel—Highway 1 just across from the Geothermal Information Centre, close to the golf course. Bar/restaurant, tea/coffee. Doubles start about NZ$120; villas NZ$170, suites from NZ$225. ☎ 374-8021.

Karaka Tree Hotel—216 Lake Terrace, residential area northeast of the harbor. Kitchens, spa, courtesy van, coffee/tea. Doubles about NZ$100. ☎ 378-2432.

Lakeland Motor Inn—Highway 1, across from the Cascades Inn. Two licensed restaurants, laundry, handicapped facilities. Doubles about NZ$85. ☎ 378- 3893.

DeBrett's Thermal Hotel—Highway 5, the Taupo-Napier road, about a kilometer from the lake. Our choice when we haven't sold a kid or two to pay for a room at the Huka Lodge. The century-old DeBrett's hotel has tons of class and creaky floors, nice bar, and free access to the thermal pools. Bar/restaurant. Also a motel and RV park. The hotel rooms are about NZ$90 double; reservations recommended. Motel units are NZ$65 double. On-site caravans are NZ$25 double, and cabins are NZ$50 double. For the hotel ☎ 378-7080; For the other units, ☎ 378- 8559.

Sunseeker Motel—Taharepa Road, just off the lakefront. Laundry, spa, tea/coffee, breakfast available. Doubles about NZ$85-105. ☎ 378-9020.

Loretta's Quality Guest House—135 Heu Heu St. center of town. B&B, laundry, BBQ, tea/coffee, dinner available (Italian a specialty). Doubles about NZ$70. ☎ 378-4927.

Suncourt Motor Hotel—Northcroft Street near lakefront. Rooms and motel units. Restaurant/bar, all rooms with bath, coffee/tea. Doubles about NZ$65. ☎ 378-8265.

Lake Establishment—Corner of Tongariro and Tuwharetoa streets downtown. A pub/hotel member housing the country's original Cobb & Co. Restaurant. Some rooms without baths, tea/coffee. Doubles with baths about NZ$50. ☎ 378-6165.

Rainbow Lodge Backpackers—99 Titiraupenga Street downtown. Popular, friendly spot, book ahead. Kitchen, dining room, sauna, laundry, BBQ, courtesy van, tour bookings. Bunkrooms NZ$15 per person; doubles NZ$40. ☎ 378-5754.

Taupo Pavlova Backpackers—69 Spa Road. Kitchen, laundry, no curfew, linen hire. Dorm or doubles available. NZ$15-18 per person. ☎ 378-9292.

WHERE TO EAT

Edgewater Room—In Manuel's Resort Hotel on the lakeshore. *One of the best in town with great lake views and award-winning cuisine,* specializing in fresh fish. Call for hours. ☎ 378-5110.

Echo Cliff—Tongariro Street near the visitors center. *Our favorite, also with nice lake views and friendly staff.* No reservations taken. Licensed or BYOB wine, good seafood. Dinner 6:30-10 p.m.; closed Sundays.

The Graham Room—In the THC Wairakei Hotel. *The place to bring those trout you caught—they'll fix 'em up.* Open breakfast 7:30-9:30 a.m.; dinner 6:30-9:30. Semidress code. Closed Sundays. ☎ 374-8021.

Whispers—Highway 1, 2 kilometers south of town. *Nothing fancy, but good fare.* Open for breakfast from 7:30 a.m.; dinner 6:30-10 p.m. Licensed. ☎ 378-3893.

Lakeside Cafe and the Italian Connection—Corner of Lake Terrace and Tongariro. A cafe by day, Italian restaurant by night. *Fairly plain decor, good Italian.* Licensed. Breakfast and lunch 7 a.m.-3 p.m.; dinner Monday-Saturday from 6 p.m.

Homestead Restaurant—Huka Falls Road on the river. *Family dining,* licensed and BYOB wine. Kids welcomed. Dinner from 6 p.m. ☎ 378-2245.

Freeman's Cafe & Bar—Tuwharetoa Street next to the Lake Establishment Hotel. Live music (often country/western) on Friday and Saturday nights. Sandwiches, burgers and their own really good pub beer, Waikato Bitter. Open from noon on; closed Sunday.

There is also a Colonel Sanders and a Pizza Hut in town.

TONGARIRO

The oldest national park in New Zealand—and one of the most beautiful—is Tongariro, fewer than 60 miles southeast of Taupo. The park, about 200,000 acres, has three active/dormant volcanoes. It is a popular tramping area in the summer and, in the winter, a major skiing area. It was established in 1887, about the same time as Yosemite National Park in California and Glacier and Yoho national parks in Canada. It's a **World Heritage area**.

The volcanoes continue to cause problems—and deaths—right up to the present day. The upper slopes of the cones are spattered with hot rocks and mud from time to time, and **Mt. Ruapehu** (at 9,200 feet, the tallest mountain on the North Island) has erupted several times since 1945. Its sister peak, **Ngauruhoe**, has had several major eruptions as well. The third peak, **Mt. Tongariro**, has not erupted in modern times. **Mt. Ruapehu**, although still active, is where the major ski runs are located.

The park is a contrast in ecosystems. On the eastern side, the area is a near desert. On the west, which gets heavy precipitation, there are lush forests. The park contains about 500 species of native plants, from conifer forests to orchids to wildflowers and vast areas of tussock.

The park is reached by driving south on Highway 1 to Turangi, then taking on Highway 47 to Highway 48. At the end of the highway (the so-called Bruce Road) are the park headquarters, the **Chateau Tongariro** and a number of chalets and lodges belonging to ski clubs. (For ski information, see the Skiing section.) The settlement here is called **Whakapapa Village**. It's also possible to take a train to the park area. Both the Silver Fern and Northerner trains stop at National Park, a small settlement about 15 kilometers from the park headquarters. The Fern leaves Auckland at 8:30 a.m. Monday-Saturday and arrives at National Park about 1:30 p.m. From Wellington, trains leave about 6:30 a.m., arriving at National Park around 1:15 p.m. The fare is about NZ$80 from Wellington, NZ$50 from Auckland. From National Park there is fairly regular bus service to Whakapapa.

Using a series of sealed state highways, it's possible to drive completely around the park, although some roads might be blocked in the winter. But the real draw in the summer is hiking. *One of the most interesting treks is to the crater lake near the summit of Mt. Ruapehu.* The lake, warmed by subterranean steam, is not suitable for swimming, but the scenery from the area is tremendous. **The lake can be deadly**, however. In 1953, the lake level rose because mud and lava blocked its exit down the mountain. When it finally broke through, the flood rushed down the slopes and swept a passenger train off the tracks at Waiouru at the south end of the park, killing 153 people. The trip to the lake and back can be made in a day—check with park headquarters about conditions and necessary equipment. There are a number of shorter walks as well, including one that goes to the spectacular Taranaki Falls east of the village. Information is also available at Turangi.

Most trails start at Whakapapa Village. Maps and other information are available from the park headquarters, located behind the chateau. There are a limited number of camping huts located on the trails around the park.

CHATEAU TONGARIRO

The park is the site of one of the country's old premier hotels, the **Chateau Tongariro**, which is of the same ilk as the grander Hermitage at Mt. Cook. The chateau, built in the 1920s, offers five-star accommodation and decent food in several restaurants, including a moderately-priced cafeteria. Rooms at the Chateau during the winter are between NZ$160 and NZ$250 (single or double, same price). In the summer, rooms are in the NZ$110-160 a night double range. It has a pool, spa and sauna and ski-drying area. The mailing address for the hotel, as well as other places in the village, is actually Mt. Ruapehu. Information on the chateau: ☎ (0812) 23-809. There is also the **Skotel**, which has a range of rooms from plain to fancy, with prices ranging from about NZ$40 double to around NZ$100. It has a spa, restaurant/bar and some chalets with kitchens. ☎ 23-719. Finally, there is the **Whakapapa RV park**, which has cabins for about NZ$30; bungalows for NZ$40, and tourist flats for about NZ$50. There are also tent sites and backpackers units. ☎ 23-897.

Information on the park is available in Taupo, as well as ranger offices in Ohakune and Turangi. Park headquarters in the valley: ☎ 23-729.

HAWKE'S BAY

One of the country's premier wine-growing areas lies along Hawke's Bay, running from the Mahia Peninsula to the Napier/Hastings area. The bay also has a fair number of good beaches and the Mediterranean-like weather makes it *a popular, but still underexposed tourist area*. There are more than a dozen small-to-medium wineries in the area, specializing in cabernets, sauvignon blanc and some good reds. These **wineries**, combined with those further to the north in the Gisborne area, are a major source of New Zealand wines, producing more than a third of the total output. (See Wine section.)

The major base for exploring the wine region is **Napier**, the self-proclaimed *Art Deco capital of the world* (look out, Miami Beach). And the town does have a large selection of Art Deco buildings, all courtesy of a devastating 7.9 earthquake that hit the city in 1931. More than 250 people died, the city was leveled and a huge chunk of marsh and swamp area (nearly 8,500 acres) was raised above sea level, in some places as much as 6 feet. The town was rebuilt in the style of the times, creating a living museum of Art Deco architecture. The city airport, by the way, is built on the earthquake-raised land. There are also some nice Art Deco structures in Hastings, 20 kilometers south, also rebuilt after the town was destroyed by the quake.

The city is so proud of its collection, in fact, that *in February it holds an Art Deco weekend*, when visitors are urged to wear vintage costumes, try a tea dance or two, take walking tours of the city and sample some regional wines. This is all part of the activities of the **Art Deco Trust**, a Napier organization that tries to keep the old relics ship-shape and attractive for the growing tourist trade. And every Sunday throughout the year, there are walking tours of the city with emphasis on the Art Deco, as well as looking at the remains of the earthquake damage. The tours leave the Hawke's Bay Museum at 2 p.m. Wednesdays and Thursdays and cost about NZ$5.

The museum—full name **Hawke's Bay Art Gallery and Museum**—is located on Marine Parade at the waterfront, and is well worth a stop. In addition to a before-and-after audiovisual show about the earthquake, *the museum houses an excellent collection of Maori art*, in this case a display designed and placed by the Maoris themselves. It's open 10 a.m.-4:30 weekdays, 1-4:30 on weekends. Admission is about NZ$3.

Another good spot on to stop Marine Parade is the **Hawke's Bay Aquarium**, said to be the largest in the Southern Hemisphere. In addition to the usual fishy features, you can see **tuataras**. Feeding time is 3:15 p.m.; hours are 9-5 daily. Admission is about NZ$8. In conjunction with the aquarium is Marineland of New Zealand with trained dolphins and sea lions. There are shows at 10:30 a.m. and 2 p.m. daily. It's open from 10-4:30 daily. Admission is about NZ$10.

And if you haven't met a **kiwi** yet, the **Nocturnal House** at the north end of the Parade is a good bet, particularly since in this case, you get to actually touch one of the beaky critters, *the only place we know of in New Zealand that allows people to get that close to them*. Hit the exhibit at 1 p.m. for the tactile program. Feeding time is at 2 p.m. The Nocturnal House is open from 11-3 daily. Admission is about NZ$4.

GANNET COLONY

One of the major tourist attractions in the Napier/Hastings area is the large colony of gannets which arrive every July to nest at **Cape Kidnappers**, a point of land about 20 miles west of the two cities. The sanctuary is closed between July and October while the birds mate and nest, but is open from October to June. There are usually around 3,000 pairs of birds, and *the best time to see them is between November and February.*

There are several companies in Napier and Hastings that do **gannet tours,** which can be booked through the city information offices. Alternatively, you can drive as far as **Clifton**, then hike to the sanctuary. Or you can take a tractor-pulled trailer guided tour. *The hike is a bit strenuous, 5 miles each way, and must be done only at low tide.* Tide tables are available at the city information offices; you have to start the trek no later than 3 hours after high tide and return no later than an hour or so after low tide. Carry water and wear good boots or hiking shoes. There is a toilet and drinking water near the gannet beach. The normal time to do the round trip is about 5 hours. You get a free permit and tide tables at Clifton where you park your car.

The easy way is to take the trailer from Burden's Motor Camp at Te Awanga, about 20 kilometers from Napier. For about NZ$15, you get a guided 4-hour trip. The trip departs daily between October and April. Reservations required. Information: ☎ 875-0400 or ☎ 875-0334. Another way to get there is to take a four-wheel drive from Summerlee Station near Te Awanga. The trip goes overland, rather than along the ocean. The daily trips from October through April depart at 1:30 p.m. The cost is about NZ$40. Information: ☎ 875-0511.

FANTASYLAND

The big draw in Hastings is **Fantasyland,** especially if you have younger children along. The park, a sort of miniature Disneyland, has rides, amusements, ice cream parlors—the usual. It's on Grove Road south of Highway 2. The park is open daily. Entrance fee is about NZ$3.

Information on the Hawke's Bay area is available from the Napier Information Centre, Marine Parade, ☎ 06) 835-7579; from the Hastings Public Relations Office, Russell Street, ☎ 876-0205; from the Hawke's Bay Tourism Board, Stortford Lodge, Hastings,

☎ 876-0497, and from the Central Hawke's Bay District Council in Waipawa, ☎ 857-8060. The Napier area code is (06).

Napier/Hastings is served by regular air service from Auckland and Wellington, as well as major South Island cities. The one-way fare from Auckland is about NZ$190; from Wellington, about NZ$170; from Christchurch, about NZ$260. The **Bay Express** train runs from Wellington to Hastings and Napier for about NZ$55. It leaves Wellington at 8 a.m., arriving in Napier at 1:30 p.m. *There are some very interesting stretches along the line as it cuts through the mountains, using a series of bridges and tunnels.* Meal service is available. Daily bus service is available to Taupo (NZ$35); Rotorua (NZ$50), and Auckland (NZ$75).

NAPIER

WHERE TO STAY

Tennyson Motor Inn—Corner Tennyson and Clive Square, city center. Restaurant/bar, tea/coffee, courtesy airport van. Doubles about NZ$105. ☎ 835-3373.

Fountain Court Motel—411 Hastings St. Best Western. Some suites with spas, handicapped facilities, pool, some kitchens, coffee/tea, breakfast available. Doubles NZ$115. ☎ 835-7387.

Marewa Lodge Motel—42 Taradale Road. Studio units, kitchens, spa, pool. Doubles NZ$100. ☎ 853-5839.

Masonic Hotel—Tennyson and Marine Parade. Art Deco structure with a Cobb and Co. restaurant. A bit run down, but hanging in there. Doubles from NZ$50 to NZ$85. ☎ 835-8689.

Pinehaven B&B—259 Marine Parade. No-smoking B&B in a grand old house converted into a hotel. Shared baths, tea/coffee. Doubles NZ$70. ☎ 835-5575.

Napier Hostel—277 Marine Parade. YHA in an old guest house. Mostly twin and family units. Kitchen, dining room, bike hire, Open 24 hours, NZ$16 per person. ☎ 835-7039.

Criterion Backpackers Inn—48 Emerson St. Former hotel, accommodations upstairs. Downstairs is a bar, cafe and pizza parlor. Dorm and twin rooms. NZ$15-18. ☎ 835-2059.

Kennedy Park Motor Park and Motels—Kennedy Road northeast of city center. Top 10 group. Kitchen, laundry, store, restaurant. Cabins NZ$30-40; tourist flats, NZ$66 double; motel units with kitchens, coffee/tea. Double NZ$80. ☎ 843-9126.

WHERE TO EAT

Beaches Restaurant—War Memorial Building, Marine Parade. Award-winning cuisine featuring lamb, venison and seafood. On the waterfront with a good view of the Bay. Lunch noon-2 p.m. Wednesday, Thursday, Friday; dinner from 6 p.m., closed Sundays. ☎ 835-8180.

Tennyson Restaurant—Corner Tennyson and Clive Square. Seafood, steaks, venison, lamb. Cocktail bar. Lunch noon-2 p.m.; dinner 5:30-9:30 p.m. Open seven days. ☎ 835-3373.

Cobb & Co.—In the Masonic Hotel. Family dining, senior discounts. Open 7:30 a.m.-10 p.m. seven days. ☎ 835-8689.

Poppa's Pizzeria—In the Criterion Backpackers Inn. Salad bar, coffee, pizza. Budget.

Bayswater Restaurant—Hardinge Road. Waterfront locale with outside dining. Monthly menu changes, but expect quality seafood, as well as lamb and venison. Homemade breads and desserts. Open lunch 11:30-2; dinner 6 p.m.-1 a.m. Closed in winter Sunday, Monday, Tuesday. ☎ 835-8517.

HASTINGS
WHERE TO STAY

Fantasyland Motel—Corner Sylvan Road and Jervois Street. Kitchens, pool, spa, tea/coffee, courtesy van. Doubles about NZ$90. ☎ 876-8159.

Town Lodge Motel—911 Heretaunga St. East, close to Fantasyland. Best Western. Some kitchens, tea/coffee, courtesy van. Doubles NZ$85. ☎ 876-5066.

Pacific Hotel—Corner Heretaunga and Market streets. Built in 1907, faded around the edges. Restaurant and four bars. Shared bath, coffee/tea, breakfast available. Doubles about NZ$45. ☎ 878- 3129.

WHERE TO EAT

Barrel Room Restaurant—At Vidal of Hawke's Bay winery, 913 St. Aubyn St. East. *One of the best in the area,* housed in a classy building with stained glass, oak decor and fireplace. A blackboard menu with seasonal specials. In the summer, eat outside. Lamb and seafood specialties. Lunch noon-2 p.m.; dinner 6-11 p.m. Closed Sundays. ☎ 876-8105.

McGenty's Licensed Restaurant—Anvil Court Motor Lodge, 1408 Karamu Rd. North. Also BYOB wine. *Specializing in Hawke's Bay seafood. Good wine list.* Lunch noon-2 p.m.; dinner 6 p.m.-midnight. ☎ 876-4122.

Lodge Brasserie and Bar—1122 Heretaunga St. Rabbit, pork, lamb, fresh area produce. Licensed or BYOB wine. Lunch noon-2 p.m.; dinner 6-9:30 p.m. Closed Sundays. ☎ 878-9039.

Rush Munro's Ice Cream Garden—704 Heretaunga St. West, as you enter Hastings from Napier. *A legend since 1926, this homemade ice cream using local fruits is a pilgrimage for some New Zea-*

landers. A secret recipe, of course. In the summer, it's open from noon to around 9 p.m.

TARANAKI

If you ever get to New Plymouth, at the central western bulge of the North Island, *you'll always remember the gracious, snow-covered cone of Mt. Egmont, or in Maori, Mt. Taranaki.* The 8,261-foot-high peak is New Zealand's Mt. Fuji, and was named by Captain Cook. The mountain is almost a perfect cone, marred just a bit by a subsidiary cone about 2 kilometers south of the main peak. Egmont is officially classed as a dormant volcano, having last erupted in the 1630s.

Surrounding the peak is **Egmont National Park**, an 82,000-acre national park that was the second established in the country. Much of it is lush bush, which like the excellent farmlands in the vicinity, owes its existence to Taranaki's volcanic ash eruptions. There are more than 320 kilometers of paths and tracks in the park, including a trail to the top of the peak. The weather on the mountain is extremely changeable and subject to frequent rain—in fact, *it's one of the wettest places in the country.* For that reason, inexperienced hikers should not try the peak climb alone.

The **New Plymouth area** is one of the major dairy regions in the country, and the Port of New Plymouth ships more cheese out of the country than any other. But the area is also the center of the nation's fossil fuel reserves. There have been oil fields worked in the area, but they dwindled. But a huge offshore natural gas field was discovered in 1969, and the energy industry is expanding again around the area.

The coast north of New Plymouth has some of the best seascapes in New Zealand, and looks like a twin to some stretches of the Pacific Coast Highway north of San Francisco. Lots of sea stacks, towering cliffs, marvelous ocean views. *Many of the beaches in the area are made of black iron—you can actually pick them up with a magne*t. The entire coastline from Wanganui to Waitara is dotted with hiking trails and scenic overlooks.

Information about the national park is available at Department of Conservation offices in Devon Street in New Plymouth, as well as ranger stations in the park itself, and at the conservation office at Stratford on Highway 3 east of the park.

The New Plymouth Vistors Centre is at 81 Liardet St.; ☎ (06) 758-6086.

WAITOMO

It's on almost every tour itinerary of the North Island, maybe as famous as the geysers around Rotorua, *easily the most popular insect attraction in New Zealand*: the **Glow Worm Grotto**, also known as **Waitomo Cave**, one of three caves open to the public in a largely unexplored underground cavern area about 100 kilometers west of Rotorua.

There are glow worm caves in many spots around New Zealand, but the caves at Waitomo are the biggest and the best. The main cave is fairly standard issue until you get on a flat-bottom boat and slide out onto an underground lake and look up. It's a sort of greenish Milky Way, dotted with thousands of lights from the insects clinging to the cave roof. The worms—actually the larval stage of a fly—emit light to attract other insects to sticky filaments they dangle to snare their food. There are two other caves on the site as well, Ruakuri and Aranui. Ruakuri, now closed to regular tours, is the largest, Aranui the prettiest. Tours of the Glow Worm Grotto run on the hour from 9-4 daily and cost about NZ$10. Smoking and photography are not allowed. **Aranui Cave** is open only from 10 a.m.-3 p.m. It's about 3 kilometers from the grotto. Tickets about NZ$15. For reservations and information: ☎ (0813) 88-227.

In recent years, the most popular way to do the caving experience is what is called "black water rafting." After a lesson or two on the nearby river, you are given a wet suit, a hard hat with lamp and an inner-tube and taken below ground on a 3-hour journey through the darkness of **Ruakuri Cave**. You climb over waterfalls, glide along underground rivers and see a cave like you've never seen a cave before. At the end of the trip, you get a hot shower and some hot soup. It's a marvelous trip, but not for folks who don't like dark, confined spaces. Tours cost about NZ$50 and can be booked at the Waitomo Museum of Caves. The trips are so popular, you'd better book ahead. ☎ 878-7640.

There is bus service to the caves from Auckland. The bus leaves Auckland at 9:15 a.m., arriving in Waitomo at 1:30. A bus from Rotorua leaves at 9:30 a.m., arriving at the caves at 1:30. Various combinations of excursions between the three points are available. Check with an InterCity agent.

If you plan an overnight at the caves, there is the very good **THC Waitomo** with some budget rooms, as well as premium rooms and suites. It has the best food in town and a friendly bar. Rooms run from NZ$45 to NZ$115; suites about NZ$300. ☎ 88-227 or 228. There are also several motels, including the **Caves Motor Inn** at the caves turnoff, about NZ$70 double, backpackers NZ$13, ☎ 873-8109; and the **Glow Worm Motel,** also at the turnoff, doubles about NZ$60, ☎ 873-8882.

WELLINGTON

If you ever catch a real San Franciscan with his guard down, you soon discover that a lot of that haughty civic pride the city is so well known for is partly bluff. Sure, he'll rave about the culture, the history, the scenic beauty, Golden Gate and all that tourism office stuff. But way deep down he also hates the place for its steep streets that ruin his brakes and tear out his transmission, an impossible city to find a parking place (especially in front of his house), insane drivers, streets choked with tourists, and high prices. And the lousy weather. Damp, foggy, and a never-ending wind. San Franciscans *say* they love the murky weather, and especially love the wind because it keeps the skies clear of the ugly smog they claim covers the rest of the ugly state.

Yeah. We heard the same sort of rumblings in *Wellington, a town often compared to San Francisco.* Lovely harbor, steep streets that ruin your brakes and tear out your transmission, a never-ending wind, metropolitan atmosphere, no place to park. The sort of things that make civic boosters swell their chests and sing out loud. Also—and this is something few residents of either city will say out loud—there is among both sets of citizens that continual deep-seated, back-of-the-brain tingle of fear about "The Big One." Both cities, you see, are sitting right on top of some very serious earthquake faults, and one of these days....

Cable Car, Wellington

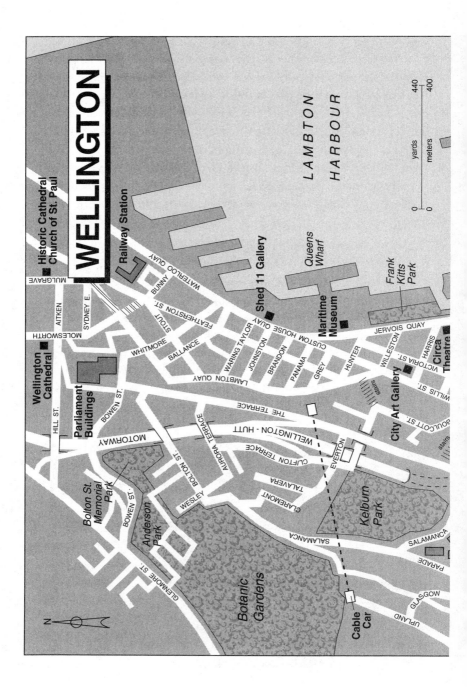

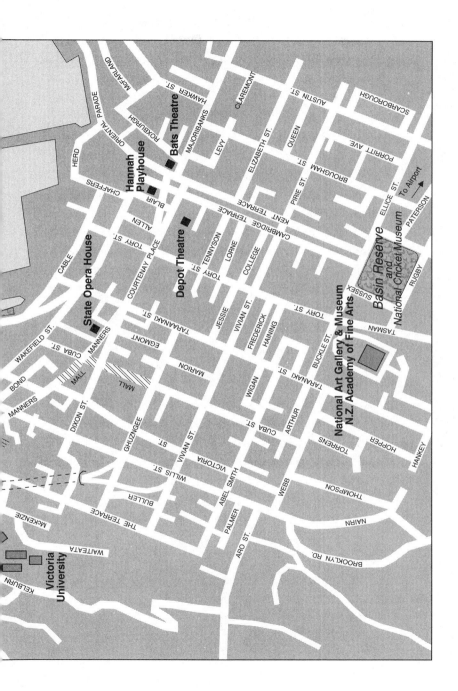

A big chunk of downtown Wellington is built on land uplifted in a huge earthquake in 1855. In fact, if you walk down the main business street—**Lambton Quay**—you're walking along the original shoreline. We can only hope that this big chunk of reclaimed land is not composed of the same sort of fill that was used in San Francisco, upon which was visited most of the damage in the big 1989 quake. But, like the citizens by the Bay, the Wellingtonians say most of the buildings around town are earthquake proof, an interesting concept depending on the magnitude of the quake in question.

Despite the cosmetic similarities, it's a bit of a stretch to call them sister cities because they have, after all, different cultures and are really miles apart in attitude. But on one thing we can agree. The weather in both cities is basically lousy.

Smog in Wellington? Never. The city's location might have been selected with clean air in mind. The only problem is that the clean air is moving past at about 50 miles an hour, courtesy of the Roaring Forties. Wellington sits on the edge of the **Cook Strait**, a channel of water that takes those mighty southern winds and funnels them right down the middle of town. Add a little rain (which can happen any minute) and you have cause to understand why folks who live in calmer parts of the country get in and out of Wellington as fast as they can. The local papers keep track of the high wind speeds the same way the Minneapolis Star keeps track of the wind chill index. *It's not uncommon to have 70-or 80-mile-an-hour-air (clean, green and nuclear free) raging down the waterfront*, blowing unwary tourists into the drink.

We'll be blunt right up front and tell you that *Wellington is not our favorite New Zealand city*. It hasn't got the energy of Auckland or the class of Christchurch. It's a pain to get around in because of the maze of one-way streets, and a major pain getting to and out of. In truth, one of the major reasons to go to Wellington—unless you work for the New Zealand government—is to get to someplace else. In fact, a lot of folks, both domestic and foreign, miss most of Wellington because the Picton ferry dock is several miles from downtown. They hop in their cars and RVs and head for Taupo or Rotorua.

Having said that, we must also say that parts of the city are very nice indeed, especially the harbor. **Port Nicholson**, as it was originally named, is the remnant of an ancient and huge volcano that collapsed and was filled by the sea. The harbor, now lined by corporate and governmental high-rises, lies at the base of low hills that terrace back into residential areas, which are themselves a blend of old and new, fairly jumbly like the neighborhoods of San Francisco but still having a distinctly New Zealand look. *The downtown area for the most part is 20th century eclectic, not particularly attractive but efficient and relatively clean.*

Wellington has been the capital of New Zealand since 1865, picked as a compromise of sorts. Auckland, even then starting to flex its muscles, was thought to be too far away from the South Island. There were loud grumblings and threats coming from down south about proclaiming a separate colony, and it was thought that putting the capital nearer the South Island would stop the secessionist plots, which it did. (It has not stopped the southerners from casting long glances down their noses toward the north, of course.) Thus Auckland finds itself in much the same position as New York City—the largest city in the country, the main financial base, but playing second fiddle to a smaller and bureaucrat-ridden city to the south.

The major tourist target for New Zealanders (and for those from abroad who like to look at buildings) is **Parliament**. There are, in fact, several other interesting buildings parked around the seat of government, which is located at the end of The Terrace, just north of Lambton Quay. The place where the legislators actually meet is a English-style marble edifice whose interior is bedecked with native woods. It was designed with two houses of Parliament in mind, but one hall is no longer in regular use because New Zealand's government became unicameral in the 1950s. The building was completed in 1922. Nearby is the **Beehive**, the executive quarters of the government. *The name comes from the shape of the building, a truncated cone of glass and metal, which was built in 1981.* This is where the prime minister and his/her cabinet do their thing. In the complex of buildings also is the **General Assembly Library**, a Gothic-style heap built in 1897. The library serves as a research facility for Parliament, as well as a sort of Library of Congress for the country. Free conducted tours of Parliament are available on weekdays. They run hourly from 9-3:30. Information: ☎ 471-9457.

Across Lambton Quay from the government center is what is said to be *the second-largest all-wood structure in the world*, the **Government Building**. If you ever wondered where all those kauri trees went, here's part of the answer. The Italianate structure, completed in 1876, used more than a million board feet of kauri and other native hardwoods. Wood was chosen because it was supposedly earthquake resistant. The huge building (about 30,000 square feet) was built on land reclaimed after the 1855 quake.

On Mulgrave Street, a few blocks to the south of the government center, stands one of the prettiest churches in New Zealand, **Old St. Paul's**. This building, too, is all of wood and was built as a temporary cathedral until a bigger stone structure could be erected. Over the years, there were attempts to tear it down or remodel it, which fortunately came to naught, and the church today is a fine example of what Gothic looks like when it's made from native New Zealand wood. The church is open from 10 a.m.-4:30 p.m. Monday through Saturday; Sunday, 1-4:30 p.m.

Wellington is best seen from on high, and the usual place to see the city is from atop **Mount Victoria**, which rises about 640 feet above the city on a peninsula at the southeast end of the city harbor. The view is the best in town. Be prepared for wind. You can either drive to the top or take a No. 20 bus from the downtown Railway Station Terminal on Waterloo Quay.

Another very popular vantage point is in **Kelburn** at the end of a cable car, yet another tie to San Francisco. It's pretty tame by Frisco standards, but almost a million people a year ride it up the hills. The total run is about half a mile. The **cable cars** are relatively new, having been installed in 1979. They replaced earlier cable cars first installed in 1902, and which were disassembled shortly before the new Swiss-designed system was opened. Catch it by walking along Lambton Quay to Cable Car Lane, about a half mile south of the Parliament buildings. A ride to the top costs about a buck. The cars run from 7 a.m.-10 p.m. Monday-Friday; 9:20 a.m.-6 p.m. Saturdays, and 10:30 a.m.-6 p.m. Sundays and holidays.

Once there, you can shop (there's a shopping center about half-mile to the left down Upland Road) or walk back down through the **Botanic Gardens**. The gardens, about 60 acres, are known for their tulips, begonias and the Lady Norwood Rose Garden, a 100-bed display, each bed with a different variety of rose. There is also the Dell, where outdoor concerts are given. The botanical gardens date from 1869.

The best way to do the oceanside thing in Wellington is to take the highway around the beaches south and east of the harbor. The road, which has a variety of names, starts at Courtenay Place and Cambridge Terrace. Turn onto Oriental Parade and just keep hugging the coast. Along the way, you pass **Oriental Bay**, a popular swimming area; Freyberg Swimming Pool, named after a hero of World War I; the Wellington International Airport; and **Shelley Bay**. Then around the tip of the Miramar Peninsula to Scorching Bay, a small fishing beach, you'll pass by **Worser Bay**, another popular beach; around past Breaker Bay and Moa Point to **Lyall Bay,** a popular surfing beach; Houghton Bay to Island Bay, where the fishing fleet hangs out, then back down The Parade to Adelaide Road and downtown once again. The entire circle is about 25 or 30 miles or so.

If you still haven't seen a **kiwi** by now, there is a nocturnal house at the **Wellington Zoo** in Newtown, about 2.5 miles from downtown. The kiwi house is open from 10-4 daily; the zoo itself, which has a collection of animals from around the world, is open from 8:30-5 daily; admission is about NZ$7. Take the No. 11 bus from downtown—it will be marked "Newtown Park Zoo."

For an excellent day trip, and a chance to see the harbor up close, *take one of the ferries that go from Queen's Wharf to Days Bay east across the harbor.* The 60-foot, high-speed catamaran carries the strange name of *Government Print I,* so named because the government printing office for some reason sponsors the boat. The 25-minute trip across the harbor costs about NZ$6 per person; there are several trips a day and hours vary. Information, East By West Ferries, ☎ 499-1273. Once across, there is a good restaurant (At Bay), beaches and a park.

If you'd like a more leisurely cruise, try Bluefin Launches, which has coffee and lunch cruises. Coffee cruises are NZ$15; luncheon cruises for about NZ$30, or a sight-seeing cruise for about NZ$20. Information ☎ 569-8203.

If you're a literary buff, you can visit the home of Kiwi writer Katherine Mansfield ("The Doll's House," "The Garden Party"). The house where Kathleen Beauchamp (her real name) was born in

1888 is on Tinakori Street near the U.S. Embassy. It's open 10-4 daily; small admission charge. In a park next to the embassy is a memorial placed there by her father.

On Buckle Street near Basin Reserve Park is a large park area where the **National Museum** and the **National Art Gallery** are located. *The museum is one of the better places to see what Captain Cook was all about.* Included in the displays are part of the collection his two on-board botanists made on his epic first voyage, as well as the figurehead from his ship, *Resolution*, which he used to explore New Zealand. There is also a large Maori collection, including a carved meeting house. In the art gallery above the museum is a large collection of mostly European and New Zealand works. There are cafes and souvenir shop—plus the skeletal remains of old **Phar Lap**, the poisoned pony. The complex is free and is open from 9-5 daily.

Next to the museum building is the **National War Memorial** with a hall of memories and carillon. Another museum worth a look is the **Maritime Museum**, which houses boat models, displays of the harbor and paintings and photographs. Check out the display of the sinking *Titanic*. The facility is located back of Queens Wharf on Jervois Quay. The museum is open from 9:30-4 Monday-Friday, and from 1-4:30 p.m. weekends and holidays. Admission is free.

THE ESSENTIAL WELLINGTON

CLIMATE

Aside from the strong winds, Wellington has almost the same summertime climate as Christchurch, meaning fairly mild. Highs will run around 70, lows around 60. Rainfall will average about 50 inches or so a year, but it's fairly unpredictable. In the winter, highs will be around 60, lows around 40.

INFORMATION

The city information center is at the Civic Square, corner of Victoria and Wakefield streets. It's open every day from 9-5. ☎ 801-4000.
The Automobile Association office is at 342 Lambton Quay; ☎ 738-738. The main post office is on Waterloo Quay near the railway station. The Wellington area code is (04).

GETTING THERE

As noted elsewhere, Wellington has an international airport for Australia, as well as service by internal airlines. In addition to flights to major New Zealand cities on both islands, there are flights to Napier/Hastings and the Nelson area. The fare to Auckland is about NZ$235; to

Christchurch, about NZ$180; to Queenstown, about NZ$400, and to Rotorua, about NZ$200.

Wellington is the terminus for two major train services, the overnight **Northerner Express** and the **Silver Fern.** The Northerner runs Sunday through Friday, departing Wellington at 8:45 p.m. and arriving in Auckland around 7 a.m. Sleeper chairs, bar and light meal service. The fare is about NZ$90. The Monday-Saturday Silver Fern leaves Wellington at 8:20 a.m., arriving in Auckland at 6:30 p.m. The service includes complimentary morning and afternoon tea and lunch. The fare is about NZ$110. Information is available from the InterCity office on Bunny Street off Waterloo Quay near the Government Buildings and the central post office. Hours are 7:30 a.m.-6:15 p.m. Monday- Friday and 7:30-11 a.m. weekends. ☎ 498-3190 or ☎ 498-3199 after hours.

Daily **bus service** is available to Auckland, Hastings, Taupo, Rotorua and other cities on the North Island. The fare to Auckland is about NZ$90; to Rotorua, about NZ$70, and to Taupo about NZ$55. InterCity buses arrive at the railway station; Mt. Cook and Newman's depart from the city bus terminal on Stout Street up from the InterCity office and the railway station.

Wellington is also the terminus for the **Cook Strait ferry service** to Picton. Free buses leave from the railway station to go to the Aotea Quay north of the city center about 35 minutes before each sailing time. For full details on the ferry service, see the *Essentials* section earlier in the book.

GETTING AROUND

Wellington City Transport buses—

The Big Red service—operate downtown and to the suburbs. The fares for a hop around downtown are about a dollar. There are two passes as well. The Day Rover lets you ride suburban trains, as well as all buses for NZ$15 a day from 9-4 and from 6 p.m. to midnight. A Day Tripper lets you ride any city or suburban bus for NZ$6.50 after 9 a.m. weekdays and all day on weekends. The passes can be purchased at WCT ticket offices at the railway station and Courtenay Place; the Day Tripper can also be purchased on any bus.

The WTC also operates a 2 1/2 hour **tour of the city** starting at 2 p.m. daily. The tour, which costs about NZ$30, takes in all the major spots and as an added bonus, they pick you up and return you to your hotel. The tour can also be picked up at the city information center. Reservations: ☎ 385-9955.

There is a **shuttle bus** service from the airport to hotels and back on a 24-hour basis for about NZ$10. Information ☎ 878-787. A taxi ride in will cost about NZ$15. Taxis don't cruise, so find a taxi rank, a big hotel or call. Capital City Cabs is ☎ 884-884; Gold & Black is ☎ 888- 888.

Information about all local transportation, including the Picton ferry, is available by calling Ridewell at ☎ 801-7000. It's operated by the Wellington Regional Council.

SHOPPING

Lambton Quay is lined with stores, in just about all sizes and tastes. One good guide, found at the tourist information center, is the free paper, **Capital Times**, which has listings of many crafts stores and other outlets, as well as current information on shows, plays and other entertainment.

The best-known leather shop in town is probably **Skin Things** at the corner of Cuba and Manners streets next to the Cuba Street pedestrian mall, which is also a major shopping area. Another popular shopping area is the underground mall at the **BNZ Centre** on Willis Street near Lambton Quay.

WHERE TO STAY

Plaza International Hotel—148-176 Wakefield St. Our favorite five-star in Wellington for its top service, proving there are still some places that treat hotel guests as guests and not chunks of cold meatloaf. Rooms include 17 suites. Two bars, two restaurants. Tea/coffee, handicapped facilities, courtesy van, baby-sitting. Standard doubles about NZ$240. ☎ 733-900.

James Cook Hotel—On The Terrace near the business district. Restaurant, piano bar. Autographs of the famous who have stayed there are on display, good view of the city and harbor. Tea/coffee, baby-sitting. Some suites. Doubles about NZ$250; suites up to NZ$550. ☎ 725- 865.

Parkroyal—Corner of Grey and Featherston streets, city center. Two restaurants, two bars. Pool, spa, sauna, health center, tea/coffee, courtesy van, baby-sitting. Some suites. Doubles about NZ$290. ☎ 722-722.

Oriental Park—360 Oriental Parade. Beachfront area. Restaurant/bar, tea/coffee. Doubles about NZ$185; suites from NZ$400. ☎ 385-9949.

Terrace Regency—345 The Terrace. Hillside location. Restaurant/cocktail lounge. Indoor pool, sauna, health club, tea/coffee, courtesy airport van. Standard doubles, NZ$175; suites from NZ$200. ☎ 385-9829.

Plimmer Towers—On Plimmer Lane at the south end of Lambton Quay. Restaurant, two bars. Tea/coffee, sauna, handicapped facilities, courtesy van, baby-sitting. Doubles start around NZ$270. ☎ 733-750.

Quality Inn Oriental Bay—73 Roxburgh St., Mt. Victoria, northeast of the city. Close to golf courses, harbor views, 15 minutes from the airport.

Indoor pool, sauna, restaurant/bar, tea/coffee. Doubles NZ$160-200. ☎ 385-0279.

Airport Hotel—16 Kemp St. near the airport. Pool, restaurant/bar, handicapped facilities, coffee/tea, courtesy van, baby-sitting. Doubles about NZ$120. ☎ 387-2189.

Sharella Motor Inn—20 Glenmore St., opposite the Botanic Gardens. Restaurant/bar, tea/coffee, courtesy van. Doubles about NZ$170. ☎ 723-823.

West Plaza Hotel—110-116 Wakefield St. Restaurant/bar, coffee/tea. Doubles about NZ$165. ☎ 731-440.

Harbour City Motor Inn—92-96 Webb St. Studio units and suites. Restaurant/bar, kitchens, tea/coffee, handicapped facilities, baby-sitting. Doubles about NZ$145. ☎ 384-9809.

St. George Hotel—Corner of Willis and Boulcott streets. Art Deco building. Restaurant, two bars. Tea/coffee, baby-sitting. Doubles about NZ$90. ☎ 373-9139.

The Tas Hotel—Corner of Willis and Dixon streets. Restaurant, tea/coffee, baby-sitting. Doubles about NZ$100. ☎ 385-1304.

Trekker's Motel—213 Upper Cuba St. One- and two- bedroom motel units. Restaurant and cafe, house bar, spa, sauna, laundry, tea/coffee. Doubles from NZ$110. Also available are budget rooms with or without baths starting at NZ$60, plus backpackers accommodations starting at NZ$16 per person. Linen hire and breakfast available. ☎ 385-2153.

Academy Motor Lodge—327 Adelaide Road, south of the city center. One- and two-bedroom units. Kitchens, spa, laundry. Doubles about NZ$90. ☎ 389-6166.

Capital Hill Apartments—54 Hill Rd., off Main North Motorway 3 near Parliament. Family and executive suites. Kitchens, tea/coffee, courtesy van to restaurant, baby-sitting. Doubles about NZ$130. ☎ 723-716.

Flanagan's Hotel—8 Kent Terrace, south of Oriental Parade. Cafe/bar, kitchenettes available, most rooms with shared baths. Breakfast available. Doubles with bath about NZ$70. ☎ 385-0216.

Victoria Bed and Breakfast—58 Pirie St., off Kent Terrace south of Oriental Parade. On a bus stop. Dining room, tea/coffee. Doubles about NZ$70. ☎ 385-8512.

Ambassador Travel Lodge—287 The Terrace. Rooms with or without bath, backpackers rooms. Tea/coffee, laundry, breakfast available. Doubles with bath about NZ$80; backpackers NZ$25 per person shared room. ☎ 384-5696 or 5697.

Bud's—40 Tinakori Rd., north of Parliament. Laundry, library, luggage storage, travel bookings, bike and car hire, courtesy van from ferry dock, dinners and snacks available, free linen and blankets, some rooms with bath, on a bus stop. NZ$18 per person. ☎ 739-312.

Hampshire House—Corner of Ghuznee and the south end of The Terrace. Rooms in guest house, also some budget apartments. Room with bath and kitchen, about NZ$75 double; shared facilities, NZ$68 double. ☎ 384-3051.

WHERE TO EAT

Pierre's—342 Tinakori Rd. A very popular place with the locals, and it is small (seats 40), so *call ahead and don't be disappointed if you can't get in.* The best bet is to show up at the door early and get your name on the list. Tinakori Road has a bunch of good restaurants. Pierre's is a BYOB and the food, as the name suggests, is French but using New Zealand products. One speciality is rabbit terrine with onion confit. Lamb and seafood are also on the menu, which changes often to reflect what's available locally. Lunch noon-2 p.m. Monday-Friday; dinner 6-9 p.m. Monday-Saturday. ☎ 726-238.

Tinakori Bistro—328 Tinakori Rd. *Popular and even smaller than Pierre's,* specializing in lamb, seafood and prime cuts. Also a BYOB. Lunch noon-2 p.m. Monday-Saturday; dinner from 6 p.m. Monday-Saturday. ☎ 499-0567.

Kiwi Rock Cafe—97 Willis St. *If you want to see and hear the newest in the Kiwi rock scene, this is the place.* The cafe is a springboard for many local groups. Cafe-style food—potato skins, burgers, steaks and ice creams. Open seven days noon-late. ☎ 472-1555.

Orsini's—201 Cuba St. Housed in an old 1900s building, and small (seats 40). But there's a *nice cocktail lounge on the second floor* where you can wait to be seated. The specials here include crab, venison and fresh fish. Lunch noon-2:30 p.m. Monday-Saturday; dinner from 6 p.m. Monday-Saturday.

Armadillo Bar & Grill—129 Willis St. Howdy, buckaroos. Yup, barbecues, steaks, ribs and other Wild West fare. *Very popular, stand-in- line place.* Licensed. Lunch from noon Wednesday, Thursday, Friday; dinner from 6 p.m. seven days. ☎ 385-8221.

Angkor Restaurant—43 Dixon St. Cambodian food, maybe the best of all the Asian cuisines. *Coconut curries, excellent noodle dishes, fish in a different way.* Lunch noon-2:30 p.m. Monday-Friday; dinner from 6 p.m. seven days. ☎ 384-9423.

Piero's Il Cavallino—13 Pirie St. Italian songs and dances Wednesday-Sunday nights. BYOB and licensed. Pastas, some Italian wines. Garden patio bar open in the summer. *Huge portions.* Lunch noon-2:30 p.m. Monday-Friday; dinner from 6 p.m. seven days ☎ 384-9040.

Mexican Cantina—19 Edward St. just north of Dixon Street. *The usual Mexican fare plus vegetarian dishes and take-aways.* Licensed and

BYOB. Lunch noon-2 p.m. daily; dinner 6-10 p.m. daily. Weekends, noon-10 p.m. ☎ 385-9711.

Cathay Restaurant—14-16 Courtenay Place. *Wellington has more Chinese restaurants than any other city in New Zealand,* many along Courtenay Place. *The fare is basically Cantonese; nothing special.* The Cathay is a *BYOB* with special Hong Kong-style lunches. Open noon until late seven days. ☎ 384-8513. A few others are the **Ping On, Uncle Chang's** and the **Casablanca**. The Ping On is at 125 Manners St. (Courtenay Place runs into Manners). **The Casablanca,** Cuba and Manners streets, has a *smorgasbord lunch* noon-2 p.m. Monday-Friday, and Uncle Chang's, 72 Courtenay Place, also has Szechuan.

Vege Garden—2-6 Courtenay Place. This claims to be the *only vegetarian Chinese restaurant in New Zealand.* The specialty is Mandarin dumplings with your choice of fillings, and the air is often full of Chinese zither music. The food is Mandarin and Szechuan. Lunch noon-2 p.m. Tuesday-Saturday; dinner 6-10 p.m. Tuesday-Saturday. ☎ 382-9579.

Baxter's Restaurant and Wine Bar—22 Brandon St. The main draw here is the *extensive cellar of New Zealand wines by the glass or by the bottle,* but you can also nibble on some tasty snacks while sipping the grapes. Or you can get light meals. Hours are 11a.m. to late; ☎ 734-608.

Beaujolais Wine Bar—11 Woodward St., a few blocks from Customhouse Quay. Light meals available. Noon to late, Monday-Friday.

Cuba Cuba—179 Cuba St. Here's an odd combination of game arcade, dance floor and cafe. *Noisy and popular.* Licensed. Sandwiches and meat/potato dishes plus breakfasts. Hours 9 a.m.-3 a.m. Monday-Saturday; Sunday 11 a.m.-1 a.m. ☎ 801-8017.

Sultan Turkish Restaurant—39 Dixon St. *Kebabish food on an à la carte menu with some vegetarian dishes* and take-aways. Lunch noon-2:30 p.m. Monday-Saturday; dinner 6-10 seven days. ☎ 801-5544.

La Casa Pasta—37A Dixon St. upstairs. *Homestyle Italian. Lotsa pasta, big portions, great service.* Licensed and BYOB. Lunch noon-2 p.m.; dinner 5:30-11 p.m. seven days. ☎ 385-9057.

Hotel Dining

Joseph Banks—In the James Cook Hotel, 147 The Terrace. *Nouvelle French and California style cuisine,* menu changes daily. Reservations necessary. Dinner 7-11 p.m. Monday-Saturday. ☎ 725-865.

Kimble Bent's Restaurant—Parkroyal Hotel, Featherston and Grey streets. *Classic French with lots of lamb and an extensive wine list.* Lunch Monday-Friday noon-2:30 p.m. dinner 6-10:30 p.m.; Sunday brunch, 10:30-2:30. ☎ 722-722. Also in the Parkroyal is the **Panama Street Brasserie,** a lively spot done in Italian decor with colorful banners, open kitchen, inlaid tile floor and casual atmosphere. Grilled meats the speciality. Open 6:30 a.m.-1 a.m.

Atrium Restaurant — Plimmer Towers off Lambton Quay. External glass elevator and *good harbor views in a light and airy decor.* Continental with a Kiwi touch. Breakfast 7-10 a.m.; lunch noon-2 and dinner 6-10 p.m. ☎ 733-750.

Flanagan's Brasserie—In Flanagan's Hotel, 8 Kent Terrace. Seafood sausages, shrimp sauces, huge charcoaled steaks. Lunch noon-2:30 p.m.; dinner 6-11:30 p.m. ☎ 385-0216.

Plantation Cafe—West Plaza Hotel, 110 Wakefield St. Dining in a plant-shrouded hotel foyer. *Vegetarian dishes* plus lamb and chicken. Open seven days: breakfast 7-10 a.m.; lunch 11:30-2:30; dinner 6-9:30 p.m. ☎ 731-440.

Crab and Coconut Bistro—Trekker's Hotel, 213 Cuba St. *Good quantity for the price, with a varied blackboard menu. Popular with the budget crowd.* Also take-aways. Lunch 11:30-2 p.m.; dinner from 6 p.m. ☎ 385-2150.

THE WINTERLESS NORTH

The northern tip of New Zealand stretches northwest of Auckland into the relatively balmy climate of the sub-tropics.

Ie Werahi Beach, Cape Reinga

The gentle climate, lack of population, magnificent beaches and unspoiled bush country make this spot a popular vacation target for New Zealanders, especially those interested in water sports.

It was in this piece of the country that European settlers first established a beachhead on New Zealand soil, and it was here that the Treaty of Waitangi was signed, ceding control of the country to the British Empire. Away from major population centers (the largest city north of Auckland is Whangarei, 45,000 population), *the region generally has the same laid-back, pastoral feel you get on the South Island.* In the winter, when the kids are in school, the roads up north are every bit as deserted as they are in the south.

The major tourist destination for Kiwis, as well as for foreign visitors, is probably the **Bay of Islands**, a lovely harbor area with good diving, a booming yacht-charter business and a growing deep sea fishing trade. It also attracts visitors for historic reasons because the Waitangi treaty was signed there. The major industry in the north is agriculture, although there is also a growing industrial base with a major oil refinery and other industries at Whangarei.

Way, way up north is the **Ninety Mile Beach** *area, one of the best day trips in New Zealand,* and at the extreme tip is **Cape Reinga**, a popular tourist spot but also a place of special significance to the Maoris.

Driving to the north is fairly straightforward, and if you have the time, you can do the area in a wide circle trip. Our choice is to take Highway 1 to Wellsford, then go east to Whangarei, up to the Bay of Islands, up through Kerikeri to Ninety Mile Beach, and then back down Highway 12 along the west coast back to Auckland. Or you can reverse directions.

WHANGAREI

The city, which calls itself the Gateway to the North, sits next to one of the deepest protected harbors in the country. It serves as the commercial and shipping center of the region. But the primary lure of the area is not the city, but the **beaches** that lie at the ocean edge of the harbor, 40 kilometers to the east.

The area, called **Whangarei Heads**, has some quite good beaches, and the drive out to the heads follows the jagged ridge of the **Manaia mountain range**. A favorite track goes to the top of **Mt. Manaia** (about **1,400** feet high) with a lovely view of the area. The road out to the heads passes several good beaches before it turns inland to cut across the headlands to the exposed length of **Ocean Beach**, a primo surfing beach. *Another popular trip is to take the heads road to Pataua South Road which leads to the nice little settlements of Pataua and Pataua South, which have great beaches.*

A popular attraction for many Kiwis is the Marsden Point oil refinery, which can be seen from many vantage points in the area. Refineries not being high on our list, we suggest you head instead to one of the most photogenic waterfalls in New Zealand, **Whangarei Falls**, which drops about 80 feet into a pool surrounded by a park area. The falls are on the Ngunguru/Tutukaka road leading from downtown (Bank Street, then Mill Road). The site is about 5 kilometers north of the city centre.

Another attraction is the **Northland Regional Museum** southwest of the city center. The museum is actually a big homestead with displays of farm animals, a historical center, a steam train, lumberjack contests and other delights. The major reason to go is the **nocturnal kiwi house,** where the wee birds are on display. To get to the museum, take State Highway 14 (Maunu Road) to Dargaville. The displays are open daily; admission about NZ$10.

Scuba Diving, Poor Knights Islands

North of the city on the coast about 30 kilometers is the fishing port of **Tutukaka**, which is becoming important as a base for fishing and diving trips to **Poor Knights Islands**, a volcanic amalgam of caves, tunnels, arches and other bizarre formations, completely surrounded by herds of sea creatures. *The islands are reputed to be the best diving in New Zealand* and, if you listen to the Kiwis, maybe the best in the world. The islands are part of the **Hauraki Gulf Maritime Park** and are protected. There are companies in both Whangarei and Tutukaka that can arrange diving, fishing or sightseeing trips. Visitor information is available at the Whangarei Visitors Bureau in Tarewa Park on Highway 1 south of the city center; ☎ (089) 438-1079. There is also an information office at the corner of Rust Road and Water Street (take Maunu Road east from Highway 1; it becomes Water Street). There is a Department of Conservation office at 154 Bank Street (the main drag) that has information about the Poor Knights Islands and other sites.

THE BAY OF ISLANDS

If you're a sailor, The Bay of Islands is one of those places, like the Greek islands, where the sailing is so easy and the scenery is so grand, you think you've died and gone to wherever it is that old salts go.

Opua Harbour, Bay of Islands

There are something like 150 islands in the bay, which sits between two headlands with a ragged coastline of about 500 miles.

In history, the Bay of Islands has seen both the pious and the profane. Early Christian missionaries arrived here in 1814, when the Rev. Samuel Marsden held the first church service in the country. Marsden, whose reputation in Australia was so bad he was called the Whipping Parson because of his treatment of convicts, was a bit kinder in New Zealand, and established missions in the area in the early 1800s. About 1820, another settlement came along, this one at a place called Kororareka, which came to be called Russell, a hangout for whalers, whores, brigands, thieves and other riffraff. Russell, after a time, came to be called the "Hell-hole of the Pacific," and was a source of much mumbling from the Christian communities nearby.

Before major settlements grew up further south on both islands, the Bay of Islands was the center of European settlement in New Zealand, and it was at Waitangi, across a harbor from Russell, that the English and the Maoris signed the treaty that started modern New Zealand history.

One of the biggest industries in the area is deep sea fishing. Thousands of fishers coming every year to try for marlin and billfish. The area was a favorite hangout for American author Zane Grey, who set down his impressions of the bay in *Tales of the Angler's El Dorado.* The bay is also noted for excellent diving.

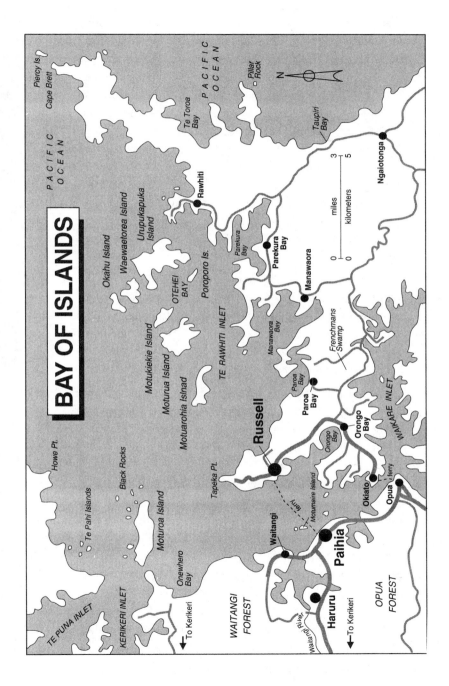

PAIHIA

Paihia, which started life as a mission station, is *the tourist center of the Bay of Islands. The ideal time to visit the area is in March or April* when the town is almost deserted and you can literally walk into any hotel or motel and get a bed. The main information offices, as well as ferry services and fishing boat offices, are located in the Maritime Building on the waterfront downtown. From here, you catch the small ferry boats that make regular runs across the bay to Russell. The Bay of Islands Information Centre on Marsden Road has the lowdown on almost any activity you want, and it can book tours; ☎ 402-7426. As befits its role in life, the city of **1,750** population has a large number of motels, holiday apartments, RV parks and restaurants. The other good news is that in the off-season, room rates drop as much as NZ$30 a night. The area code for the region is (09).

One of the most popular trips, nationally famous, is the so-called **"Cream Trip,"** operated by the Fullers company. The launch for years served as a mail and provision boat for folks scattered around in remote settlements around the Bay of Islands, and *today the 5-hour excursion is probably the best single experience in the area—unless, of course, you're on your own sailboat.*

The trips leave from the Maritime Building in Paihia at 10 a.m. daily from November through May, and at 10 a.m. on Monday, Wednesday, Thursday and Saturday from June to October. If you're staying at Russell, the launch stops there at about 10:15. The boat then returns to Russell at 3:15 p.m., arriving back at Paihia at 3:30. The tour includes a stopover at **Otehei Bay** on Urupukapuka Island, where Western author Zane Gray had a marlin-fishing camp. Here you can sunbathe, swim or take a ride on a 30-passenger underwater-viewing boat over reefs, caves and the ocean floor. Or you can chow down at the local eatery—the Zane Grey Restaurant (what else?). The boat has bar service, running commentary on the sights and, on a sunny day, provides a wonderful view of the bay. The price is about NZ$50 per person (lunch not included) and the excursion can be booked at the Fullers office at the Maritime Building.

Fullers also has a trip out to the scenic **Hole in the Rock**, a water-carved rock at **Cape Brett**, the southeastern headland of the Bay of Islands. The four-hour trip also stops at Otehei Bay. There are two daily trips. From November-May, the catamaran leaves Paihia at 9 a.m., Russell at 9:10 a.m., and then goes back to Russell at 12:50 p.m., and Paihi at 1 p.m. From June to October, the trip is only 3 hours, with no stops at Otehei Bay. The fare is about NZ$50. Information: toll free ☎ (0800) 653-339.

Just across a causeway north of town is the road that leads to the **Waitangi Treaty House** and the **Waitangi National Reserve**. As noted in the section on the history of the Maori, *this is not a place to be every year on Feb. 6 if you don't like crowds*. Here is where New Zealand's national day is celebrated with pomp and circumstance, much pressing of noses and many hakas (war dances). The queen shows up from time to time, and there are usually thousands of Maoris to either protest or support the anniversary of the treaty. In less frantic times, the reserve and historic building afford an opportunity for a nice stroll through grassy lawns and hikes through the bush surrounding the area.

The place to start is the visitors center, where you can view an audio-visual program on the treaty, as well as see copies of the document written in both English and Maori. There is a souvenir shop with some nice Maori carvings. **The Treaty House** (actually the home of James Busby, the British official who signed the treaty) is *one of the oldest surviving colonial buildings in the country*. It was prefabricated in Australia, then shipped to New Zealand in 1833. The rooms in the buildings have been restored and furnished in colonial style.

Outside, across a wide sweep of lawn, are a flagpole and plaque marking the spot where the treaty was signed, and to the side is *the beautiful carved Maori meeting house, one of the finest in the country*. (Take your shoes off when entering.) A path from the treaty house leads to **Hobsons Beach** and the **Canoe House**, *which contains the largest war canoe in the world*, a Maori craft with the ungodly name of Ngatokimatawhaorua. The canoe, 123 feet long, was crafted from two kauri trees. The bow and stern pieces came from a chunk of tree 3 meters across. The boat was built for the 1940 centennial of the treaty signing and carries 80 warriors. It is launched every Feb. 6. Trails around the preserve go on a coastal walk, through mangrove swamps and native bush, an area of about 1,250 acres in all . It costs about NZ$5 to enter the preserve, open 9-5. Information: ☎ (09) 402-7437.

WHERE TO STAY

PAIHIA

Abel Tasman Motel—On the waterfront. Kitchens, coffee/tea, spa, courtesy van, baby-sitting. Doubles NZ$120. ☎ 402-7521.

Ala Moana Motel—Waterfront. Kitchens, tea/coffee, spa, courtesy van. Doubles about NZ$120. ☎ 402-7745.

Autolodge Motor Inn—Marsden Road, close to the beach. Bar/restaurant, spas in suites, tea/coffee, pool, spa, sauna, games room, bike and dinghy hire, laundry. Doubles about NZ$115. ☎ 402-7416.

Swiss Chalet Lodge—3 Bayview Rd., close to beach. Kitchens, one- and two-bedroom units, tea/coffee, handicapped facilities, spa, BBQ, boat and windsurfer hire, courtesy van, breakfast available, baby-sitting. Doubles NZ$110-NZ$195. ☎ 402-7615.

Cook's Lookout Motel—Causeway Road off Yorke Road, Haruru Falls. Take the Kerikeri road, a few miles out of town. Great view of the bay. Kitchens, studio units, tea/coffee, pool, spa, BBQ, laundry, breakfast available. Doubles NZ$90. ☎ 402-7409.

Casa Bella Motel—3 McMurray Rd. Spanish-style units with kitchens, some suites. Restaurant/bar, tea/coffee, tour desk, laundry, pool, spa, courtesy van, breakfasts available. Doubles from NZ$90. ☎ 402-7387.

Abba Villa Guest House—21 School Rd. B&B, coffee/tea, no smoking, tour bookings, breakfast available. Doubles from NZ$75. ☎ 402-8066.

Mayfair Lodge—7 Puketona Rd., end of Marsden Road. Dorms and doubles. Open 24 hours, kitchen, BBQ, spa, tour desk. NZ$15 per person and up. ☎ 402-7471.

Lodge Eleven—Corner McMurray and Kings Road. Dorms and doubles with baths, linen hire, open 24 hours, kitchen, BBQ, tour desk, courtesy van. From NZ$15 per person. ☎ 402-7487.

Panorama Motor Lodge and Caravan Park—Old Wharf Road, Haruru Falls off Puketina Road. Our choice, for rooms or **RVers**. The facility sits on a lake near the falls. Very friendly managers, good food, very tranquil spot. Studio and family units, spa, swimming pool, bar/restaurant, BBQ, laundry, charter boat for fishing, dinghy and paddleboat rental, courtesy van. Doubles from NZ$50. RV spaces are NZ$10 per person. ☎ 402-7525.

WAITANGI

THC Waitangi Resort Hotel—Just across the bridge from Paihia. Two restaurants and the Zane Grey Bar. Adjacent to golf course. New wing has better units. Boardwalk to Haruru Falls, pool, tea/coffee, courtesy van. Doubles from NZ$130; suites NZ$250-500. The main restaurant is the Governors Room, featuring Bay of Islands seafood, plus lamb and venison. Dinner 6:30-10 p.m. Monday-Saturday. Expensive. The hotel also has **Waitangi Backpackers** with single and double rooms, some with private baths. Tavern, bistro, Sunday smorgasbords. NZ$24 per person with bath. Phone for hotel and restaurant ☎ 402-7411.

WHERE TO EAT

Bistro 40—40 Marsden Rd., in the Baywater's Inn. Blackboard menu, specializing in bay goodies, including Russell oysters, prawn chowder and crayfish; also *award-winning lamb dishes.* Dinner from 6 p.m. seven days. ☎ 402-7444.

La Scala—Selwyn Road. Seafoods with a European influence. Speciality of the house is The Extravaganza, a selection of seafood—NZ$85 a couple. Reservations necessary, *extensive wine list.* Dinner 6:30- 10:30; ☎ 402-7031.

Ferryman's Restaurant and Bar—Opua Store Wharf, 6 kilometers south of town. Housed in an old sailing bark with a window in the floor to watch the fishies swimming by. Blackboard menu, as well as à la carte. *The special here is The Fish Kettle—scallops, mussels, oysters, prawns, squid and fish cooked in a cream chowder and baked in an iron pot.* NZ$60 a couple. Also lamb and venison. Breakfast 8:30-noon; lunch noon-2:30, and dinner from 6 p.m. seven days; ☎ 402-7515.

Tides Restaurant—13 Williams Road. *Perennial award winner for its menu.* Seafood, beef and venison, *discounts for early birds* (before 7 p.m.). Dinner from 6:30 p.m. Closed for periods during the winter; ☎ 402-7557.

King's Progressive Dinner—On the Party Bus. The bus picks you up around 6, you then visit four local restaurants and return home about 10:30-ish. NZ$60 per person; ☎ 402-8171.

Alby's Bistro—Lighthouse Tavern, second floor. Licensed, *light meals* such as Thai chili lamb and nachos. Daily specials. Lunch noon-2 p.m.; dinner from 6 p.m; ☎ 402-8324.

Cafe Over the Bay—Waterfront opposite the Maritime Building. *Country cooking with an Italian tilt.* Light meals all day, daily specials. BYOB. Lunch from 11 a.m.; dinner from 5:30 p.m. ☎ 402-8147.

RUSSELL

There ain't much to Russell, but, as Spencer Tracy used to say, what there is, is cherce. *It's a little bayside village with a couple of good hotels, a nice waterfront, lovely scenery and a sort of Bahamian away-from-it-all atmosphere.* The bad attitude types who hung around here in the 1820s wouldn't recognize the place today and probably wouldn't hang around, either. *Russell makes its living off the daytrippers who come across on the ferry from Paihia and the eager fishermen who come down to pursue the wily marlin.*

The Strand, or waterfront, once had more than 20 hotels, and stacks of grog shops and bawdy houses. There are still a few hotels and groggeries around, including the venerable old **Duke of Wellington Hotel**, which lays claim to holding *the oldest liquor license in New Zealand* (July 14, 1840). The beach in front of town is not very good, but if you walk about a kilometer over the hill behind town, you come to a really nice stretch of sand, **Long Beach** on Oneroa Bay.

If you walk out the front door of the Duke of Wellington and turn right, you will come to Wellington Street. Take that to the top of Maiki Hill where one of our favorite Maoris did his thing. The hill is also called **Flagstaff Hill**, and therby hangs a tale.

In the middle 1840s, there was in the Russell area a Maori notable named Hone Heke. The local British administration, always ready to make a buck, enacted a port duty, which caused visiting ships not to visit so often, cutting into the revenue given by ships' captains to the local Maoris. Heke put up with this loss for a few years, and then one day he marched to the top of Maiki Hill and chopped down the flagstaff, British flag and all. The Brits, having noticed what unpopular taxes had led to in Boston, rescinded the order and the flagpole was replaced. Legend has it that an American living in the village persuaded Heke that such acts of independence against the British were noble, indeed, so the lad chopped down the flagstaff again. The English retaliated by placing guards around the staff, but Heke snuck in and chopped it down a third time. The flagpole was replaced and, just in case, wrapped with iron to stop would-be axers from attacking. But Heke managed to hack it down a fourth time, after which he and his tribe attacked the town, chased the residents out to sea, and proceeded to relieve the grog shops of most of their stores. From that day on, Russell faded into obscurity until tourism came along to revive it.

At the south edge of town is the **Pompallier House**, which started life in the 1840s as a printing plant for a Catholic mission, and which still carries musket-ball holes from Heke's attack. The house, one of the oldest in the country, now houses a small museum and is open daily; admission about NZ$4. More bullet holes are also evident in the walls of **Christ Church**, *the oldest church in New Zealand*. In the church cemetery are the graves of several seamen killed in Heke's 1845 attack. Most of the town was destroyed, by the way, by naval bombardment from offshore English ships.

Also in town is the small **Captain Cook Memorial Museum** with some interesting exhibits of the great explorer's voyages. It's open from 10-4 daily; admission NZ$2. Next to the museum is the **Bay of Islands Park Information Centre.** The park, which encompasses many of the islands plus onshore areas, has hiking trails, huts, camping areas and wildlife walks. The centre has maps and other information about activities.It has an audiovisual program and is open daily 9-5. Information: ☎ 403-7685.

The main information office for Russell is on the boat dock where the ferries tie up, and there is a Fullers office near The Strand.

If you don't want to walk to see the sights of Russell, you can take a van tour with Russell Mini Tours. The 1-hour tour costs about NZ$10 and hits all the high spots. The vans depart from the wharf and can be booked at the Fullers offices in Paihia or Russell. Information: ☎ 403-7891.

If you want to take a car or camper to Russell, you should take the car ferry from Opua, south of Paihia. There is a road to Russell, but it's rough and long. The ferry runs every 10 minutes, starting at 6:50 a.m. and ending at around 9 p.m. It lands at Okiato, about 10 minutes by car from Russell.

The passenger ferry from Paihia (there are actually two companies) runs about every half hour starting at 7 a.m., last trip at around 10 p.m. The Waimarie charges NZ$3 one-way; Fullers *Bay Belle* is $2.50. Both can be booked at the Maritime Building.

As noted earlier in the book, it's possible to book a wide range of fishing activities while staying in the Russell area. But you can also arrange Bay of Islands fishing trips from North America through Shoreline International, a California-based, New Zealand-owned company.

For example, a 5-day trip starts in Kerikeri and offers 3 days of big game fishing and 2 days of light saltwater tackle. Luxury accommodation is in a resort hotel, as well as aboard the sportfishing boat, and includes most meals and all equipment. The trip runs about US$1200. Also includes a rental car. More- and less-expensive packages are available. Contact Shoreline International, ☎ (800) 932-5055.

WHERE TO STAY

Russell has two upscale lodges to supplement the old **Duke of Marlborough**, which is starting to sag a touch.

Kimberley Lodge is a white mansion sitting atop a hill not far from downtown. It was built in 1989, using lots of kauri wood. It's relatively small (four double rooms and a studio), and comes *with all the goodies you'd expect from a world-class hideaway.* It has a pool/spa on a deck overlooking the ocean, and some of the rooms have spa pools as well. There are gardens, a lounge with a grand piano, and a family-style dining room with huge kauri-wood table and chandelier. It also comes with a fireplace, video equipment and a courtesy van. Full breakfasts are included in the tariff, and you can opt for a five-course formal dinner or a more casual feast. Doubles are NZ$545, which includes morning and afternoon tea and refreshments; ☎ 403-7090.

The Okaito Lodge also sits on a hill with a sea view. It has a spa pool and a menu featuring lamb and New Zealand seafood. The nightly rate includes all meals, wine, liquor and transfer from the airport at Kerikeri. *A very elegant place.* Room for only eight guests. Take the barge from **Opua**—about a 10-minute ride. Doubles are about NZ$600; ☎ 403-7515.

OTHERS

Duke of Marlborough—The Strand. As noted, a little long in the tooth. The rooms are small and, if you have a choice, make sure you get an ocean view. The bar almost makes up for the whole hotel—it's plumb elegant and plumb comfy. **Somersets restaurant**, overlooking the harbor, is a favorite dining spot. The Duke will be full most of the summer, especially when the marlin are running between December and April. Rooms, all of which have baths, range from budget to suites. Doubles start about NZ$80; suites NZ$150; ☎ 403-7829.

Duke's Lodge—Next door to the Duke of Marlborough. Once part of the Duke, this motel-style unit is now under separate management. Good views of the bay. Kitchens, pool, sauna, gardens, BBQ, laundry, breakfast available. Units from NZ$85 to NZ$150; ☎ 403-7899.

Te Maiki Villas—Flagstaff Hill. Nine villas, two- and three-bedroom units. Spa, laundry, coffee/tea, courtesy van. Doubles from NZ$150; ☎ 403-7046.

Motel Russell—Matauwhi Road, three blocks from The Strand. Kitchens, pool, spa, BBQ, laundry, courtesy van. Doubles NZ$65-95.

Russell Lodge—Corner Chapel and Beresford streets near the post office. Family units and cabins, some with kitchens, all with private bath.

Tea/coffee, BBQ, laundry. Owned by the Salvation Army. NZ$20 per person; NZ$80 for a family unit; ☎ 403-7640.

Orongo Bay Lodge and Holiday Park—On the road between Russell and the Opua/Okiato ferry dock. YHA accommodations, as well as cabins, tent sites and RV sites. Kitchen, pool, BBQ, bike hire, laundry, tour bookings, camp store, linen hire. Lodge, NZ$15 per person; cabins without kitchens, NZ$30 double; ☎ 403-7704.

Russell Holiday Park—Long Beach Road, up Wellington Street east of The Strand. A Top 10. Kitchens, laundry, store, BBQ, linen hire. Tourist cabins NZ$35 double (NZ$14 per person shared for back-packers in the off season); ☎ 403-7826.

WHERE TO EAT

The Gables—On The Strand—Located in a house built in 1847 with whalebone as foundation and pit-sawn kauri throughout the interior. *It creaks and tilts, but it's elegant.* Seafood, steaks, daily menu. Check out the asparagus pancakes or the Grand Marnier mousse for dessert. Lunch hours vary; dinner from 7 p.m. seven days. ☎ 403-7618. Check for hours during off season.

Somersets—In the Duke. *Excellent views, formal dining.* Seafood, lamb and beef. Lunch 11:30-2:30 p.m.; dinner 6:30-9:30 seven days. ☎ 403-7829.

Quarter Deck—The Strand. Outside dining in the summer. Fresh sea-food, salad bar, steaks. Dinner from 6 p.m. ☎ 403-7761.

Duke of Marlborough Tavern—Behind the Duke hotel. The pub is *pretty seedy*, but the family dining room is seperate. Lunch noon-2 p.m.; dinner from 6 p.m.

KERIKERI

Kerikeri is an agricultural base at the north end of the Bay of Islands. *It's a big kiwi fruit producing area, and you can buy them by the ton for cheap when the harvest is on in May and June.* There's not much to do, but the town is a good base for exploring the area. And the Bay of Islands airport is here with daily service from the rest of the country.

Of some note is the **Stone Store**, *the oldest stone building in the country,* dating from 1835. Kerikeri was the site of the second mis-sion station in the bay area, dating from 1819. The store was used by missionaries to store goods. It was purchased by the New Zealand Historic Trust in 1975, and still is operated as a store. There's a small museum on the second floor. The small wharf next to the river is hip deep in ravenous ducks. Across from the store is a reproduction of a

Maori village with displays of plants and buildings. There's a small admission fee. Next to the store is the **Kemp House**, built in 1821, the *oldest surviving building in New Zealand*. You can take a tour from 10-12:30 and 1:30-4:30 for NZ$3.50.

Information about the Kerikeri area is available at the information center in Paihia. Mt. Cook Airlines flies daily to Kerikeri from Auckland for about NZ$200 one way. There are also flights to Wellington (NZ$440); Christchurch (NZ$490), and Rotorua (NZ$290), as well as to several other cities.

Among the Bay of Islands tours available are those offered by Vanway Tours in Auckland. A two-day tour, which includes the Waitangi Reserve, Russell, the Cape Brett boat trip, breakfasts and accommodation, is about NZ$240 per person double. A three-day tour adds a trip to **Cape Reinga**. The tours pick you up and return you to your hotel in Auckland. Information: Vanway Tours, 15a Scotsdoun Place, Glen Eden, Auckland, ☎ (09) 817-8046.

Or you can take a shuttle bus that leaves Auckland Tuesday, Thursday and Sunday and that has door-to-door service between your Auckland address and your hotel in Russell, Paihia or Kerikeri. The shuttle leaves Auckland at 6:45 a.m., returns from Kerikeri at 3:30 p.m. The round trip fare is about NZ$70. Information: Bay Shuttle, ☎ 366-3566 in Auckland.

From Paihia or Kerikeri, you can also organize a day trip to Cape Reinga and Ninety Mile Beach. The trip, which includes lunch, is about NZ$70 from both towns. The trip can be booked in Paihia, Russell, Kaitaia or Mangonui.

WHERE TO STAY

Colonial House Lodge—178 Kerikeri Rd. between the Stone Store and town. Kitchens, saltwater pool, BBQ, tour desk, handicapped facilities, courtesy van. Doubles about NZ$115; ☎ 407-9106.

Abilene Motel—Kerikeri Road. Studio and one- and two-bedroom units, kitchens, private patios, spas, pool, tea/coffee. Doubles NZ$75; ☎ 407-9203.

Homestead Motel—Homestead Road, 11 kilometers from Stone Store. Restaurant, two bars, pool, spa, some rooms without baths, tea/coffee. Doubles NZ$85 with breakfast. ☎ 407-8421.

Kerikeri YHA Hostel—Close to Stone Store. Kitchen, laundry, store, tour desk, bike hire, hot meals available. NZ$15, NZ$18 non-members; ☎ 407-9391.

Aranga Holiday Park—Banks of the Puketotara River close to town. Top 10 facility. Kitchen, laundry, BBQ, canoe hire. Cabins NZ$35 double; tourist flats, NZ$50 double; backpackers bunkroom, NZ$12 per person; ☎ 407-9326.

WHERE TO EAT

Janes Licensed Restaurant—State Highway 10. *Olde English decor.* Fireside dining, poolside in the summer. Chicken, lamb, steaks. Dinner from 6 p.m.; ☎ 407-8664.

Adam and Eve Restaurant—Waipapa Road, off State Highway 310. *French cuisine in a spacious garden setting.* Licensed, cocktail lounge. Dinner from 6 p.m. Wednesday through Sunday; ☎ 407-8094.

Stone Store Tearooms—Across from the Stone Store. Indoor and outdoor seating. Open from 9 a.m.-4 p.m.

A fisherman displays his prize catch at the Bay of Islands

TOP OF THE NORTH

Four-Wheel-Drive Tours, Mt. Tarawera

Cape Reinga is not actually the northernmost point in New Zealand; that honor falls to North Cape, across the tip of the country to the east. But Reinga is the easiest to get to and has the added advantage of being next to Ninety Mile Beach. At the cape, there is a lighthouse and small souvenir shop. From the base of the lighthouse, you can look out and see a swirling mass of water where the currents of the Pacific Ocean and the Tasman Sea collide. *It's a windy vantage point and one of the prettiest in the country.*

The tip of the cape is also of religious significance to the Maoris. Here stands a gnarled old pohutukawa tree which, according to Maori legend, is the place departing souls leave New Zealand. The spirit goes down the roots of the tree to the seabed, rises again on one of the offshore **Three Kings Islands**, says goodbye to New Zealand and then heads for the ancient Maori homeland of Hawaiki. *The tree is supposedly 800 years old.*

Tours of the **Cape Reinga** area normally start in the Paihia area and go up the center of the island to Kaitaia, then on to the cape. Depending on tides, the tour buses either go up the road and down **Ninety Mile Beach** or vice versa.

A lot of the land in the extreme north is reclaimed sand dunes. In fact, when Cook sailed by on his first voyage, he described the area as a desert. Once there was a huge kauri forest here, but successive ice ages raised and lowered the sea level and the area was inundated several times, killing the trees and creating vast expanses of sand. The few trees that survived were almost wiped out by loggers after colonization began. The government has planted thousands of fast-growing pine trees and flame trees to stabilize the dunes. The tour also takes you through the remains of the gum fields—which further destroyed the land. The gum, a resin that accumulated at the base of kauri trees, was used as a varnish and, for years, extracting it was a major industry. But to get the resin, the ground had to be torn up, and there are still vast areas that haven't recovered.

The top of the North Island is predominantly agricultural, with banana plantations, macadamia nut groves, avocados and a growing cultured mussel industry. You'll also see sheep and cattle and wild turkeys. A popular stopping place on the tour is at **Houhora Heads**, at the head of a bay on the east side of the island. Located here is the **Wagener Museum**, an eclectic collection of New Zealand antiques, Maori war clubs, chamber pots and stuffed possums (including stuffed baby possums). There's also a Maori war canoe at the bayshore if you want to try your hand at paddling.

Along the way, you also pass Great Exhibition Bay, so named by Captain Cook because of the display put on for *Endeavor* by a pod of dolphins. This is a major nesting area for migrating birds, especially godwits. There are also shellfish farms in the area, especially for abalone.

Once at the cape, you'll notice that here the wind tends to blow a lot. This is the spot on tours where you are given a box lunch, and the trick is to find someplace out of the wind to eat. It's only a small hike to the lighthouse, where you get wonderful views of **Cape Marie van Dieman** to the west and, off in the distance, **Abel Tasman's Three King Islands.** Close to the concession stand, there is also a hill that offers great views.

Ninety Mile Beach is not, of course. We got estimates of between 56.6 miles and 69.4 miles, depending on where you start measuring. But whatever, it's a great drive. Whichever direction you're going, try to sit on the ocean side; the windows on the land side tend to get covered with sand and saltwater.

The beach is a clammer's haven. No commercial fishermen are allowed within 1.5 miles of the low-tide mark, but the public can take up to 150 clams a day each, so it's a popular area. The traditional method is to wiggle your toes in the sand to find them.

The bus drivers generally drive straight down the beach but swerve from time to time to miss wet spots. It's not really smart—or legal—to drive a rental car onto the beach. *The tour buses pass the remains of several cars that have bogged down and had to be abandoned.* If you lose a car that way, you pay for the whole car. The tour starts by going down a quicksand-ridden stream bed on the **Te Paki River,** and a scene right out of *Dune.* It's hard to tell you're in clean, green New Zealand. As noted, you can book Cape Reinga tours in Auckland or the Bay of Islands area, as well as Kaitaia. During the summer, *there are special nighttime drives with barbecues and trips to glowworm areas.* If you stay up north, the tour buses will stop and pick you up.

If tour buses are a bit too calm for you, try one of the four-wheel-drive trips offered by Sand Safaris in Kaitaia. The vehicles get off the beaten path and go to kauri forests, look for wild horses, go over and around huge sand dunes, and generally spend the day getting away from it all. The trips are about NZ$50 per person, a real deal, and light lunch is included. Booking information: ☎ 408-1778, 24 hours.

KAITAIA
WHERE TO STAY

Orana Motor Lodge—**238** Commerce St. Bar/restaurant, pool, tea/coffee. Doubles about NZ$80; ☎ 408-1510.

Best Western Wayfarer Motel—231 Commerce St. Kitchens, tea/coffee, pool, spa, courtesy van, breakfast available. Doubles NZ$85; ☎ 408-2600.

Arondale Motel—88 North Rd., off Commerce toward the cape. One- and two-bedroom studios with kitchens, pool, spa, tour desk, BBQ. Doubles NZ$75; ☎ 408-3300.

Sierra Court—65 North Rd. Studio and family size units with kitchens, laundry, pool, tour desk, BBQ, courtesy van, all meals available. Doubles about NZ$75; ☎ 408-1461.

Kaitaia Hotel—15 Commerce St. Restaurant, three bars. Coffee/tea. Doubles about NZ$40, laundry; ☎ 408-0360.

Kaitaia Hostel—160 Commerce St. Twin and family rooms available. Kitchen, BBQ, laundry. NZ$15 per person; ☎ 408-1840.

Main Street Hostel—235 Commerce St. Kitchen, laundry, tour bookings. NZ$14 per person; ☎ 408-1275.

FURTHER NORTH

The Park/Ninety Mile Beach—At the Waipapakauri Ramp entrance to the beach, 18 kilometers north of Kaitaia. Restaurant/bar, kitchen, laundry, shop, nice family service. Tourist and budget cabins, some with baths. Doubles NZ$35-45. Food at the restaurant on demand; just let them know. The speciality is lamb on a spit. Many tour buses stop here for morning and afternoon teas; ☎ 406-7298.

Houhora Heads Campgrounds—Next to the Wagener Museum. RV park only, no power, no hot water. Toilets, BBQ, showers, boat ramp. There is a snack bar at the musuem. NZ$8 per person; ☎ 409-8850.

Pukenui Motor Camp—On the Aupouri Peninsula 45 kilometers north of Kaitaia near Houhora Heads. Kitchen, laundry, tourist flats, backpackers bunkhouse. Close to shops and licensed restaurant. On-site caravans, NZ$15 double; tourist flats, NZ$40 double; bunkhouse, NZ$13 per person; ☎ 409-8803.

WHERE TO EAT

Beachcomber—222 Commerce St. Licensed and *BYOB*. Salad bar, daily specials. Local oysters and scallops, as well as lamb and venison. Lunch 11:30-2:30; dinner from 5 p.m. Closed Sundays; ☎ 408-2010.

Garden Restaurant—185 Commerce. As the name suggests, candlelight dinners in a garden setting. Avocado shrimp a speciality. Dinner 6-9 p.m.; ☎ 408-0910.

INDEX

Introducing the 1994 Fielding Travel Guides—fresh, fascinating and fun!

The travel guide series that started truth in travel is back.
An incisive new attitude and an exciting new look! All-new design and format. In-depth reviews. Fielding delivers travel information the way frequent travelers demand it—written with sparkle, style and humor. Candid insights, sage advice, insider tips. No fluff, no filler, only fresh information that makes the journey more fun, more fascinating, more Fielding.

Australia 1994	**$16.95**
Belgium 1994	**$16.95**
Bermuda/Bahamas 1994	**$16.95**
Brazil 1994	**$16.95**
Britain 1994	**$16.95**
Budget Europe 1994	**$16.95**
Caribbean 1994	**$16.95**
Europe 1994	**$16.95**
Far East 1994	**$16.95**
France 1994	**$16.95**
The Great Sights of Europe 1994	**$16.95**
Hawaii 1994	**$16.95**
Holland 1994	**$16.95**
Italy 1994	**$16.95**
Mexico 1994	**$16.95**
New Zealand 1994	**$16.95**
Scandinavia 1994	**$16.95**
Spain & Portugal 1994	**$16.95**
Switzerland & the Alpine Region 1994	**$16.95**
Worldwide Cruises 1994	**$16.95**
Shopping Europe	**$12.95**

To place an order: call toll-free
1-800-FW-2-GUIDE
add $2.00 shipping & handling, allow 2-6 weeks.

FIELDING'S
TRAVEL
SECRETS

For Travel Insiders Only!

FIELDING'S TRAVEL SECRETS is the insider's travel guide, available only to travel professionals and a very limited number of Fielding Travel Guide readers. Created by Fielding's experienced staff of writers and released in six bi-monthly installments per year, the insider's report is packed with timely travel information, trends, news, tips and reviews. Enroll now and you will also receive a variety of significant discounts and special preview information.

Due to the sensitive nature of the information contained in these reports, subscriptions available to non-travel industry individuals are limited to the first 10,000 subscribers. The annual price for all six installments is $60. This offer also comes with an unconditional money-back guarantee if you are not fully satisfied.

To Reserve Your Subscription
1-800-FW-2-GUIDE

Favorite People, Places & Experiences

ADDRESS:	NOTES:

Name

Address

Telephone

Name

Address

Telephone

Name

Address

Telephone

Name

Address

Telephone

Name

Address

Telephone

Name

Address

Telephone

Name

Address

Telephone

Favorite People, Places & Experiences

ADDRESS:	NOTES:

Name

Address

Telephone

Name

Address

Telephone

Name

Address

Telephone

Name

Address

Telephone

Name

Address

Telephone

Name

Address

Telephone

Name

Address

Telephone

Favorite People, Places & Experiences

ADDRESS:	NOTES:

Name

Address

Telephone

Name

Address

Telephone

Name

Address

Telephone

Name

Address

Telephone

Name

Address

Telephone

Name

Address

Telephone

Name

Address

Telephone

Favorite People, Places & Experiences

ADDRESS:	NOTES:

Name

Address

Telephone

Name

Address

Telephone

Name

Address

Telephone

Name

Address

Telephone

Name

Address

Telephone

Name

Address

Telephone

Name

Address

Telephone

Favorite People, Places & Experiences

ADDRESS:	NOTES:

Name

Address

Telephone

Name

Address

Telephone

Name

Address

Telephone

Name

Address

Telephone

Name

Address

Telephone

Name

Address

Telephone

Name

Address

Telephone